The Social Co

The Social Contexts of Schooling

Edited by

Mike Cole

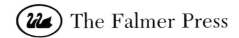 The Falmer Press

(A member of the Taylor & Francis Group)
London ● New York ● Philadelphia

UK   The Falmer Press, Falmer House, Barcombe, Lewes,
East Sussex. BN8 5DL

USA   The Falmer Press, Taylor & Francis Inc., 242 Cherry Street,
Philadelphia, PA 19106–1906

First published 1989

British Library Cataloguing in Publication Data
The Social contexts of schooling.
   1. Schools. Social aspects
   I. Cole, Mike
   370.19

   ISBN 1–85000–450–1
   ISBN 1–85000–451–X (pbk)

Library of Congress Cataloging-in-Publication Data

The Social contexts of schooling/edited by Mike Cole.
     p.   cm.
   Bibliography: p.
   Includes index.
   ISBN 1–85000–450–1. — ISBN 1–85000–451–X (pbk.)
   1. Discrimination in education — Great Britain.   2. Educational
equalization — Great Britain.   I. Cole, Mike, 1956–   .
LC212.3.G7S65   1989
370.19′34′0941 — dc20   89–32550
                                                CIP

Jacket design by Caroline Archer

Printed in Great Britain by Taylor & Francis (Printers) Ltd, Basingstoke, Hants.

Contents

Contents

Introduction

Mike Cole

This collection has arisen out of my work at Brighton Polytechnic. Apart from two years' absence on exchange to Canada and Australia, I have been teaching sociology to BEd (Bachelor of Education) students there for the last thirteen years and to BA (Social Administration) students for the last eight years. The book aims to fill what I perceive to be a gap in the literature. Its purpose is to enable readers to undertake a comprehensive introductory analysis of class, 'race'[1] and gender and their relation to schooling *in a single source* rather than having to sift through the diversity of texts which characterize that literature. As such, it should prove to be of interest not only to students, but to all those interested in the social contexts in which schooling takes place.

The term 'schooling' is used both here and in the title of the book to distinguish it from education. By schooling I refer to a narrow process in which young people are socialized into their perceived future roles in society, perceived that is by those who control the education system. As Kenneth Baker put it at the 1987 Conservative Party Conference, 'Our first national priority must be to educate the young of today for the jobs they'll have tomorrow'.[2] The contributors to this volume argue that the society in which we live, including the occupational structure, is rigidly stratified on lines of class, 'race' and gender. Because of this, 'schooling for jobs' necessarily entails the reproduction of the social inequalities of the labour market on account of its focus and the reproduction of social inequality elsewhere because of its exclusive concern with jobs.

By education I mean a wider more all-embracing and liberating process which centralizes both excellence and equality. As Michael Stoten has argued:

> The fundamental aims of educational progress and improvement must always be the same: to raise standards, attainment and life chances. In other words, to promote excellence ... Without equality excellence can only be partial and the divide between

those who have success and those who don't will become greater. Without excellence those who suffer from inequality will not be able to play a full part themselves in combating and redressing discrimination and disadvantage . . . All learners are of equal value and have unlimited potential for development . . .[3]

Such an approach will necessarily involve attempts to undermine class, 'race' and gender inequalities and to promote equality. It is not the primary purpose of this book to suggest guidelines for such attempts but rather to shed light on the process in which inequalities are reproduced and hence to inform practice. A companion volume,[4] however, deals specifically with *practical* advice on education for equality from pre-school to higher education.[5]

This introduction is, of necessity, brief since the proceeding chapters are introductions in their own right. Chapter 1 is a much requested introduction to sociology and to the sociology of education which makes use of 'the sociological imagination' to attempt to understand current crises and responses. This is followed in chapters 2 and 3 with a comprehensive history of mass schooling from the early days to the 1980s. Next, in response to student demand, chapters have been provided which deal with class, 'race' and gender per se before relating them to schooling (Chapters 4–9). The rationale for this is the difficulty in looking at say, social class and schooling, before examining the meaning of social class in the context of British society. Similarly without an understanding of 'race' or gender the manifestations of racism and sexism in schools are more difficult to comprehend and therefore to combat.

No book would be complete, in the present political climate, without a chapter on testing and this is the content of Chapter 10. The book concludes with a comparative analysis of schooling in Australia (Chapter 11).

Acknowledgement

I would like to thank Tara Jungkunz for her very helpful comments on an earlier draft of this Introduction.

Notes

1 While the term racism clearly has substance, 'race' as a concept is problematic and for this reason is in inverted commas. Robert Miles argues against the notion that there exist distinct 'races' since: (a) the extent of genetic variation within any population is usually greater than the average difference between populations; (b) although the frequency of occurrence of different alleles (possible forms taken by genes) does vary from one 'race' to another, any particular genetic combination can be found in almost any 'race'; and (c) owing to inter-breeding and large scale

migrations, the distinctions between 'races' indentified in terms of polymorphic (dominant gene) frequencies are often blurred (MILES, R. (1982) *Racism and Migrant Labour*, London, Routledge and Kegan Paul, p. 16). A good example of Miles' last point can be demonstrated in the black population of the United States (HERSKOVITS, M. (1958) *The Myth of the Negro Past*, Boston, MA, Beacon Press) (see also McKellar's discussion in chapter 6).

2 BAKER, K. (1987) Speech to the Conservative Party Conference, 7 October, Conservative Central Office.

3 STOTEN, M. (1987) *Equality and Excellence — A Framework for the Development of the Education Service in Brent*, Brent Education Department, 25 June.

4 COLE, M. (Ed) (1989) *Education for Equality: Some Guidelines for Good Practice*, London, Routledge.

5 It is not by any means suggested in that book that education per se can create equality. The relationship between schooling's role as a reproducer of inequality and the potential of education to resist such reproduction and promote equality is problematic. See COLE, M. (1989) 'Class, gender and "race": From theory to practice' in COLE M. (Ed) *ibid* for a discussion.

Part 1
Analytical Framework

Chapter 1

What is Sociology? What is the Sociology of Education?

Peter MacDonald

Introduction

I am staring out the window as I sit in front of my computer wondering what on earth I am going to say to you. It is very cold outside, transforming the snow into a crunchy, frozen mass. I live in New Brunswick, a small Canadian province located on the East coast. I am terribly aware of the sheer impossibility of the task confronting me. I am to tell you of sociology; when I have managed that, I am to tell you of the sociology of education — all within the space of a single chapter. When you realize that there are at least two broad schools of sociological thought — consensus (functionalism) and conflict (including Marxism), and that there are two levels of analysis — macro and micro — you see that their combination gives at least four varieties of sociology. And each variety propogates its own sociology of education. Clearly this chapter cannot be a survey of the discipline.

What is to be done? Clearly I shall have to make some hard choices, hopefully on your behalf. I propose to teach you one sociology and to teach you more about schools than about the sociology of education. Let me elaborate.

Beginning with the one sociology, I shall explain the notion of the sociological imagination as advocated by C. Wright Mills (1959). Since its publication thirty years ago it has acquired something of a cult status. I shall speak more about this later; for now, note that it represents more of an ideal to be approached than a specific programme of analysis or a specific sociology, though it does imply conflict sociology conducted at the macro level. This will be covered in the section 'What is sociology?'.

Turning now to the sociology of education, I stated above that I wish to deal with some of the current issues confronting schools from the perspective of sociology rather than with the sociology of education *per se*. Instead of attempting to survey the discipline to give you some sense of it, I believe that it is more useful in these circumstances to talk about schools themselves. So the focus is not to be on the discipline but instead on schools. By the end of this chapter, I would like you to be able to think about schools together with some of their fundamental problems just as a sociologist would. I believe that readers, many of whom will be teachers or student teachers, will find this strategy more useful than a review of the discipline.

As I am sure you are aware, there has been and are hints of crisis surrounding education. Much has been made of the recent 'failures' of education; much is being proposed (and implemented) to counter these supposed failures. We are living in interesting times. I would like to provide an account of these interesting times as a focus for our sociological discussion of schools. Some themes I consider to be important include the organization of, and conflict over, the utilization of time, the closely related theme of schools as jails (and jails as schools), and the question of the commodification/privatization of schools both as places and as sets of social relationships. Though these may be puzzling to you now, I shall explain what I mean, drawing from newspaper accounts and similar sources. Though these may seem disparate to you now, I do think there is an underlying unity to these themes in that they are expressions of the single crisis that I mentioned above. More on this to follow; for now, let me say that they have something to do with the current transformation of the welfare state within the context of neoconservativism.

Let me conclude this introduction by giving you a highly selective list of books you may wish to consult; needless to say, they are my favourities. For sociology as a discipline, look at Lee and Newby (1983), Collins (1982), and Giddens (1982). For the sociology of education, any of the materials published by the Faculty of Educational Studies of the Open University rank at the top. Finally, books that are good to read because they themselves are so good (even though they have little to do with the concerns at hand) that they serve as exemplars: Hall *et al.* (1978) and Stanley Cohen (1985). Enjoy reading them.

What is Sociology?

As I mentioned above, I wish to base my explanation of sociology on Mills' exposition of what he calls the sociological imagination. Again, as I mentioned above, this exposition has acquired something of a cult or quasi-religious status. In practice, this means that all sociologists of all proclivities pay homage to it, but they do so by imposing on it their own particular predispositions and biases. Varieties of interpretation of a single statement are the result. I am no different; I shall impose my predispositions in producing my particular variety of explanation. You are entitled to know that my particular bias, expressed in terms of the four varieties of sociology mentioned in the introduction, is towards macro conflict theory.

Let me begin with a deceptively simple statement. Sociology is the study of society. Society is comprised of a configuration of institutions each impinging on others. Depending on one's theoretical stance, some of these institutions are thought to be more central than others in that they do most of the impinging. For instance, the state is central to the understanding of schools for it secures their existence by means of compulsory attendance laws.

Institutions are configurations of social relations independent of the specific individuals who are inserted in them. For example at a very prosaic level, students are expected to appear at a certain place at a certain time. At a less prosaic level, students are expected to produce a demeanor of deference to the teacher. Further, this deference extends to the knowledge embodied in the school curriculum. More subtly still, students are expected to pass and to fail, to be good and to be bad, to require and not to require counselling, and the like. These too are components of the social relations of schools which, in a sense, produce through their everyday operations passing and failing, goodness and badness, and so on.

Now to the tricky bit. Though the social relations mentioned above are independent of particular individuals, individuals are not simply objects inserted into them. Rather, it is the confrontation of individuals with social relations that produces the daily social activity of schooling. Individuals try to 'make do' on a daily basis, but do so not simply as they please. They do so in the context of the pattern of social relations which defines the nature of schools.

To understand the social activities of people in schools requires us to see how individuals cope with this institution. To understand this institution requires us to locate schools within the institutional configuration of society. So what appeared as a relatively simple point of departure (sociology is the study of society) is in reality rather more complex. The sociological imagination is a means of dealing systematically with this complexity. Mills tells us that this imagination '. . . enables its possessor to understand the larger historical scene in terms of its meaning for the inner life and the external career of a variety of individuals' (p. 5). This is the genuine purpose of sociology — to enable those who utilize its perspective to make sense of their fates by seeing these fates within the framework of the history of their society. In light of this goal, one realizes it by grasping '. . . history and biography and the relations between the two within society' (p. 6). So we have three components to deal with: society, history and biography. Moreover, we must concern ourselves with the connections among the three.

Let us begin with society. As I mentioned above, society is constituted by a configuration of interrelated institutions. It follows that one must identify these institutions and determine the nature of their inter-relationships. One is, of course, schools. Given this, others include the state as I noted above. And, given my own bias, I want to include the economy by which I mean the organization of the production of goods and services. I will make much more of this in the next section of this chapter.

Now on to history. For our purposes, history is not a narrative of events or a record of great figures and their accomplishments. Rather, it is the study of changes in the social structure – the institutional configuration – of society. Important questions here include when and why a particular institution first appears (for example, state schooling), how the structure of that institution has been transformed, and how its relations have changed with other central institutions of the society. As you can see, we have already related two of the components of the sociological imagination — society and history. We have done so in order to try to understand where an institution is in terms of its pattern of development. By examining the past, by identifying the developmental pattern, one may be able to make some sense of the future by projecting this developmental pattern.

On to biography — another tricky bit I am afraid. Mills speaks of varieties of people, of human nature, '... selected and formed, liberated and repressed, made sensitive and blunted ...' (p. 8) by society. Mills is suggesting here that the sorts of individuals that exist have much to do with the social types provided for by society at a given stage in its history. For instance, one can no longer be a feudal noble, no matter how much one may wish to be. One can no longer be an owner of slaves no matter how much one may wish to be. Conversely, one can (perhaps) be an entrepreneur, an option not available to those who lived in preindustrial society (indeed, their social structure could not provide their even think-ing of that option let alone attempting to pursue it). I think this is the sort of thing Mills is attempting to get at with his notion of individual bio-graphy — people trying to be (or not to be) one of the varieties of individuals provided for by a given social structure at a given point in history.

The trick is to comprehend our own destinies by utilizing all of the above, to try to make sense of our own lives through the use of the sociological imagination. This leads me to the final set of concepts pro-posed by Mills, the notions of personal troubles and public issues. Personal troubles are just that — difficulties that all of us face as a part of our daily lives. These may range from the abstract like a generalized sense of malaise to the concrete like being unemployed, or being subject to sexual or racial harrassment. Public issues, on the other hand, tend to be matters characteristic of society as a whole. Often they are aggregations of personal troubles (for example, a high unemployment rate, patriarchy, or institu-tional racism) but — and this is the point — they are brought about by structural difficulties in the larger historical society. Our private troubles are, in a sense, delivered to us by the dilemmas or contradictions of our social structure. Thus individuals, caught up in their personal troubles, are only able to make sense and perhaps to do something about them by confronting the source of the public issue. The key is for individuals to be able to make the connection between their private troubles and public issues. Making this connection is the job of the sociological imagination — of being able to see how our personal biographies are shaped through the historical development of our society.

The sociological imagination provides us with an agenda for our discussion of schools. We must commence with schools as one of the institutions comprising society. We must locate schools as part of the institutional matrix; as I noted above, I think the most important are the economy and the state. We must locate schools (together with their connections with the economy and the state) within the historical pattern of development. Doing so should reveal the foundation of some of the public issues comprising what seems to be something of a crisis in current education. Doing so should reveal something of the nature of the biographies available to individuals in today's schools. Doing so should reveal something of the connection of the private troubles of today's pupils and students with the public issues of educational debate and conflict.

Let us try to follow this agenda.

What is the Sociology of Education?

I said earlier that education appears to have been in something of a crisis state for the past few years. Certainly there has been much complaining about the supposed failure of education and almost as much debate about what should be done. All this has been characterized as the 'noise' of crisis. I should like to begin by saying a little about this noise.

In the 1 February 1988 issue of *Time Magazine* the cover story deals with a black Principal of an essentially black school in New Jersey. The substance of the story discusses how he brought order and discipline to a drug-ridden, violence-prone inner city school. Noting that he was a former army sergeant, the article explains that he solved the discipline problems in a totally authoritarian way. Travelling the school's corridors with a baseball bat and a megaphone, he banned loitering, locked the doors against drug pushers, gave tardy students latrine and graffiti-scrubbing duties, much as one would find in an army boot camp.[1] But he did much more than this. He suspended 300 students in a single day for being tardy, and tossed out 'hundreds' more in the next five years. Teachers too are expected to toe the line. One hundred teachers have left in six years including a basketball coach '. . . who was hustled out by security guards for failing to stand at attention during the singing of the school alma mater'.

7

What is one to make of this? A point that I consider to be very important is this man's fame. Though I know that everyone is supposed to be famous for fifteen minutes, this seems to be pushing Warhol's epigram a bit far. Here is a man who has made the cover of *Time* (appropriately weilding a baseball bat, the model name of which is 'Big Stick'), has been offered a White House post as policy adviser, has appeared on TV talk shows, and has had the rights to his life story bought by Warner Bothers. The man's philosophy and behaviour should not be stuff from which fame is made. In the course of events, these verge on the trivial. I would like to suggest that the times (no pun intended) have made him famous. Yesterday he would never have been famous; tomorrow he may not be. But there is something about the current situation that has given to him this fame. A key question then becomes what is it about the current situation?

This fame is all the more bemusing given that he is a manifest failure. I submit that one ought to have an orderly school if one expels those students whose behaviour constitutes disorder. But one would also anticipate that if disorderly students tend to get lower marks, and if these students are systematically removed, the average mark would increase. However, whilst math scores are up 6 per cent, reading scores have 'barely budged' and remain in the bottom third of American high school seniors. Moreover, the dropout rate has increased from 13 to 21 per cent. So in terms of the most widely acceptable criterion of success — student achievement — the man and his school must be judged a failure. Yet he and his practices, his transformation of social relations among himself and teachers and students, have acquired fame. The foundation of his fame lies in his success in instilling discipline and order by means of transforming his school into a jail. Doing so has made him famous at this juncture in the historical development of American society. Why?

If schools ought to become like jails, perhaps it would be equally good for jails to become like schools. In the 7 January 1988 issue of the Toronto *Globe and Mail* one can read an account of alternative prisons in Georgia. Referred to in the article as shock centres, they are intended for youth (ages 17 to 25) without a prior record and without psychological problems. They live under highly regimented conditions and within very authoritarian social relations. The experience resembles an army boot camp and many of the prison guards are ex-military men. The centre is located adjacent to a regular prison replete with 'hardcore inmates' to which these youth can be transferred at the discretion of the guards. The fear of this in conjunction with the regimentation of their daily experiences in order to instill self-discipline is supposed to be responsible for the success of these shock centres. Again, success is a relative term. The failure rate is 20 per cent in spite of the care taken over selection (youth with no prior record) and release, where their return to society is supervised for 'an extended period'.

You will have noticed the parallels between the high school in New

Jersey and the shock centre in Georgia. The reforms I have described have transformed these institutions in a direction such that the boundaries separating schools and jails have become indistinct and blurred. It becomes more difficult to know which is what. Change and fame, schools into jails, jails into schools, all are symptoms of some quite fundamental changes in the direction of the historical development of social structure. What are these changes?

The final example of 'noise' I wish to discuss highlights more the biography component of Mills' triumvirate. Again this is taken from the *Globe and Mail* of 30 November 1987. The article describes a private tutoring centre in Toronto, part of a franchise chain (Sylvan Learning Centres) headquartered in Alabama. Being private it charges fees — $295 Cdn per month for two lessons per week. It is based on what the franchisers call a 'reward oriented programme'. In practice students are awarded poker chips for achievement (as one might expect) and for non-academic activities such as arriving on time (as one may not expect). These chips are placed in a savings account which pays interest. Cheques can be written on these chips to purchase goods from a store 'crammed with toys and books'. The article notes that students often count their tokens, at times hoarding instead of spending them to see their assets grow.

A number of points are relevant. First, this is private education — education for profit. Another way of saying this is that education in this example has become a commodity, a good exchanged in the market. Second, the actual process of education has too become commodified. Whether intentionally or not, children are transformed into consumers by means of education. Learning becomes a means rather than an intrinsically worthy end. This is the variety or social type of individual available to the children to become. Finally, knowledge itself tends to become a commodity in such circumstances. I will say more about this later; for now note that knowledge to be experienced (i.e. knowing) is transformed into information to be instilled.

Perhaps this technique is not so terribly new but surely this carries it further than ever before. And the idea of education through private franchised centres is new, apparently becoming ever more popular. Why? Why now?

Thus we have three instances of the 'noise' of crisis, all of which have become public issues. I think these instances are symptoms of a hidden dilemma, hidden because the source of the dilemma lies outside of the institution of education. Education reflects, expresses within itself in the form of a variety of public issues, an underlying problem or 'disease'. These issues together constitute a syndrome in which each is a component of a larger unity. Our task is to 'read' these symptoms to be able to diagnose the disease. Only then will we be able to comprehend the nature of the issues from a sociological perspective, issues that structure the daily lives of teachers.

Peter MacDonald

Education and Production

Stating that the source of these issues is located outside the institution of education means that we must begin by locating education within the institutional matrix of society, just as Mills would have us do. To do this, I want to introduce you to the theory of the correspondence principle formulated by Bowles and Gintis in *Schooling in Capitalist America* (1976). This theory asserts a systematic relationship between schooling and the economy (more specifically, the organization of work) such that schools, in their classrooms, replicate/reproduce the social relations characteristic of work. It follows, then, that the social nature of schools depends on the social relations of production at a given point in time; in other words, education is related to production relations such that the latter have priority. It also follows that crisis occurs when this 'reproductive fit' does not obtain due to changes in work organization. This, of courses, raises the question of history as Mills defined it. Issues like those noted above are symptoms of the absence of correspondence, the source of which is rooted in the changing relations of production.

This is a first statement about where education fits in the institutional matrix of society; let us now work out the correspondence principle in more detail. First, a word on what the correspondence principle is not. When thinking of schools, one has a tendency to concentrate on the overt curriculum, about what is ostensibly being taught and presumably being learned. The correspondence principle does not address these issues, considering them to be of lesser significance. Rather, its concern is with the social structure of schools in the sense in which Mills intended the term.

By social structure I mean the patterned social relations which obtain between teachers and students, among students themselves, and between both and the knowledge which constitutes the curricula. These social relations may be comprehended through such concepts as power and authority, discretion and autonomy, control and alienation. For now we can observe an asymmetry in authority relations, the circumscription of student autonomy, and the like. In short, schools tend to be bureaucratic. Why schools are patterned in this way is the question with which the correspondence principle attempts to grapple.

Bowles and Gintis argue that schools integrate youth into the economic system by means of the structural correspondence between its social relations and the social relations of production. Youth are prepared for the work place, the shop floor, not so much in terms of the knowledge and skills acquired as a consequence of schooling, but rather in terms of what could be referred to as social skills necessary to adequate job performance — a predisposition to submit to authority, a willingness to be cooperative, and other aspects of personal demeanor. These specific skills are acquired not because they are didacticly taught but rather as a result of the structuring of youth experiences in the school setting. Bowles and Gintis put it better than I:

> ... the social relations of education ... replicate the hierarchical division of labor. Hierarchical relations are reflected in the vertical authority lines from administrators to teachers to students. Alienated labour is reflected in the student's lack of control over his or her education, the alienation of the student from the curriculum content, and the motivation of school work through a system of grades and other external rewards rather than the student's integration with either the process (learning) or the outcomes (knowledge) of the educational 'production process'. Fragmentation in work is reflected in the institutionalized .... competition among students through continual and ostensibly meritocratic ranking and evaluation. By attuning young people to a set of social relationships similar to those of the work place, schooling attempts to gear the development of personal needs to its requirements. (p. 131)

As you can see, schools are structured the way they are because of their particular role in the institutional configuration of society. Their social structure is 'delivered' to them by the organization of production relations in the economy. To understand schools, then, is to understand that they replicate — correspond to — production relations.

Because they are hierarchical, production relations are constituted by a variety of levels. Given the logic of the correspondence principle, one would suppose that schools would be organized to reproduce this hierarchical division of labour. It seems that they are. One can point to different types of schools (private, grammar and secondary modern schools), and to the practice of ability grouping or streaming within schools. Each of these levels is characterized by their particular pattern of social relations. Each tends to feed students into the variety of locations in the division of labour (or, if you prefer, the class structure). Bowles and Gintis refer to a study of the types of social relations in higher education in which junior colleges, state universities and private universities were examined. The results indicated that those institutions that tended to enrol working class students emphasized behavioral control and external compliance together with docility to authority. The elite schools emphasized the internalization of norms and innovation together with leadership skills. The former are geared to lower level jobs in the production hierarchy whilst the latter to the higher level jobs requiring organizational and leadership abilities.

Finally, Bowles and Gintis note that while correspondence is primarily a structural matter, they feel that it spills over into character or personality development as well. In their study of a senior class of a New York state high school, they found a positive association between grade point average and such traits as perseverance, dependability and consistency. Equally, they found a negative association between grade point average and the traits of creativity, aggressiveness, and independence. Though not wittingly, grades were rewarding those qualities of personality compatible with the hierarchical division of labour and vice versa.

The correspondence principle, then, meets one of the strictures set for us by Mills. It purports to explain the social structure of schools by locating education in the institutional configuration constituting society. More specifically, school structures are accounted for by seeing them as replications of the structures of production. Moreover, the theory seems to say that schools possess very little autonomy from production relations, that schools must be organized the way they are. Finally, if they are not, we are likely to experience a crisis manifesting itself as a crisis in education, the resolution of which will be the reorganization of education to re-establish correspondence.

With their correspondence principle, Bowles and Gintis made quite a splash in the sociology of education.[2] As you can well imagine, much controversy was produced. Some were critical of the aforementioned implication of the lack of any autonomy for schools. Others stressed that the principle, in concentrating on the reproduction of class inequality, marginalized the ways in which schools reproduce gender and 'race' inequalities. Notwithstanding these major reservations, most critics were sympathetic to their overall project — that of capturing the unequal nature of schooling. And their theory also stimulated some further studies, some far more empirically grounded than theirs. One very interesting study was done by Anyon (1980), a study I would like to address now.

Anyon, through observational research, sought to demonstrate many of the points theorized by Bowles and Gintis. She systematically studied five different grade 5 classes all located in different schools. Because American schools tend to be neighbourhood schools, and because American neighbourhoods tend to be relatively homogeneous in class composition, the schools themselves reflect this class homogeneity. Thus, Anyon was able to identify what she labelled two working class schools, one middle class school, one affluent professional school, and one executive élite school. Finally, the overt curriculum in all classrooms was very similar; all used the same maths texts and all had available at least one set of individualized reading programmes.

In spite of the curricular similarities, Anyon found very significant differences in the everyday social practices constituting these five classrooms. In attempting to summarize these differences for you, I shall utilize the dimensions of labour process and social control. By labour process I mean the social activities constituting the teaching-learning process. By social control I mean the social activities constituting the attempts by teachers to direct the activities of students as well as students' response. I should emphasize that Anyon does not employ these analytical categories; I do so in the interest of summarizing complex material briefly and hopefully in a meaningful way.

Anyon found the nature of the labour process of the two working class classrooms to be mechanical and rote. Directions were given with little explanation, and students were expected to follow them precisely, such that the following of them became an end itself. The work was fragmented with little attempt to place its bits in a coherent context. For the dimension of social control, Anyon noted that it was often capricious in nature with no consultation by the teacher with the students. Finally, social control was characterized by a constant struggle and student attempts to sabotage.

The labour process of the middle class school placed much greater stress on students obtaining the correct answer; directions and procedures, instead of being an end themselves, were presented as a means useful to achieving the answer. Though somewhat mechanical in that creativity or innovation was not encouraged, procedures, unlike the working class schools, were seen as a means to an end instead of being of intrinsic merit themselves. Social control in this classroom was based on external rules carefully formulated and presented and even more carefully followed; there was little of the caprice characterizing the working class schools.

The labour process of the affluent professional school encouraged individuality, creativity, and independence. Teachers placed emphasis on students expressing and illustrating their ideas which meant that the products of student labour were highly valued. In terms of social control, there was little attempt to control pupil movement. Rather than issuing direct orders based on external rules, teachers negotiated with students over appropriate social activities.

Finally the executive élite classroom's labour process placed a great deal of emphasis on developing analytical capacities. To achieve this, teachers emphasized concepts in their instruction and actively encouraged independent research. Much more important than correct answers was the reasoning process used by students to arrive at them. Social control was characterized by the relative freedom of student movement and stress on student presentation of self where each student was required to be a student teacher.

Anyon concludes her analysis by arguing that the working class schools prepare their students for routine and mechanical wage labour on the factory floor. The middle class school prepares students for the tasks and relationships appropriate to the middle ranges of bureaucracy. The affluent professional school prepares future technical experts and intellectuals through the acquisition of symbolic capital. Finally, the executive élite school cultivates in its students the ability to manipulate systems by means of analysis and conceptualization, thereby facilitating the role of leadership.

In spite of a similar curriculum, and in spite of the similar geographical location of the five schools, Anyon found very real differences in the social structure of these five classrooms, differences which appear to be accounted for by Bowles and Gintis' correspondence principle. Through its highlighting of the social relations of schooling, the correspondence principle accounts for how children are both prepared and placed for future insertion in the social relations of production. It shows how schools reproduce production relations and, in so doing, why they possess the pattern of social structure that they do. But is social reality quite so neat as this?

Recall my discussion of social control in the working class schools. Student practices included resistance and even attempts to sabotage work being conducted (asking irrelevant questions and the like). Though authority is not often directly challenged, there is incessant struggle against the directions and control the teacher is attempting to exercise. Often this manifested itself over the use of time (the need for some relief from the omnipresent routine) and space (the movement of pupils). Though Anyon appears unaware of it, this poses something of a contradiction in the correspondence principle. One wonders how this is appropriate preparation for the destination of the production relations of the shop floor. In Bowles and Gintis' terms, this seems a description of the failure of schools and, perhaps, the failure of the correspondence principle.

To deal with this anomaly, I should like to turn to a fascinating study done by Willis (1977) of a small group of working class boys attending a secondary modern school. First I shall recount Willis' description of the culture of the shop floor which will then put us in a position to juxtapose this description to the social relations of schooling. Doing this will 'save' the correspondence principle from the anomaly noted above but in a highly ironic way.

Shop floor culture arises from the material reality of production. Its conditions are set by others, often in the most routine and boring way. Given the absence of intrinsic interest and enjoyment, the organization of time and space assumes problematic status. In the endeavour to impose meaning in the attempt to derive satisfaction, workers constantly confront the constraints imposed on them by others. Shop floor culture, then, has an oppositional, confrontational quality about it which provides the medium through which attempts are made to derive meaning and enjoyment.

More specifically, Willis identifies some basic themes which constitute this culture. The first is the element of physical bravery historically arising from the doing of difficult, heavy work. Respect from others and a sense of self-accomplishment is acquired from success in this. This is the source of the concept of masculinity characteristic of working class culture (and equally the source of much of its sexism). The next constituent theme revolves about the attempt to gain informal control of the work or labour process. This, naturally, generates a pervasive (though often latent) conflict between workers and management and serves as the foundation for oppositional attitudes toward official authority so characteristic of the working class. Finally, the culture of the working class reflects its material experience in that it glorifies practical, useful knowledge and ability whilst denigrating theoretical, intellectual knowledge. This splitting of manual from mental knowledge has corresponded with the appropriation of mental knowledge from the working class by capital as the organization of production has been historically transformed.

These themes which define the essential elements of shop floor culture have been generated by, and are rooted in, the material reality of the shop floor. That, however, is not to say that this culture is somehow bounded by the shop floor; it pervades all arenas of working class life from the family to leisure to political action to the school. Elements of toughness, of opposition to authority, and of the devaluation of mental knowledge define for working class boys their place relative to schooling. But note that this is a place the boys themselves choose (this sounds overly voluntaristic for they choose within the context of their culture) rather than schools imposing their choice on the boys.

As you can imagine, there is, rooted in the shop floor culture, an inherent, structured resistance by (at least some) working class boys to the culture of the school. There is opposition to official school authority manifested in the attempt to gain informal control over primarily the use of time and in sabotage of official school plans. There is the rejection of mental knowledge on which the school curriculum is based. There is the celebration of masculinity and toughness, again realized through opposition. All of this coalesces around a vibrant, anti-school culture through which the boys realize their culturally defined ideals. This is rather a different picture from that portrayed by Bowles and Gintis in their formulation of the correspondence principle.

In living and affirming this school counter-culture on a daily basis, 'the lads', as Willis describes them, do not do well at school. From the school's point of view, they are disruptive and troublesome; indeed, they are failures. But note that the school has also failed. In contraposition to Bowles and Gintis, the lads have not been transformed into docile, dependable workers ready to be inserted in production relations. Rather, they have challenged and sabotaged the social relations of education and, one would presume, by dint of their disruption have severed the reproductive link between education and production that the correspondence principle casts in such a salient role.

But, as Willis stresses so correctly, there is a fundamental irony here. Precisely through their celebration of their counter-culture, the lads voluntarily deliver themselves to the shop floor. By failing in school, their occupational destination is working class. In this ironic way, the school does indeed reproduce the class structure and does so with the willing

15

compliance of what might be called its victims. And the school does this through its ostensible failure. This is in stark contrast to the 'successful school argument' set forth in the correspondence principle.

At issue here is the nature of the connection between the social relations of education and the social relations of production. The correspondence principle argues a direct functional relation conjoining the two. Willis proposes a much more dialectical sort of relation in which the direct functional link is broken. Education and production are bound together in a contradictory, oppositional unity. Each derives its structure and content in antagonism with the other. The shop floor culture developed in opposition to capital, providing the context for cultural socialization and, with it, the cultural resources utilized by the lads in the reconstruction of the counter-culture. Through the creation and recreation of this counter-culture, the lads freely deliver themselves to the unfree conditions of the shop floor.

For me, Willis presents the more persuasive argument. But you should realize that his argument is based on a study of a relatively small portion of white working class boys and not on girls at all. This neglect or marginalization of gender and 'race' is a failure of sociology in general (recall the critiques of the early Bowles and Gintis above) and traditional sociology in particular. Only in recent years has this failure begun to be repaired (see the other chapters of this book, particularly 7–11). Willis discusses a group the lads call 'ear 'oles', those for whom the school has been relatively successful from the perspective of the correspondence principle. Moreover, as one ascends the class structure, one might argue the correspondence principle also ascends in its validity.

There is another matter I wish to address. The primary constituent of the shop floor culture (and the school counter-culture) is the theme of opposition. Though the lads are inserted into the shop floor by schools, they carry with them the qualities of conflict and opposition they have acquired at school. In an era in which the labour process is being ever more rationalized and bureaucratized, we have, perhaps, the germ of crisis founded on presumably increasing opposition on the part of the working class. More on this later, but I did want to sensitize you to this now.

Thus far, we have achieved part of Mills' charge to us. We have situated education partially in the institutional matrix of society by showing its connections with production. Moreover, we have done so through the concept of social structure again in keeping with Mills. However, we have yet to complete this task for there is another institution of critical importance to the comprehension of schools. This is the state; the schools we are considering are, above all, state schools.

Education and the State

I wish to begin with a very brief and generic history of the founding of state schools. Willis' account makes clear the great divide between schools and at least some of their students. This can be partially understood by examining the history of state schooling. My interest here is quite limited; for a broader and more detailed historical analysis, see chapters 2 and 3.

An outstanding feature of this history is that it is simply one element of the 'great incarcerations' which developed in the nineteenth century. Stanley Cohen (1985) describes the process as follows: '... thieves into prisons, lunatics into asylums, conscripts into barracks, workers into factories, children into school ...' (p. 25). Two themes are important here: the significance of understanding schools as one of the institutions of incarceration, and the reasons underlying the great incarcerations which transformed the organization of education.

As with the other institutions of incarceration, the schools of this era were established by the state. This is to say that their existence was secured and guaranteed by the power of the state, primarily by means of compulsory attendance laws (on which grounds I count schools as incarceral institutions). As they evolved, schools — because of state control — became increasingly bureaucratic and centralized. As a result, schools became increasingly separate and distinct from the communities of which they nominally were a part. Moreover, given the presence of a (more or less) non-voluntary clientele, they were, and are, characterized by an unbridgeable gap between authorities and clientele (or inmates). This gap, structured into state schools from their conception, gave and gives rise to an inherent tension between the two, characterized by opposition and conflict. This resistance, so carefully documented by Willis, is a social fact of all such institutions, manifesting itself in greater or lesser degrees depending upon the extent to which the clientele is voluntarily present. Compulsion — the hard edge of the state — reproduces itself as resistance in the school.

Schools as a member of the larger group of institutions of incarceration developed at approximately the same historical moment as industrial capitalism. This observation has led many to talk of the necessity of inculcating discipline in, and control of, the newly-created proletariat. I do not wish to dwell on this; rather, I would like to talk about the changing nature of the state and the location of education within this vital institution.

I shall begin with the ending — the welfare state. I very much like Giddens' (1982) account which uses Marshall's seminal work as a point of departure (chapter 3). Marshall portrays the evolution of the modern welfare state through the progression of three types of what he calls citizenship rights — rights which define the relation of the individual to the state.

The types of citizenship rights are civil rights, political rights, and social rights. Civil rights refer to formal equality before the law and of access to the legal system. Political rights include the universal franchise and accompanying rights (freedom of assembly, speech, and the like). Social rights are of two sorts; the rights of trade unions and the rights of social welfare.

Now Marshall argues that each type of right provided the stage for progression to the next type of right, culminating in our modern welfare state. For instance, civil rights, established in the early phase of capitalism, were necessary for its development. People had to be free to leave the land, enter the labour market, to be able to 'choose' their occupation, and so on. The law of contract had to be enforced; markets had to be 'free'. To ensure that the state was responsive to these requirements, it had to be made responsible to the citizens who needed them (see MacPherson, 1965). This led to the development of political rights in which the relation between the citizen and the state was constituted by the formation of political parties. This in turn supposes the freedom of assembly, of speech and the franchise. Various classes could now make the state responsive to their interests via the political arena. The logic of political rights was such that they could not be denied to the working class; after decades of struggle and conflict the male members of this class too won the franchise and its associated freedoms of assembly and speech. Utilizing these rights the working class formulated its own political party representing its own interests. This culminated in the acquisition of social rights — the formation of trade unions and the establishment of social welfare. According to Marshall, this resulted in the institutionalization (i.e. the routinization and containment) of class conflict. Given that the engine (class conflict) of progression from one stage of citizenship right to the next has run out of petrol, the welfare state signifies the culmination of development. The welfare state has altered the nature of class divisions by muting class conflict. Giddens, as we shall see, has something to say about this; for now, ask yourself what a crisis in the welfare state (that all seem persuaded is occurring) means in terms of Marshall's theory of citizenship rights. Indeed, ask yourself how such a crisis could even occur.

Marshall's history can be understood as a process whereby the state does become increasingly neutral in terms of its responsiveness to class interests, especially with the stage of welfare rights. Giddens criticizes Marshall for envisioning the welfare state in this way. He argues that in light of state dependence upon the wealth generated by capital investment, it must maintain 'investor confidence', to be especially responsive to the interests of capital. Even more significantly, given that the state's primary function is the maintenance and reproduction of the system, of necessity it will be tilted towards the interest of capital. Giddens points out that civil/legal rights provided the mechanism for exploiting the working class by means of wage-labour — individuals were freed from feudal bonds to turn them into a pool of 'free' labour. He notes that these rights do not provide for control by workers over the labour process, nor do political rights extend into the industrial sphere. He further argues that each progression in the stages of citizenship rights had to be struggled for. This expansion of types of rights was the achievement of the working class accomplished, he argues, in reaction to their lack of power in the sphere of production. With no formal rights of participation in the labour process, workers have defensively coped by struggling for social rights. The welfare state is the consequence of the absence of worker rights in production.

In light of these origins of the welfare state, one can better comprehend current problems. The confrontation of what was essentially a white male working class with dominant classes over social rights produced a particular definition of these rights. The very idea of welfare became entwined with the welfare of the British nation as a whole instead of a specific class. Welfare was intended to promote Britain both in competition with other capitalist nations and in its project of empire maintenance. These acquired racist overtones manifested ideologically in the presumed superiority of the British 'race' in the context of the British Empire, and in controls over who was eligible for welfare programmes in terms of the 'foreigners' then present and control over who might be eligible in the future by immigration restrictions (Steve Cohen, 1985).

If Giddens is correct (and I find his argument persuasive), the welfare state is the manifestation of the power of the working class at a given point in time. Rather than being the enduring institutionalization of class conflict that Marshall would have us believe, it is a reflection of working class power in society at a given point in time. As such, it is a fragile creation depending on the capacity of the working class to wage its defensive struggle. If so, then the notion of a crisis in the welfare state assumes an entirely different meaning as compared to Marshall's formulation.

Education is one of the key institutions of the welfare state. To try to see where education fits, I wish to turn to an article by Finn, Grant and Johnson (1978). Their argument fleshes out in particular the role of the working class by examining both the role intended for education and the nature of the groups who, together with the working class, established this role.

The activities of the Labour Party must loom large in this discussion. Because of their faith in parliamentarianism (which Finn *et al.* define as a belief in the neutrality of the state and in the ability of its institutions to achieve social equality and resolve social problems), the Labour Party attempted to change the existing apparatus of education to provide for equality of opportunity. In this context, the pragmatic question became that of access and expansion, especially to secondary education, which led to concentration on the forms of secondary education (and ultimately the introduction of the secondary modern school). Questions of curriculum and control were largely absent from this consideration. This absence

permitted teachers to capture the void in the name of increasing professionalism (which, of course, presupposed greater autonomy). In
conjunction with expansion, teachers realized their occupational interests. Finally, intellectuals increasingly documented the inequality of
the old forms of education, providing justification for the Labour Party
programme.

These forces — the Labour Party in the name of the working class,
teachers and intellectuals — coalesced to bring about a reorganized
and expanded system of education that was an integral component of
the welfare state. Underwritten by these interests, this system was to
provide opportunity for the working class and to overcome its historical
resistance to education; in short, it was to reflect the interests of the
white, male working class. Concerns about black and white, female members of the class came far later. Whether it was a triumph for the working
class in the pursuit of welfare rights as Marshall's analysis would lead us to
believe, or simply an historical moment symbolic of the defensive struggle
by the working class as Giddens would argue is answered by the current
crisis in the welfare state. More on this later.

I wish to conclude this section by returning to Mills. In following his
charge concerning social structure, I have attempted to situate education
in the institutional configuration constituting society. We have seen how
education became an increasingly crucial institution in a particular form of
state — the welfare state; as such, it was increasingly integrated into the
apparatus of the state. In so doing, we have portrayed it as the primary
means for the realization of welfare rights. We have equally noted the
possibility that it is a temporary rather than an enduring phenomenon.
Whatever, it is impossible to make sense of education without locating it
relative to the welfare state.

I have also attempted to situate education relative to production
which led us to concentrate on the structure of the social relations of
teaching and learning. Logically, I suppose, we ought make mention of
the relation between production and the state, of how the two together
provide for education its structural location in society. In our discussion of
the state, I pointed out that Giddens sees the state biased in favour of
capital. This suggests that generally the state provides the sort of education supportive of capital, of the social relations of production. Another
way of saying this is that the state provides for correspondence between
the two (even if this correspondence is, in some instances, of the dialectical variety). But remember, this sometimes does not occur. When it does
not, we have, according to Bowles and Gintis, a crisis only resolved when
correspondence is reconstructed. It is very important to understand here
that while the crisis lies in the nature of the relation between production
and education, it appears as a crisis in the state itself. The crisis in the
welfare state is derivative. Please realize that I can only make this argument by following Mills' mandate, by comprehending education as a part

of an institutional matrix. Whatever merit the argument has (reserve judgment until we complete the next section) is a tribute to the sociological imagination.

I have not said much about Mills' second dimension of history (of social structure). But the element of history has permeated our discussion of the relation of education with the state. In proper analysis, history and social structure are inseparable. I trust you will find this to be especially true in the section below.

Education and the Current Crisis

What does a crisis in the welfare state look like? How do we know when it is happening? And, how can we explain why (and when) it is happening?

I would hope that what I have written this far will provide you with some clues on how to proceed. Near the beginning, I spoke of the noise of crisis. When exceptionally harsh discipline brings national fame and when education for profit becomes highly popular, the times are exceptional. From your own personal experience you know that education has been on the receiving end of vehement rhetorical attack and that far-reaching changes have been proposed and carried out. For a discussion which locates these changes in the particular context of Thatcherism, see Cole (1989). We are living in an extraordinary era.

Gough (1979) discusses the crisis in terms of the reorganization of the welfare state. In keeping with the tradition voiced by Giddens, he conceives of the state acting in the long-term interests of capital by ensuring the receiving end of vehement rhetorical attack and that far-reaching population. The first he refers to as the function of accumulation, the latter as the function of maintaining social legitimacy. Depending on the patterns of capital development these twin functions may be contradictory, resulting in a crisis of the state. I shall say more of recent patterns of capital development later; for now I wish to review Gough's ideas about the resolution of crisis.

These days we hear much about the cutting back of the welfare state. Gough argues that understanding these changes as a dismantling of the welfare state is highly misleading. Instead, a rather different phenomenon – restructuring – is occurring Policies supportive of accumulation are pursued by the state whilst those which are supportive of 'human needs' (social legitimacy) are cut back.[3] Instead of a single-minded reduction in the role of the state, it is reorganized to render it more compatible with the requirements of capital. This may take a variety of specific forms. Gough speaks of the adjustment of policies to adapt the labour force more in line with the needs of the labour market. The social security system is likely to be harmonized with the labour market in terms of minimum wage levels, rates of welfare, and the like. The social services sector will be made more efficient according to market definitions of efficiency. Finally, pressure for the reprivatization of aspects of welfare services will appear. This is a point Giddens mentions as well, though he does so in slightly different terms. Observing that the removal of social relations from the market is the essence of the welfare state (what might be termed decommodification), he argues that commodification (for example, the sale of council flats) represents its retreat. The shifting balance of commodification/decommodification is indicative of crisis.

These are techniques useful for seeing a crisis in the welfare state. We will wish to utilize them when we discuss the changes in education but now I want to deal with the sources of the crisis.

We can begin with the process whereby the legitimacy possessed by schools came to be questioned, especially by the popular classes in the comprehensive system of education created by the Labour Party. Here I wish to return to the analysis of Finn, Grant and Johnson who demonstrated the class coalition that underwrote that expansion. One could assume that that particular configuration of interests broke apart, and with it the sort of education system that represented its interests.

The crisis, which began in the late 1970s, arose from the attempt to maximize equality of opportunity within a larger commitment to reform (rather than to change) capitalism. The emphasis on opportunity by the Labour Party failed as it had to do given the momentary failure of capitalism at that time. Opportunities could not be expanded at the very time they were being reduced by this economic crisis. As a result, the entire justification for the expansion of education demonstrated itself to be a failure. The Labour Party became the emperor with no clothes.

These limits to social democracy in an era of crisis revealed themselves in massive levels of unemployment, most especially for working class youth. Naturally, fundamental questioning of the utility of education arose, particularly among those for whom it manifestly did not work. These questions assumed the form of complaints over the irrelevance of not simply education, but particularly the sort established by the Labour Party. Coupled with this were attacks on teachers, leading to an inevitable questioning of their autonomy. The importance of this lay in the fact that teachers were a significant component of the coalition of interests underlying the expansion of education.

With the economic crisis, things fell apart. This disintegration took the form of an attack on progressivism in education. The outstanding feature of this process was the disruption of the class coalition; one would anticipate an attack from capital but here much of that attack came from within the working class itself whose interests were supposedly embodied in progressivism.

Because this loss of popular support was such an outstanding feature of the educational crisis, I want to discuss it in a bit more detail. One very useful analysis in this respect is that done by Sharp and Green (1975).

They examined both the theory and the practice of progressive, child-centered education paying special attention to its effects on working class children.

A brief review of the philosophy of child-centered education may be in order. Its key concept is learning readiness which means that children are physiologically unable to learn abstract concepts until the appropriate developmental stage is reached. This occurs at different ages for different children. The key educational question then becomes the particular developmental stage given children have achieved. This can only be ascertained through the observation of children in appropriate settings. Specifically, this translates watching children as they play at specific activity centres in a comparatively unstructured environment.

Sharp and Green provide a fascinating account of how stratification (or class bias) is produced, even in a system that was intentionally designed to avoid such outcomes. But for our purposes, I wish to concentrate on their discussion of the philosophy of progressivism and its relation to working class 'common sense'.

The concepts of progressivism — learning readiness, stages of development, play — are highly ambiguous, even to teachers let alone to working class parents whose only knowledge of school is based on their own now dated (and possibly distasteful) school experiences. Progressivism grants to teachers an autonomy from parents based on a seeming esoteric expertise. Though parents may be prepared to accept or to submit to this as long as education appeared to be working, it was bound to be called into question when it appeared not to be. This is precisely what happened, generating the rhetorical attack revolving around themes of laxity, frivolity and indiscipline — all of which appeared to be integral elements of the open classroom to the untrained outsider. Moreover, the key feature of play (through which pupils manifested their learning-readiness) proved to be antithetical to the very culture of the working class. As Bernstein (1975, chapter 6) has argued, the working class — more than any other class — characteristically has a very strong boundary separating play from work. The two are very different sorts of activities done in very different times and places. This is a consequence of the nature of their work; because it is by nature alienating, play is understood as a compensation. To the working class, then, schools are places to work. Children playing at school is an anathema, especially if education is viewed as a route to upward mobility. Being told by the teacher (as I once was) that one's child 'plays well' causes, at the very least, utter confusion and at worst, complete loss of confidence in the school.

Writ large, this example drawn from Sharp and Green is indicative of the pervasiveness of the loss of popular support. Progressive education created by the Labour Party in retrospect can be seen as a disaster waiting to happen. When the system failed in response to the economic crisis, the disaster did happen. It provided the counterpoint for the nature of the criticism which occurred: the irrelevance of the curriculum, the decline in necessary skills of literacy and numeracy, of the immorality and indiscipline of youth, and the like. It equally provided the counterpoint for the changes suggested by those purveying this rhetoric: 'toughening' the curriculum by reducing choice and forcing the basics, lessening the autonomy of teachers, increasing selectivity in streaming, all of which I expect you are quite familiar with.

Thus far in my discussion the idea of the economic crisis has remained in the background. Now is the time to bring it to the foreground, though only briefly, and to bring this section of the chapter to a close.

In recent decades, capital investment has become increasingly international in scope so that now there is an international system of production with an international division of labour. Where capital is invested in this system is determined by the relative rates of profitability, itself largely a reflection of wage rates. Here what has been termed superexploitation (rates less than that required for the physical maintenance of labour) of third world men and women is a highly salient factor. To turn this around, one could equally say that national economies are now subordinate to this 'world system'. In such a conjuncture, the accumulation role of the state becomes the task of aligning the national economy to the world market to ensure the maximum amount of production in the nation. National economies must be structured to attract the flow of capital. To put this in more popular terms, national productivity/competitiveness must be enhanced. The hard consequences of this strategy include the elimination of unprofitable lines of production and the support of profitable lines. Elimination means unemployment. Ironically, support of profitable lines also means unemployment. Such support typically increases productivity which results in a decrease in the need for workers (unless this larger number of products can be marketed, but note that other national economies are engaged in precisely the same strategy greatly increasing competitiveness). The result is that national economies are less able to develop full employment policies. Simultaneously, the state has even less resources to devote to social services and welfare. Here we have the crisis in the welfare state discussed in reference to Gough's work above.

The result is unheard of levels of unemployment, particularly for youth. The nonsense of education increasing opportunity becomes obvious to all, not the least of whom are these youth. This is one principal aspect of the crisis. But there is another as well, more hidden because it manifests itself at the level of the labour process. To increase productivity is to increase management control of the production process. Work is more carefully planned; the discretion over space and time available to workers is reduced. The entire process becomes much more bureaucratized. Given this, those aspects of labour unpalatable to workers are reinforced and increased. One would predict that this would engender and enhance the oppositional elements of the shop floor culture (though I should note that massive levels of unemployment provide a disciplining factor). To the extent that this is true, the very strategies utilized to enhance productivity may well result in undermining it. The management solution to this conundrum is to increase the supervisory ingredient of the production process. By definition, however, supervisors are non-productive; this too tends to undermine the endeavour to increase productivity.

This contradiction in the labour process together with the dramatic increase in especially youth unemployment is the face of economic crisis. Schools which provide the context against which oppositional youth culture evolves (see Willis above) and which fail to reproduce the social relations of production (see Bowles and Gintis above) are no longer in correspondence. This is the conjuncture of the present crisis, a crisis rooted in production that appears at the level of the welfare state in general and in, for our purposes, education in particular. This historical/ structural analysis, mandated by Mills' definition of good sociology, provides the context according to which we can attempt to account for the quite dramatic changes which are transforming the nature of education. In the next section we will examine some of these. These extraordinary times cast up marine drill sergeants as principals and education for profit.

Education and the Resolution of Crisis

As you well know, some quite fundamental changes have been occurring in education in the past few years. Above I have attempted to provide a context to enable you to comprehend some of these changes. In this final section, I should like to discuss some of these, seeing them as responses to the economic crisis. I would also like to suggest to you that even if I do not cover the changes you find particularly intriguing, you should be able to interpret them for yourself utilizing the context I have provided. Moreover, if I have been successful, you ought to be able to do the same for changes which have yet to occur.

The dominant rhetorical theme used to marshall the forces for change has been the notion of 'toughness' which, to be properly appreciated, must be juxtaposed to the rhetorical theme of 'permissiveness' historically used to marshall the forces for the expansion of progressive education by the Labour Party. The notion of toughness is a two-edged sword used to attack both the supposed indiscipline and moral laxity of youth on the one hand and the autonomy of teachers on the other. As you now know, the former has been placed on the agenda by the twin phenomena of youth unemployment and problems of control in the labour process, the latter by the loss of popular legitimacy suffered by progressivism in schools. This rhetoric of critique contains as well a manifesto for change propagated by what is often called the neo-conservative right. I should like to discuss the basic contours of these changes. Not being intimately involved in the

British scene, I shall depend on two newspaper reports: 'Baker sets out plans for education' in the *Guardian Weekly*, 29 November 1987 and 'A radical proposal for English schools' by Stuart Maclure in The Education Life Section of the *New York Times*, 8 November 1987 (see also Cole, 1989).

Maclure describes the English system as '... on the threshold of a revolution' (p. 57), which is precisely the point I have endeavoured to make. The tools of revolutionary transformation are founded on '... the centralization of power in the Department of Education and Science' (*ibid*). The proposed uses to which this power is to be put is best understood in terms of two key dimensions. The first is the implementation of a national core curriculum (in which foundation subjects would take up 90 per cent of the week), and national assessment and testing at ages 7, 11 and 14. The second has to do with the local governence of schools. Each school is to have a board of governors including representatives of parents. This board is to have authority over spending and the power to opt out of the local authority (whilst being financially maintained by the central government). There is to be open enrollment, giving parents the choice of school for their children to attend. Finally, there is to be a complaints procedure available to parents who feel their children are not being taught the National Curriculum.

These are radical proposals indeed, though I should hasten to add, not unique to the British social landscape. With variations, such plans are being implemented in both the United States and Canada (and, I expect, in most of the Western democracies). I am intrigued by both the breadth and similarity of these educational transformations, which suggests a common response to an economic crisis that is international in scope (recall my discussion of the internationalization of capital above).

Let us now discuss these changes in light of the economic crisis. The centralization of control is a prerequisite for a national core curriculum and national assessment. This centralization of education will purge the system of its progressive, child-centered elements. The core curriculum will on the one hand eliminate 'frivolous' courses (for example, anti-racist and anti-sexist education) and on the other, ensure emphasis on the 'old fashioned' standards (for example, language and maths). National testing will maintain adherence to the curriculum, as well as constructing an élite of high achievers. This is one aspect of the toughness mentioned earlier, an intellectual toughness founded on tough standards which only 'tough' students can be expected to meet. Students are to shape-up, both intellectually and morally. They are to be better equipped to meet the needs of the labour market which is to say the requirements of the capital that will employ them.

Centralization has particular implications concerning the capacity of education to engender anti-sexist and anti-racist practices. By means of central control and the complementary decline of LEAs, both the conceptions and the significance of gender and 'race' as seen by the state become embodied in the system. The phenomenon of Thatcherism is partially constituted by an almost Victorian notion of the family and thus of gender; its stance on non-white immigration, on law and order vis-a-vis inner-city uprisings, speaks volumes about the question of 'race'. These attitudes are incorporated via the means of central control, perhaps as much by the official silence which tends to see such questions as frivolous or irrelevent in terms of the more conventional curriculum as by the advocacy of curricula of a particular bent (for example, the maintenance of mono-cultural education at worst and, at best, tolerance of multicultural rather than genuinely anti-racist education) (see chapter 7). Those local author-ities who feel that they must confront these issues, will increasingly be unable to do so. The fate of the Inner London Education Authority has a special poignancy in this context. I know that I have said very little on matters on which much needs to be said; later chapters will give these questions the attention they deserve.

But as well as this centralization of education, there simultaneously is its contradictory 'localization', not to the local authorities but to the school's board of governors. Given national curricula and assessment, one might reasonably wonder what is available for this board to control. The answer is teachers. Based on the popular dissatisfaction by parents of progressive education, this could prove a mechanism for the reduction of the professional autonomy of teachers (they will have the power to hire and fire staff).

These changes, then, are intended to attune education to the new melodies played by capital. Indisciplined youth in production and unruly unemployed youth roaming the streets are to be replaced by their oppo-sites. Capitalist production relations are to pervade more nearly the social relations of schooling; the loss of correspondence is now to be found. Quite strikingly, this is to be done with the popular support of the working class as they underwrite the restrictions on teacher autonomy. This revolution in education, then, is a response to economic crisis that re-establishes correspondence between the changing labour process and the curriculum (both overt and hidden) of schools.

Though you might suppose we are finally finished, there remains the third element of the sociological imagination – individual biography, the conjunction of social structure with history to provide for certain varieties of individuals. By way of conclusion, I wish to talk of the variety provided for by this revolution in education, focussing both on students and on teachers.

There is the theme of privatization. Recall in our discussion of the welfare state that one of the modes of restructuring in response to crisis is partial or complete privatization, what we termed recommodification or the placing of services in the market. Now opting out provisions (from the local authority) that are to be available to local schools in conjunction with parental choice of school are likely to create schools responding to private-ly expressed demands in a sort of market logic. *The Guardian* article noted above envisions the best schools being 'captured' by articulate, middle class parents creating the best for their children while leaving local authorities with poor schools in poor areas producing poor education with poor resources. If it is right, two varieties of students are made available — the best and the poor.

This example finds its logical conclusion in the private, franchised learning centres I discussed when we were talking of the noise of crisis. Through the utilization of the private market, parents were attempting to give their children a 'leg-up' on their fellows. Never forget that partici-pation in the private market depends on the ability to purchase, on income. Turning education into a commodity inevitably differentiates between those who are well able to participate and those who are not. As well as the rich and poor varieties of students, overlaying this are the competitive and non-competitive varieties.

The privatization process extends beyond simply the capacity to participate into the very nature of teaching and learning itself, for there is a kind of double commodification at work. I refer here to the commodifi-cation of knowledge and its acquisition. In those private learning centres the acquisition of knowledge was accomplished through the earning of tokens which either could be accumulated (with interest) as an intrinsic end or could be spent on desirable goods (toys). The social relations structuring education have become identical with the social relations of market consumption. Another variety of student then is the student as consumer in a private market.

The commodification of knowledge tends to transform the very nature of knowledge. I like to make the distinction between knowledge and in-formation. Information is straightforward, right or wrong, true or false. Knowledge, however, tends to be rather ephemeral, uncertain, imper-manent. Information can be learned by rote and ascertained by objective tests (for example, multiple choice). Knowledge can only be understood, acquired through genuine thinking, reflection, argument with others, and ascertained by subjective tests (for example, essay type questions in which students demonstrate their skills in developing and defending a point of view). With the former, students may be thought of as empty containers who merely have to be topped up. With the latter, students are individuals who learn by integrating it with their very selves.

There seems to be a strong association between the commodification of knowledge and the commodification of schools, the double commodifi-cation I spoke of earlier. The franchised learning centres certainly are oriented to the acquisition of information by their clientele. Given its organization, one must know whether an answer is right or wrong (how else is the incentive system to work?). With information, this is certain; with knowledge, this is not always obvious for the process of reasoned argument can produce unanticipated results. The skill lies in the ability to develop an argument rather than having the right answer. So another variety of student is being encouraged, one for whom knowledge is comprehended as information, as a commodity.

What of the variety of teacher being shaped by this particular historical/structural moment? I should like to digress for a moment to mention the new technologies being introduced to the practice of pedagogy.

Items like reading laboratories have been around for some time. These are individualized reading programmes designed to be self-taught and self-paced. They consist of colour-keyed reading cards at a variety of levels of difficulty. Students select a card, read the selection, and answer a self-administered test designed to measure comprehension. If they pass, they continue to the next card and on up the hierarchy of colours; if they fail, they are returned to an easier colour. The reason I mention this is because the logic of computer assisted instruction, so much the current fad, is identical. And I might point out, this technology transforms knowledge into information (again, there must be right and wrong answers that can objectively be measured).

Apple (1982) has assessed the change in the role of teachers brought on by these technologies. He argues that they have totally restructured pedagogical practices. Teachers have been transformed into administrators of computer programmes to students, and mediators of student movement. This learning structure reduces both the initiative and flexibility available to teachers, their autonomy to practice varieties of pedagogy. In this sense, their occupation is being deskilled. This trend is reinforced by the introduction of systematic external objective testing, which inevitably is interpreted as an assessment of teacher performance. This is the social type available for teachers to be.

People have choices over whom to be. When students and teachers confront the historically shaped structural setting, there is always some autonomy available. But some choices are ever so much easier than others for they are in concert rather than in opposition with historical development of social structure. I think this is what Mills had in mind when he talked of the varieties of individual biography.

Conclusion

I said at the beginning that the task of teaching you the sociology of education as a discipline in a single chapter is impossible. So I did not try. Instead, I felt it better to introduce you to the significant issues confronting contemporary education, analyzed from a sociological perspective. My goal was to try to make sociology useful for you, in the sense that you will be able to interpret the circumstances in which you find yourselves. I want you to have that sense of mind that Mills calls the sociological imagination in the hope that you can connect the private troubles you inevitably face with the larger public issues.

Have I succeeded? Though you are the best judge of that, if you have a different and more profound understanding of the three newspaper articles I told you of at the beginning than you did on first hearing them, then some measure of success has been achieved.

But what of future changes in the educational system that you are likely to experience if you are a member of the teaching profession? In the near future, I think they are likely to occur within the broad parameters that I have sketched above which is to say more of the same. They are likely to be more evolutionary than revolutionary in nature. If that is true, you will be able to make use of this analysis in your quest for understanding.

But at some point the investment of capital at the point of production will bring about a new set of conflicts and contradictions. Willis has shown us that the working class is never totally incorporated by capital in the labour process, that elements of opposition are structured into the capital-labour relation. At some point the social relations of production will no longer coincide with the social relations of education. Again we shall all be caught up in the throes of crisis. Then the question of progressive change will be on the agenda with its potential enhanced. Until that time, I trust you will be able, using the concepts and logic — the sociological imagination — I have introduced you to in this chapter, to make your own sense of the situation and to avoid being caught up in the rhetoric of crisis. I would also like to believe that, for those of you intending to teach, the sociological imagination will enhance empathy with your pupils/students.

I hope that you have found this chapter to be more a joy than a chore. I also hope that it will prove to be at least a bit helpful if and when you confront the everyday life of teaching.

Notes

1 A boot camp is the place where basic training of new recruits takes place.
2 Seminal works by definition generate controversy. For a sense of the controversy, see COLE (1988b). This includes a reply by Bowles and Gintis to their critics. In their later writings, they have paid much more attention to gender and 'race'. However, they have also changed their theoretical orientation from Marxism to post-liberal democracy. For a review of the changes in position by BOWLES and GINTIS, see COLE (1988a).
3 This notion of restructuring (instead of a straightforward roll-back) of the welfare state is nicely exemplified in the article 'The bill for the Bill', *Guardian Weekly*, 7 August 1988, p. 12. In it Government policy towards teachers and police are compared in terms of pay, autonomy and popular control.

References

ANYON, J. (1980) 'Social class and the hidden curriculum of work', *Journal of Education*, **162**, 1.

APPLE, M. (1982) 'Curricular form and the logic of technical control: Building the possessive individual', in APPLE, M. (Ed) *Cultural and Economic Reproduction in Education*, London, Routledge & Kegan Paul.

BERNSTEIN, B. (1975) *Class, Codes and Control: Towards a Theory of Educational Transmissions*, Vol 3, London, Routledge & Kegan Paul.

BOWLES, S. and GINTIS, H. (1976) *Schooling in Capitalist America: Educational Reform and the Contradictions of Economic Life*, New York, Basic Books.

COHEN, STANLEY (1985) *Visions of Social Control*, Cambridge, Polity Press.

COHEN, STEVE (1985) 'Anti-semitism, immigration controls and the welfare state', *Critical Social Policy*, **13**, summer.

COLE, M. (1988a) 'From reductionist Marxism and revolutionary socialism to post-liberal democracy and ambiguity: Some comments on the changing political philosophy of Bowles and Gintis', *British Journal of Sociology*, **39**, 3.

COLE, M. (Ed) (1988b) *Bowles and Gintis Revisited: Correspondence and Contradiction in Education Theory*, Lewes, Falmer Press.

COLLINS, R. (1982) *Sociological Insight: An Introduction to Non-obvious Sociology*, New York, Oxford University Press.

FINN, D., GRANT, N. and JOHNSON, R. (1978) 'Social democracy, education and the crisis', in CENTRE FOR CONTEMPORARY STUDIES (Eds) *On Ideology*, London, Hutchinson.

GIDDENS, A. (1982) *Sociology: A Brief but Critical Introduction*, London, Harcourt Brace & Jovanovich.

GOUGH, I. (1979) *The Political Economy of the Welfare State*, London, Macmillan.

HALL, S. *et al* (1978) *Policing the Crisis: Mugging, the State and Law and Order*, London, Macmillan.

LEE, D. and NEWBY, H. (1983) *The Problem of Sociology*, London, Hutchinson.

MACPHERSON, C. (1965) *The Real World of Democracy*, Toronto, CBC Publications.

MILLS, C. (1959) *The Sociological Imagination*, New York, Grove Press.

SHARP, R. and GREEN, A. (1975) *Education and Social Control*, London, Routledge & Kegan Paul.

WILLIS, P. (1977) *Learning to Labour*, Farnborough, Saxon House.

Part 2
History

Chapter 2

The Rise of Mass Schooling

Clive Griggs

Introduction

It may seem that it would be simple enough to chart the facts of the development of mass schooling and find historians arguing only about their interpretation. This, however, is not so and one of the reasons is because there are disagreements as to the validity of the statistics collected relating to schooling in the first half of the nineteenth century. Moreover, although we may use similar words such as school, teacher or subjects taught, they are often applied to experiences which were very different from one period to another. Even the most basic comparison between schooling during the mid-nineteenth and mid-twentieth centuries will emphasize this point. In the former period the majority of children did not attend school regularly; in the latter they did. Most teaching staff were unqualified in the 1850s and had not attended a college course; almost all teachers were two- or three-year college trained by the 1950s whilst those leaving college in the 1980s were all graduates. During the nineteenth century hardly any children from average or below average income families attended secondary schools; after 1944 all children received secondary schooling. The school leaving age was 10 in 1876, 14 in 1918 and 16 in 1972. The elementary school curriculum as laid down by the 1862 Revised Code was basic and narrow; it had been transformed by the second half of the twentieth century. Hardly any children gained formal qualifications in the nineteenth century, about 15 per cent did in the 1950s but only 15 per cent did not by the 1980s. There was a substantial reduction in class size with numbers nearing the fifty mark in some classes at the turn of the century but nearer to thirty in most classes by the 1980s.[1] Schools in general became happier more humane places and the relationship between pupils and staff more friendly and part of this was a result of the move away from rote learning to an emphasis on the need for children to understand what they were being taught.

Whilst there were always those who looked back nostalgically to their own schooldays and claimed that standards had fallen official surveys concerning examination results proved to the contrary that standards had continued to rise.[2] There were critics who argued against changes within the education system; some for genuine educational reasons although others used education language, such as 'parental choice' or 'falling standards' to hide political views which longed to restore the social privileges of a past era.

The general changes listed above need to be charted but more detail is needed in order to understand both the complexity and significance of many of these moves. Acts of Parliament are useful markers to developments in schooling, such as the 1870 or 1902 Education Acts but it must be realized that they are often the culmination of many years of argument by conflicting pressure groups in society and that their interpretation will owe much to the climate of opinion in succeeding years. Attitudes are more difficult to measure although even here there are common themes which can be traced throughout the period being studied. There were always those who believed that providing education for all children was too expensive and that the majority needed only a limited schooling; limited by the kind of work they would be required to do later in life. There were claims that some teachers might be a dangerous threat if they held non-conformist ideas concerning religion, politics or life-style as well as concern that too much education might make youngsters discontented and unwilling to take on some of the more mundane lower paid jobs. Conversely, there were also groups who sought to improve the quality of education for all children and who argued that social conditions needed to be improved too if children were to make the best use of the schooling provided; hence the demands for school meals, medical inspection and treatment, and subsidized transport in rural areas.

Some believed only a minority should be well educated because only a small proportion were capable of understanding complex ideas and the nation could only afford advanced schooling for a few; others argued that for economic, political as well as humane reasons the nation needed to provide a good broad education for all its children and that training for work was something which should be delayed and probably provided by colleges and employers later. Just how far these themes can be traced can only be determined by looking at the period in greater detail.

Education for the Masses Prior to 1870

It is possible to argue that this period witnessed both the rise of considerable school provision for the masses and the realization that voluntary efforts alone could not cope with the scale of schooling needed for the growing population. There had been schools in Britain at least as far back as Roman times[3] but well down into the nineteenth century schooling was always limited to a minority of children. For the majority of children in the two generations prior to 1870 the schooling available was likely to be through one of the following: attendance at a Sunday school, a charity school, a dame school or one of the monitorial schools of the two major religious societies.[4] The Sunday school movement was popularized by Robert Raikes in the 1780s although he was not the first to run such a school. The main purpose of the Sunday school was to teach children the Bible, say the Church Catechism and prayers; the hidden curriculum was to teach the 'lower classes' to be pious, industrious and to know their place in society. Charity schools went back to at least the Reformation but most had their roots in the eighteenth century. A benefactor would establish an endowment from which the salary of a teacher or even the cost of a school would be provided and local prominent citizens encouraged to make contributions to the upkeep and resources of the school. From the beginning of the eighteenth century the Society for the Promotion of Christian Knowledge (SPCK) helped to support such schools by encouraging church collections for this purpose. These schools were intended for the poor and whilst reading and writing were taught there was much emphasis on 'moral and religious discipline and social subordination. In the hymns they sang, the prayers they recited and sermons they had to listen to, the charity children were constantly reminded of their low estate and the duty and respect they owed their betters'.[5] Dame schools varied widely but most seem to have taken place in the house of a teacher, usually female, who minded children for a few pence a week and often taught the alphabet and perhaps some basic elements of the 3Rs. Further consideration of their place in nineteenth-century education will be given later.

The Monitorial Schools

The most significant development of the early nineteenth century was the monitorial schools established by Joseph Lancaster and Andrew Bell. Arguments as to who was the originator of the idea need not concern us here. Lancaster, a Quaker, opened a school for poor children in 1798, and in 1814 the British and Foreign School Society was established which took over from Lancaster, whose organizational powers did not match his enthusiasm for the idea. Bell, an Anglican member of the clergy is credited with starting the monitorial system in Madras in the 1790s and in 1811 the Church of England established the National Society for Promoting the Education of the Poor in the Principles of the Established Church. These two societies were in competition and whilst this led to the building of numerous schools, with the latter having the largest number, the rivalry also prevented attempts to develop a national system of elementary education for much of the nineteenth century.[6] A teacher would be put in charge of 150 or more children who would be divided into groups of ten or twenty, each in turn supervised by a monitor about 11 years of age. The teacher taught the monitors who in turn presented the material to the children. It was in fact the application of factory production methods to schooling and its main virtue, as far as the higher income groups were concerned, was its cheapness. Only one teacher was required, rote learning was the order of the day and discipline was kept by the teacher and monitors who used canes to 'encourage' pupils to obey their every instruction. The three Rs, the Bible and sewing for girls formed the basic diet. The 1831 manual of the BFSS prepared for their elementary schools gave detailed instructions for the teacher to follow every part of the day, including the manner in which the children should enter, the orders for children to prepare to write on their slates, to wipe them clean, to put on hats, all in the form of drill-like commands. Such methodology reinforced the ethos of children as products to be processed so that they might respond mechanically more like programmed robots rather than as pupils capable of independent thought.

There were exceptions to such a pattern, and the outstanding example was the school organized by Robert Owen at the New Lanark Mills which he managed in the early nineteenth century. Here children were offered a wider curriculum which included geography, history, dancing and singing, in classroom surroundings which contained pictures and where there was an emphasis on the moral development of children encouraged by a more sympathetic attitude to young children. Owen's support for socialist ideas and his hostility to organized religion were partly responsible for a decline in his reputation as a pioneer educator for much of the nineteenth century[7] although his ideas lived on among the Chartists of the 1840s and his infant school at New Lanark was the inspiration for Samuel Wilderspin's Infant School Society established in 1824.[8]

The pattern established in most elementary schools during the first half of the nineteenth century and continued in varying degrees down to the end of that century helped to establish a folklore of schooling still acted out in many twentieth century comics, pantomines and young children 'playing at schools', in the form of dunces' caps, bullying teachers and constant caning. Whilst four main types of schools have been mentioned this hides a myriad of attempts at schooling in the nineteenth century which makes it difficult to talk of a system of even elementary schooling. Laissez-faire attitudes in a society which did not see it as the province of the state to intervene in the health, education or social well-being of its citizens resulted in disparate educational provision in which the quality of the teachers, teaching, school buildings or spaces where schooling took place varied so widely that generalizations can be very misleading. The very least that can be said with any certainty for the first half of the nineteenth century is that there were insufficient places for those of school age to have attended if they had all wished to do so.

Resistance to an Elementary School System

One might have expected that the nation which was the leader of the Industrial Revolution would also be a leader in the education and welfare of its citizens but this was not the case for a variety of reasons, many of which were to do with one form or another of vested interest. The technology of the early industrial revolution was very basic and the inventions produced by people with practical workshop skills rather than theoretical knowledge. To that extent only a limited education was necessary in order to make initial progress in industrialization[9] and even when Britain became the leading commercial nation a mere 100,000 clerks administered the system. Whilst it might make sense to look for educational reasons behind the promotion of schooling it is just as likely that economic and political reasons were at least of equal significance.

Hostility to schooling arose from a number of groups. Compulsory schooling would mean an end to child labour and that was resented by employers who saw both women and children as a cheaper form of labour than men. Thousands of children were employed in factories, especially the textile mills. On the land some worked in gangs under sub-contractors who negotiated a price with the farmer for harvesting a crop and paid their gangs a pittance. Children worked as part of the migrant canal boat population and thousands provided casual labour in the towns running errands, selling small items such as matchboxes on street corners at late hours, or acting as beaters for local hunts in rural areas. Such employers were an effective pressure group resisting the introduction and extension of both elementary and secondary education for all children. There were parents too who supported such a stance; some out of ignorance, others out of economic necessity where the few pence earned by their children kept the family budget just above the subsistence level in a society where social security was unknown. Initially there were those who argued against the provision of schooling for the masses in the belief that they might read revolutionary material such as Tom Paine's *Rights of Man* (published in 1791); later it was possible to argue that education carefully structured could act to deter revolutionary thoughts among the people.[10]

Schooling According to Social Class

The divisions of social class in Victorian Britain were not only starkly visible in terms of consumption, dress, living accommodation and social well-being but permeated almost every aspect of society. The ranking of people forms the back-cloth to the work of so many of the great novelists writing within this period from Charles Dickens (1812–70), and Elizabeth Gaskell (1810–65) to John Galsworthy (1867–1933) whilst official reports openly referred to social class; hence the first serious attempts by Parliament in 1816 to assess the provision of basic schooling was entitled 'Reports of the Parliamentary Committees on the Education of the Lower Orders in the Metropolis and Beyond'.[11] Similarly later reports considering secondary education for the middle classes were just as frank; the Clarendon Report of 1864 dealing with the major public schools[12] naively claimed that 'men of all the various classes that make up English society, destined for every profession and career, have been brought up on a footing of social equality, ...'[13] a claim even less valid in the nineteenth century than it is today when 85 per cent of those who attend the Clarendon schools come from social classes 1 and 2.[14] The Taunton Report of 1868 dealing with those secondary schools other than the famous nine claimed that there were three grades of these schools and the distinction was not in the ability of the pupils but in the social class of the fathers which determined the future expectations of the boys' life chances; hence the schools could be classified according to differences in the curriculum and the school leaving age of 14, 16, or 18.[15] The piecemeal development of schooling, the rivalry of the two major religious societies, the variety of places offering 'education', many of them short-lived, to say nothing of the low standard of most teaching in mid-Victorian Britain, brought an increasing awareness of the need for some kind of regular system of elementary schooling. The Education Department was set up in 1856 as an administrative part of the Committee of Council and two years later set up a Royal Commission 'To enquire into the present state of popular education in England, and to consider and report what measures, if any, are required for the extension of sound and cheap elementary instruction to all classes of people'. In spite of the mention of all classes 'The Commission interpreted the terms of reference to mean the education of the independent poor, but it also made enquiries into the education of pauper, vagrant and criminal children...'.[16] This attempt to gain a comprehensive picture of the provision of schooling concluded that 2,535,462 out of 2,655,767 of the poorer classes were in school but the statistics were considered to be a gross exaggeration of the situation at the time and have been a point of controversy ever since. The Commission supported the continuing monopoly of the denominational societies in schooling and that schooling should be neither compulsory nor free, except to the poorest children. The request to consider the provision of cheap elementary schooling was in line with the thinking of the Victorian middle classes who resented paying taxes or providing for the welfare of children in families less prosperous than their own. It was up to each family to fend for itself and not expect help from the State although some charities might occasionally be able to help the poor. This strain of Victorian thought has remained strong in Britain and resurfaces from time to time, most recently in the 1980s.

Usually the different social classes attended different schools as surely as they lived in separate neighbourhoods but at least one interesting exception can be traced in the Liverpool College founded in 1840 and opened with much public ceremony and acclaim. It catered for three different social classes and whilst they could all be said to attend the same school they had little internal contact; they used separate staircases, rooms and playgrounds. Even the assembly hall in which they all met guaranteed separation as each social rank sat in a different tier so that they could all see the stage but not each other. On the landing iron railings ensured that the children should not mingle and the ending of schooltime was staggered so that parents and children should not be embarrassed by meeting those from a different social grouping. It was social apartheid with a vengeance.[17]

Schooling for Working Class Girls

There can be no doubt that nineteenth century Britain was a patriarchal society in which women faced discrimination in education, careers and legal rights. Yet this needs some qualifying in terms of the schooling and occupation of working class girls. As a generalization they received the same limited and inadequate schooling as working class boys and whilst it is true that sewing and cookery were given to girls while boys did more arithmetic the outcome was of less consequence than might at first be considered. The majority of boys and girls were destined for work associated with the local community; girls into domestic service (there were about 1.4 million domestic servants in 1871, mostly female), shops, cotton mills or agricultural work. Boys went into the coal mines, docks, railways and also agriculture. The education received was largely irrelevant. Ben Pickard (1842–1904) later to become a leading trade unionist, attended Kippax Grammar School but he still left school at 12 years of age and went into the pits.

In Victorian Britain women were not fighting for the right to work; working class women had always worked. The main struggle towards the end of the century was of a minority of middle class women who wanted equal access to the kinds of careers which men of similar social standing were able to pursue. Such women wanted to be doctors rather than nurses, university lecturers not elementary school teachers. The wider differences in the curriculum between boys and girls were to be found in the single-sex fee-paying schools of the middle classes rather than in the co-educational elementary schools provided for the masses. This is not to say that gender did not play a part but it was always subordinate to social class. In any case to suggest that a boy of twelve or fourteen going underground in a coal mine, where fatal accidents were running at 1000 per annum in the 1890s, was better off than a girl of similar age going into domestic service is doubtful.

Balancing the danger of one against the hardship of the other is a futile exercise.[18] In general the work of boys and men was more dangerous as the accidents in mines, the docks and the railways make clear. However, health and life chances varied more between social classes than male and female, as they still do today. The curriculum in physical education for boys and girls began to diverge in the 1890s with boys still concentrating on military drill whilst girls moved over to Swedish Drill. The result for many of the boys was the terrible carnage of the 1914–18 war. It is true that many men were always concerned that women would be used to do 'their work' at a reduced rate of pay; a concern born of bitter experience. It must also be said that there were always men who struggled to remove women and children from some of the dirtiest and dangerous jobs not for fear of rivalry but out of genuine concern for their health and safety, for it was their wives and daughters most likely to be at risk.

Payment by Results

Whilst the findings of the Newcastle Commission were largely ignored the one thing that was seized upon was the revision of the Code by which schools received grants because these had risen from £20,000 in 1833 when they were first introduced to £125,000 by 1849. Shortly afterwards the enormous expense of the Crimean War (1854–56) had to be met and economic stringency in expenditure on education was in the mind of the Government. The result was the introduction of the Revised Code of 1862 by Robert Lowe, which became known as 'Payment by Results' because a teacher's pay was related to the results obtained by the pupils. From now on, for a school to obtain a grant, it must employ a certificated teacher, pupils must attend at least 200 times (morning and afternoon were counted as two separate sessions) and the pupils had to pass a required standard at an annual examination carried out by one of Her Majesty's Inspectors. Initially there were six standards but a seventh was added later in 1882 by which time children were beginning to stay on at school longer. Lowe's oft quoted remarks in the House of Commons promising that if the system 'is not cheap it shall be efficient; if it is not efficient it shall be cheap' was illustrated well by the reduction which followed in the Government grant for education to the religious societies from £813,441 in 1862 to £636,806 in 1865.

By introducing annual tests it was believed that standards of education would rise because teachers would be forced to pay more attention to pupils deemed as less able as their salary would be related to the academic performance of such children. The Code was bitterly resented by most teachers primarily because they had little influence upon school attendance, especially in rural areas. A major problem at least down to the 1890s was the irregular attendance of many pupils because in many hard pressed families schooling was not afforded first priority. Children were frequently required to stay at home; girls often to nurse a sick member of the family or do household chores, boys to help with some form of paid employment.

Illness was a constant source of absenteeism. There were the usual ailments of influenza, sore throats and chilblains but more frightening were epidemics such as measles, scarlet fever and diptheria in which attendance was affected by parents keeping their children at home for fear of contagion or the school being closed because of the severity of the outbreak. The rapid spread of epidemics was a subject in most school log books, a form of school diary made compulsory in 1863. Aldingbourne Village in West Sussex provides a typical example when the Medical Authority instructed the school to be closed on 3 December 1883 and it was to remain so until 14 January 1884. The entry for the first school day of 1884 read, 'Several deaths have occurred and parents as well as children have been smitten by the disease'.[19] On a less dramatic scale infections such as ring worm and head lice were common features of school life until the School Medical Service, introduced in 1907, began to tackle the causes of such parasites in a methodical manner. In these situations the taunts of class mates brought considerable embarrassment to the children concerned.

In rural areas the major cause of irregular attendance was inclement weather. Torrential rain or falls of snow meant that 'unmade roads' became impassable and poor children who only possessed one pair of shoes and sometimes no topcoat at all were kept at home. For those living nearer or more prosperous who made the journey to school their clothing would be set to dry around the fire bringing a smell that was a common feature of rural school classrooms. Infrequent attendance made school progress difficult. A child might begin with one area of work, be away for a week or more only to find upon their return that the class had moved on so that he or she was now behind in their work. Another period of absence could mean that the pupils forgot what they had learned earlier. For some children school was a place to go only if no other demands were placed upon their time by parents. Even those on school management committees, especially in rural areas, tended to ignore school absence when children were working for a local landowner or, in the case of older girls, helping with the housework at the vicarage or squire's residence.[20] Teachers' incomes became related to the area in which they taught; in poor urban or remote rural areas where attendance was low and academic standards depressed the teachers found this reflected in their pay so that they were encouraged to move to better urban areas where the catchment zone of the school ensured a situation in which more affluent parents were willing and able to send their children to school regularly. The Code dominated school life for a generation falling into general disuse in the 1890s and being finally terminated in 1898.

It has been argued that at first the Code did raise standards at least in the 3Rs but it was considered to have a narrowing effect on both the school curriculum and methods of teaching in which rote learning became reinforced so that children might be able to repeat the correct answers at the annual HMI visit.

The State Intervenes: The 1870 Education Act

The 1870 Education Act can be seen as the major landmark in mass schooling in the Victorian Age. It was, like much legislation, a compromise in an attempt to establish an elementary school system in the face of a variety of conflicting interests and this explains the form it took. It did not make schooling compulsory. This would have been impossible as there were not enough school places for all children, some employers would have resisted such moves and so would some poor families. There was in any case a justified suspicion among many working class people of any Government attempt to provide a social service for the most enduring example, and one which was to haunt generations of working class families, was the workhouse system, an earlier Government 'initiative' in 1834 to deal with unemployment, pauperism and old age as cheaply as possible.

The Act did not make education free. It was believed that the State could not, and should not, provide schooling for children with the possible exception of the very poor, and the religious schools which charged fees would not have accepted a rival system of free schooling. Yet the Act did argue that after a generation of effort the religious voluntary societies had failed to provide a sufficient number of schools and therefore the State had to intervene. It did so by allowing an area lacking in school provision to set up a school board which would comprise between five and fifteen members, according to size, who would be elected on a cumulative system triennially by the burgesses and ratepayers of the community. Hence, if there were eight candidates each voter had eight votes. Women had equal rights with men in the election as both voters and candidates and the schools were to be financed by the rates. Religious bodies were to be given a year's grace to get in applications for building a school before a school board could be established. The result was that whereas such applications from the Church of England had numbered 226 in 1869 they suddenly shot up to 3003 in the last six months of 1870. Whilst it is possible to suggest that a system of elementary education did come into being after 1870 it was one which was divided, often bitterly, between the national schools of the Church of England and the growing number of board schools. Battle lines were drawn up with the Conservative Party fully supporting the church schools whilst most non-conformists, Liberals and members of the growing Labour movement supported the board schools.[21] Hence the 'Church Party' put up candidates and captured some school boards whose activities they were able to curtail to avoid any threat that might be posed to their own schools. Elsewhere non-conformists and supporters of non-denominational religion won elections and enthusiastically provided good resources for the new schools. The London School Board became a powerful leader in the provision of good elementary education and the Bradford School Board, under the inspiration of Margaret McMillan, pioneered supporting social services in the form of school meals, baths and medical inspection. By the turn of the century the quality of mass elementary education had risen dramatically and much of this had been to do with the resources provided by school boards who were in general able to provide superior buildings, better teaching resources and offer higher rates of pay than the voluntary schools of the Church of England and comparatively small number of Roman Catholic Schools.

Education for Social Control

It is worth pausing here to consider how far the system was set up with the intention of 'controlling' the working class so that they would accept the values of Victorian society. Inevitably all societies attempt to socialize the young according to the belief and value system of the dominant group and to that extent education provided from above, whether it be by the church or the State, will have features of social control. How conscious these moves were is not easy to show because frank statements spelling out such a motive were not made frequently. They can be found, however, as in the case of Sir James Kay Shuttleworth when he was referring to the approximately 50,000 children in workhouses in need of schooling:

> The great object to be kept in view in regulating any school for the instruction of the children of the labouring class, is the rearing of hardy and intelligent working men, whose character and habits shall afford the largest amount of security to the property and order of the community.[22]

Robert Lowe's concern was that of many Victorians: that the working class should know their place in the social hierarchy. 'If the lower classes must now be educated to discharge their new duties, they must also "be educated that they may appreciate and defer to a higher cultivation when they meet it".'[23] Long before Bowles and Gintis had made the correspondence principle popular[24] H.G. Wells had written that, 'The Education Act of 1870 was not an Act for a common universal education, it was an Act to educate the lower classes for employment in lower class lines'.

Writers of varying ideologies have argued that the State stepped in to take control of education because they were unhappy with the influence of different agencies providing education. E.G. West has claimed that if left alone enough religious schools would have been built within a decade or

Clive Griggs

so to complete the system. West's main argument is that the 1870 Education Act enabled a State monopoly to arise in elementary schooling.[25] However, his alternative would have led to a religious monopoly for a population many of whom were sharply divided along established church and non-conformist lines, with a significant Roman Catholic minority in certain areas such as Lancashire, whilst many of the population were indifferent to the denominational disputes. Religious societies did see their schools as a means of gaining converts and they resented rival schools. Canon Sanderson expressed such views at a ruri-decanal conference at the turn of the century:

> '... the Church was losing its influence over a vast number of children that were being brought up and taught in this country and was allowing these children either to fall into religious indifference or to subsist on a colourless religious teaching as implied by the term undenominational religion.[26]

Alongside the spiritual message went a social message buttressing the class system of Victorian Britain justified in the words of the well known hymn *All Things Bright and Beautiful*:

> The rich man in his castle,
> The poor man at the gate,
> God made them high and lowly
> And ordered their estate.

Laquer has suggested that Sunday schools for the first half of the nineteenth century were largely attempts by the working class to fulfil their own specific needs providing a culture of self-help and improvement but that they were gradually taken over by the middle classes.[27] Whilst allowing for a few exceptions this idea does not fit in with the general picture of schools which did provide some teaching of basic literacy but always alongside a conformist view advocating the maintenance of the status quo.[28] In similar vein Gardner has argued in great detail that dame schools were in effect working class private schools which were perceived as a threat by the State so that pressure was put upon them until the majority went under. That the working class attended these schools is true and a few did provide a basic schooling for infants. To that extent they were accommodating the working class but they were not designed by the working class. It is a romantic view of working class history, tantamount to saying that because poor people lived in slums they were part of their culture and should have been preserved as such. There were cases of good infant teaching among the great variety of dame schools but because they accommodated the life styles of the working class, allowing children to come and go as their parents pleased, this does not mean they were part of any positive political ideology of that class. In general the teacher lacked any specific training in education and there was a low level of

46

educational intention and achievement whilst the accommodation which might be a bedroom, workshop or cellar was hardly conducive to serious learning. In Liverpool for example,

> With few exceptions, the dame schools are dark and confined; many are damp and dirty, more than one half of them are used as dwelling, dormitory, and school room, accommodating, in many cases, families of seven or eight persons. Above forty of them are cellars.[29]

The testament of trade unionists who attended them as children credit them with little more than teaching the alphabet.[30] It may be considered neither fashionable nor radical to suggest that the State stepped in to provide elementary schooling because whatever the past efforts of Sunday schools, dame and voluntary schools may have been they were inadequate in providing elementary education for the school population of England and Wales. Moreover, there is plenty of evidence to show that most leaders of the labour movement welcomed state intervention in terms of school boards, free and compulsory education because they had experienced the inadequate provision of schooling by various other agencies in their own school days.[31]

However much the State may have wished to design a limited education for the masses, the structure it created, the school board system, enabled those committed to improved education and welfare of all children to develop a system which was far better in terms of teaching, school buildings and resources than that which prevailed prior to 1870. The boards succeeded in attracting talented people who were able to promote good practice knowing that the funding could and would be met by the rates. Within the next generation schooling was transformed for most children as attendance committees and officers began to check up on children and their parents when repeated absence arose. The action taken by magistrates varied and was probably less effective in rural areas where a combination of tradition and squirarchy were likely to prove too powerful a combination to defeat. However, the improvement in attendance encouraged by Mundella's 1880 Act making schooling compulsory up to the age of 10 and the 1891 Act which removed most elementary school fees enabled considerable progress to be made. So much so that a VIIth standard was added to the Code in 1882. Moreover in some areas children deemed as able, often from homes of artisans, shopkeepers and clerks in which strong encouragement was given to success at school, extra 'higher grade' classes were provided for work beyond standard VII. At Sheffield in 1876 a higher grade school was established to bring such children together and soon progressive school boards in other towns such as Barrow, Bradford, Birmingham, Nottingham, Leeds and Brighton began to follow this pattern. London did not take up the idea until the 1890s. These schools which charged up to 9d (4p) per week were in effect secondary schools in all but name for working class children, yet their very success led to their downfall.

Some of those hostile to the boards for different reasons have been mentioned. In addition there were the grammar schools which were concerned about the competition provided by higher grade schools at only a fraction of the fees they charged for secondary education. Ratepayers were easily roused against the boards which were considered to be extravagant as indeed they were in comparison with voluntary schools to which members of the community could choose whether to contribute or not.

It is quite possible to argue that by the late 1890s the provision of elementary education was in administrative chaos with board and denominational schools, and at least three organizations, the Education Department, the Science and Art Department and the Charity Commissioners having some say in the organization and funding of various aspects of schooling. This muddle was largely a result of the compromise to reform which had needed to take into account numerous vested interests. What cannot be in doubt is that the school board system had provided education for the masses on a scale hardly envisaged a generation earlier. It is possible too to suggest that it was providing education of a much higher standard than was considered desirable by some higher income groups. An added irritant was the democratic nature of the school boards which were elected. When the Tories were returned to power in 1895 they were determined to destroy the school boards and they did this by a familiar tactic. They used the courts. They demonstrated that the London School Board was providing education above that of an elementary nature for which they had been originally established.[32]

Creating an Imperial Nation

Imperialism has been defined as:

> an ideological cluster which formed out of the intellectual, national and world wide conditions of the late Victorian era, and which came to infuse and be propagated by every organ of British life in the period. It was made up of a renewed militarism, a devotion to royalty, an identification and worship of national heroes, together with a contemporary cult of personality, and racial ideas associated with Social Darwinism.[33]

There are elements mentioned here which could be traced back to the Crimean War, and for those who believe that the kind of sentiments expressed in the years covered became extinct with the discrediting of militarism after World War I the scenes depicted on television and the jingoism fostered in the newspapers during the 1982 Falklands Conflict made it clear that some of the ideas merely lay dormant.

Imperialist views were propagated in varying forms to British youth both outside the school and within. Outside a whole range of paramilitary organizations were established for boys including the Boys' Brigade, Church Lads' Brigade, Army and Naval cadets and the Boy Scouts, with sister groups for girls, such as the Girl Guides and the Girls Life Brigade.[34] The Scouts developed directly out of Baden Powell's wartime experiences although in time it became the least militaristic. Uniforms, band parades and drill formed a staple diet and at numerous events and imperial celebrations such organizations were always in evidence. The leading officers of the movements were usually ex-officers from the armed services or members of the Volunteer Force, National Service League, teaching profession or clergy. These organizations served many purposes including the provision of organized activities for the leisure time of working class youth, most of whom were recruited to these movements from the homes of artisans and clerical workers, but they also reinforced the need to be prepared to defend the Empire against other nations, as outlined in the chapter entitled 'How the Empire must be held' in the last edition of Baden Powell's *Scouting for Boys*.[35]

Within the schools imperialism took several forms. The fee-paying schools had developed team games in the nineteenth century and linked them to war, which was made to appear as a kind of game.[36] The socially privileged pupils attending private schools spent time in the Officer Training Corps to ensure that they would be leaders in both civil and military roles within the Empire. Those destined to be led from the elementary schools were partly prepared by the introduction of military drill which was a major feature on the school curriculum.[37]

The extent of indirect and direct teaching as to the virtues of the Empire can be found in the former through popular literature typified by Robert Ballantyne's (1825–94) output of over 100 stories including *Coral Island* and *Martin Rattler*, and John Buchan's (1875–1940) adventure stories including *Prestor John*, *The Thirty Nine Steps* and *Greenmantle*. Alongside the fiction were biographies of British heroes of the Empire from Robert Clive to Cecil Rhodes and numerous cheap magazines with titles like *Boys of the Empire* and *Boys Champion*, many of which lasted a few years, went out of publication, only to be replaced on the bookstalls by similar titled periodicals.

The school textbook was the most direct form of teaching about Britain's imperial role. History and geography were the main vehicles for the message which lasted so long because many went into numerous editions and because sets of texts remained in school departments for years, partly due to the lack of funds to replace them but also because the ideology contained went almost unnoticed as it was the accepted view.

49

For this reason it also went unchallenged for so long. One of the most well known was Fletcher and Kipling's *A History of England* with such statements as 'to serve king and country in the Army is the second best profession for Englishmen of all classes; to serve in the Navy, I suppose we must all admit, is the best'.[38] Suggestions of abolishing the House of Lords or granting independence to India were described as 'reactionary' and direct racism fostered by passages like the one referring to the decline in prosperity in the West Indies since the abolition of slavery:

> The population is mainly black, descended from slaves imported in previous centuries, or of mixed black and white race; lazy, vicious and incapable of any serious improvement, or of work except under compulsion. In such a climate a few bananas will sustain the life of a negro quite sufficiently; why should he work to get more than this? He is quite happy and quite useless, and spends any extra wages which he may earn upon finery.[39]

According to MacKenzie 'Geography texts were the prime purveyors of racial ideas'[40] and one text described the African as 'an overgrown child, vain, self indulgent, and fond of idleness ... he has never developed the qualities of industry, self denial, and forethought'.[41] Social Darwinism and ecological determinism were applied to explain the comparative technological backwardness of some nations and the contrasting superiority of the British. Wallcharts and posters stressed the value of the Empire as a source of raw materials for Britain from the rubber of Malaya to the cocoa of West Africa, all well managed by Europeans. In return the civilizing influence of Britain was stressed through medical services and engineering, both important but not the only source of influence exported from the motherland.

Between the two World Wars the picture of British military heroism in the fight to impose the 'benefits' of Empire upon other lands was reinforced for children and adults by both British and American films such as 'Sanders of the River' (GB, 1935), 'The Four Feathers' (US, 1929; GB, 1939) and 'Lives of a Bengal Lancer' (US, 1934). Permeating so much of life were the advertisements in magazines or on hoardings featuring products from the Empire, often showing a contented native population working on tea plantations or rolling barrels of rum in the West Indies. As radio developed so this form of communication served to boost the Empire from the monarch's opening address broadcast from the Empire exhibition at Wembley in 1924 to the first Christmas message in 1932 and the jubilee celebrations in 1935.

In the post-World War II period the stories of Empire still formed the basis for radio, television programmes and new films, such as *Zulu* (GB, 1964) and *Khartoum* (GB, 1966) although greater empathy for the other side now came through. Britain was by no means unique in fostering patriotism, nationalism or even imperialism. One has only to consider the record of Nazi Germany between the two world wars to put things into perspective. One legacy, however, of British imperial propaganda has been the difficulty for so many British people to accept that the loss of Empire has reduced their power in terms of resources and that other countries are more likely to judge them in terms of their industrial performance rather than upon the size of their military budget or their possession of a seat on the United Nations Security Council, one more reflection of a past era.

Children in schools today are still grappling with the contradiction of the way in which people from different countries are depicted in books, films, advertisements and other forms of the media in comparison with their everyday experience of living alongside children whose parents or grandparents came from such lands. The necessary adjustments for all children are not always easy to make.

Notes

1 In 1986 75.1 per cent of primary school and 90.7 per cent of secondary school classes had thirty or fewer pupils (*Social Trends*, 1988, 18, table 3.6, p. 53, London, HMSO).

2 The percentage of boys and girls passing five or more 'O' levels (grade A to C) and two or more 'A' levels increased between 1975/76 and 1985/86. Moreover, the older members of the public were in general less well qualified formally than young adults (*Social Trends*, 1988, 18, tables 3.12 and 3.13 respectively, p. 57, London, HMSO).

3 For early developments in schooling see LAWSON, J. and SILVER, H. (1973) *A Social History of Education in England*, London, Methuen; and SIMON, J. (1986) *Education and Society in Tudor England*, Cambridge, Cambridge University Press.

4 For details about these years see LAWSON, J. and SILVER, H. (1973) *op cit*, chapters 7 and 8; and SIMON, B. (1960) *Studies in the History of Education 1780–1870*, London, Lawrence & Wishart.

5 LAWSON, J. and SILVER, H. (1973) *op cit*, p. 184.

6 A stream of bills were defeated by one religious group, or a combination of several if there was a hint of secularism; Graham's Factory Act 1843, W. J. Fox's Secular Bill 1850, Russell's Bill 1855, etc.

7 See SILVER, H. (1983) 'Reputation and the educational system: The case of Robert Owen' in SILVER, H. (Ed) *Education as History*, London, Methuen.

8 Wilderspin's reputation also suffered from his opposition to the Established Church and the stereotyping of the rote methods he recommended in one of his earliest publications. For a detailed study of Wilderspin's experience as an infant teacher and his contribution to the establishment of infant schooling in Britain see McCANN, P. and YOUNG, F.A. (1982) *Samuel Wilderspin and the Infant School Movement*, Beckenham, Croom Helm.

9 HOBSBAWM, E.J. (1968) *Industry and Empire*, London, Weidenfeld & Nicolson, chapter 2.

10 'Of all the arguments that were used to persuade the propertied classes to subscribe to the building of schools, that of the need to avert revolution was the most effective. Chartist leaders, albeit unintentionally, were more successful in loosen-

ing the purse strings of the charitable than were the incumbents of the throne.'
(HURT, J. (1972) *Education in Evolution*, London, Paladin.)

11 MACLURE, J.S. (Ed) (1986) *Educational Documents*, London, Methuen, p. 18.

12 These were Eton, Charterhouse, Harrow, Merchant Taylors, Rugby, St Pauls, Shrewsbury, Westminster and Winchester.

13 MACLURE, J.S. (1986) *op cit*, p. 87.

14 HALSEY, A.H., HEATH, A.F. and RIDGE, J.M. (1980) *Origins and Destinations*, Oxford, Clarendon Press, pp. 202–3.

15 MACLURE, J.S. (1986) *op cit*, pp. 92–5. There is little evidence to show that the Taunton Report, which in theory should have dealt with the schooling of girls in all schools other than elementary, really paid much attention to them. It divided the education required according to the leaving age of pupils but all the examples I have been able to locate refer exclusively to boys.

16 The Newcastle Report of 1861; MACLURE, J.S. (1986) *op cit*, p. 71.

17 See DIGBY, A. and SEARBY, P. (1981) *Children, School and Society in Nineteenth Century England*, London, Macmillan, pp. 125–7.

18 This is a controversial area in the history of education. For example, see GOMERSALL, M. (1988) 'Ideals and realities: The education of working class girls 1800–1870' and HORN, P. (1988) 'The employment of working class girls 1870–1914' both in *History of Education*, **17**, 1.

19 Aldingbourne School Log Book 1884, p. 88, Chichester Public Record Office, ref E/12/1.

20 See EDWARDS, B. (1974) *The Burston School Strike*, London, Lawrence & Wishart, pp. 51–3 for an account of a teacher's dispute with a local landowner over child labour which resulted in the former appearing in court.

21 For examples of local disputes over school boards see ELLIOT, A. (1981) 'The Bradford School Board and the Department of Education 1870–1902: Areas of conflict', *Journal of Educational Administration and History*, **XIII**, 2; FIDLER, G.C. (1980) 'The Liverpool Labour movement and the school board: An aspect of education and the working class', *History of Education*, **9**, 1; GRIGGS, C. and WALL, D. (1984) 'Eastbourne and the school board era that never was', *History of Education*, **13**, 4.

22 SHUTTLEWORTH, SIR J.K. (1838) 'A utilitarian view of workhouse education', *Journal of the Royal Statistical Society*, **1**, quoted in DIGBY, A. and SEARBY, P. (1981) *op cit*, p. 118.

23 LOWE, R. (1867) 'Primary and classical education', 1, pp 8–10, quoted in SIMON, B. (1960) *op cit*, p. 356.

24 The correspondence principle posits that schooling performs the function of allocating pupils/students to their future roles in the hierarchy of capitalistic production. This is facilitated by a structural correspondence between the social relations of schooling and those of production. According to Bowles and Gintis these social relations (the hidden curriculum) are far more influential than the actual or formal curriculum. See chapter 1 for a full discussion of the correspondence principle. See also, BOWLES, S. and GINTIS, H. (1976) *Schooling in Capitalist America: Educational Reform and the Contradictions of Economic Life*, London, Routledge & Kegan Paul; and COLE, M. (Ed) (1988) *Bowles and Gintis Revisited: Correspondence and Contradiction in Educational Theory*, Lewes, Falmer Press, particularly the Prologue.

25 West has tried to argue that voluntary efforts could have provided enough schools so that there was no need for the State to build schools. Hurt has argued that West provides an oversimplistic interpretation of nineteenth century statistics, a view that was shared about the Newcastle Commission's statistical evidence by Forster (1816–86) who commanded HMIs to make further surveys, the results of which conflicted with those of the Commission's in terms of school attendance. For

contrasting interpretations of the evidence see the articles by West and Hurt in DRAKE, M. (Ed) (1973) *Applied Historical Studies*, London, Methuen.

26 GRIGGS, C. and WALL, D. (1984) *op cit*, p. 281.

27 LAQUER, T.W. (1976) *Religion and Respectability: Sunday Schools and Working Class Culture 1780–1870*, Boston, MA, Yale University Press.

28 DICK, M. (1980) 'The myth of the working class Sunday school', *History of Education*, 9, 1.

29 GARDNER, P. (1984) *The Lost Elementary Schools of Victorian England*, Beckenham, Croom Helm, p. 153.

30 GRIGGS, C. (1983) *The Trades Union Congress and the Struggle for Education 1868–1925*, Lewes, Falmer Press, p. 219.

31 *ibid*, pp. 213–23.

32 The full story of the intrigue to destroy the school boards, an intrigue which included members of the Conservative Party and the Webbs, has been told in EAGLESHAM, E.J.R. (1956) *From School Board to Local Authority*, London, Routledge & Kegan Paul.

33 MACKENZIE, J.M. (1984) *Propaganda and Empire: The Manipulation of British Public Opinion 1880–1960*, Manchester, Manchester University Press, p. 2. This detailed study covers the numerous ways in which imperialism permeated so many aspects of British life, often beginning with school.

34 See BLANCH, M. (1979) 'Imperialism, nationalism and organised youth' in CLARKE, J., CRITCHER, C. and JOHNSON, R. (Eds) *Working Class Culture*, London, Hutchinson University Library.

35 SPRINGHALL, J. (1977) *Youth, Empire and Society*, Beckenham, Croom Helm, p. 18.

36 MANGAN, J.A. (1985) *The Games Ethic and Imperialism*, Harmondsworth, Viking.

37 GRIGGS, C. (1981) 'The attitude of the Labour movement towards drill in elementary schools 1870–1925', *Bulletin of Physical Education*, 17, 2.

38 FLETCHER, C.R.L. and KIPLING, R. (1911) *A History of England*, Oxford, Clarendon Press, p. 162.

39 *ibid*, p. 240.

40 MACKENZIE, J.M. (1984) *op cit*, p. 184.

41 *ibid*.

References

BOWLES, S. and GINTIS, H. (1976) *Schooling in Capitalist America: Educational Reform and the Contradictions of Economic Life*, London, Routledge & Kegan Paul.

CHANCELLOR, V. (1970) *History for Their Masters: Opinion in the English History Textbook 1800–1914*. Bath, Adams & Dart.

CLARKE, J., CRITCHER, C. and JOHNSON, R. (Eds) (1979) *Working Class Culture*, London, Hutchinson.

COLE, M. (Ed) (1988) *Bowles and Gintis Revisited: Correspondence and Contradiction in Educational Theory*, Lewes, Falmer Press.

DICK, M. (1980) 'The myth of the working class Sunday school', *History of Education*, 9, 1.

DIGBY, A. and SEARBY, P. (1981) *Children, School and Society in Nineteenth Century England*, London, Macmillan.

DRAKE, M. (Ed) (1973) *Applied Historical Studies*, London, Methuen.

EAGLESHAM, E.J.R. (1956) *From School Board to Local Authority*, London, Routledge & Kegan Paul.

EDWARDS, B. (1974) *The Burston School Strike*, London, Lawrence & Wishart.

ELLIOT, A. (1981) 'The Bradford School Board and the Department of Education 1870–1902: Areas of conflict', *Journal of Educational Administration and History*, **XIII**, 2.

FIDLER, G.C. (1980) 'The Liverpool Labour movement and the school board: An aspect of education and the working class', *History of Education*, 9, 1.

FLETCHER, C.R.L. and KIPLING, R. (1911) *A History of England*, Oxford, Clarendon Press.

GARDNER, P. (1984) *The Lost Elementary Schools of Victorian England*, Beckenham, Croom Helm.

GOMERSALL, M. (1988) 'Ideas and realities: The education of working class girls 1800–1870', *History of Education*, 17, 1.

GRIGGS, C. (1981) 'The attitude of the Labour Movement towards drill in elementary schools 1870–1925', *Bulletin of Physical Education*, **XVII**, 2.

GRIGGS, C. (1983) *The Trades Union Congress and the Struggle for Education 1868–1925*, Lewes, Falmer Press.

GRIGGS, C. and WALL, D. (1984) 'Eastbourne and the school board era that never was', *History of Education*, 13, 4.

HALSEY, A.H., HEATH, A.F. and RIDGE, J.M. (1980) *Origins and Destinations*, Oxford, Clarendon Press.

HIGGINSON, J.H. (1974) 'Dame schools', *British Journal of Educational Studies*, **XXII**, 2.

HOBSBAWM, E.J. (1968) *Industry and Empire*, London, Weidenfeld & Nicolson.

HORN, P. (1978) *Education in Rural England 1800–1914*, London, Gill & Macmillan.

HORN, P. (1988) 'The education and employment of working class girls 1870–1914', *History of Education*, 17, 1.

HURT, J. (1972) *Education in Evolution*, London, Rupert Hart-Davis/Paladin.

HURT, J. (1979) *Elementary Schooling and the Working Classes 1860–1918*, London, Routledge & Kegan Paul.

LAQUER, T.W. (1976) *Religion and Respectability: Sunday Schools and Working Class Culture 1780–1870*, Boston, MA, Yale University Press.

LAWSON, J. and SILVER, H. (1973) *A Social History of Education in England*, London, Methuen.

MCCANN, P. and YOUNG, F.A. (1982) *Samuel Wilderspin and the Infant School Movement*, Beckenham, Croom Helm.

MACKENZIE, J.W. (1984) *Propaganda and Empire: The Manipulation of British Public Opinion 1880–1960*, Manchester, Manchester University Press.

MACLURE, S. (Ed) (1986) *Educational Documents 1816 to the Present Day*, London, Methuen.

MANGAN, J.A. (1986) *The Games Ethic and Imperialism*, Harmondsworth, Viking.

MANTHORPE, C. (1986) 'Science or domestic science? The struggle to define an appropriate science education for girls in early twentieth century England', *History of Education*, 15, 3.

MARCHAM, A.J. (1980) 'Lies and statistics: A note on the Newcastle Commission', *History of Education*, 9, 3.

SILVER, H. (1983) *Education as History*, London, Methuen.

SIMON, B. (1960) *Studies in the History of Education 1780–1870*, London, Lawrence & Wishart.

SIMON, J. (1966) *Education and Society in Tudor England*, Cambridge, Cambridge University Press.

Social Trends, **18** (1988) London, HMSO.

SPRINGHALL, J. (1977) *Youth, Empire and Society*, Beckenham, Croom Helm.

Chapter 3

The Rise, Fall and Rise Again of Selective Secondary Schooling

Clive Griggs

Secondary Schooling for the Few; The 1902 Education Act

The 1902 Education Act of the Conservative Government abolished democratically elected school boards and replaced them with appointed local education committees. Higher grade schools inevitably disappeared in the process. The religious schools received favoured treatment; they were to provide the buildings whilst the newly established local education authorities paid for their upkeep. The majority of the managers were to be provided by the religious society and in turn they would appoint the staff whilst the LEA paid their salaries. The 1902 Act led to a storm of protest and large-scale demonstrations by the major forces opposed to it; nonconformists were furious that they would now be forced to contribute to church schools whilst the majority of Liberals and those in the Labour Movement were angered by the change from elected to appointed bodies to run the schools.

One of the key developments arising out of the Act was the establishment of local authority secondary schools but just as in the nineteenth century there was no progression from elementary to secondary school with the exception of the minority of children who gained a free place. For almost the first half of the twentieth century the majority of children were excluded from secondary schooling which remained largely the preserve of fee-payers. Elementary and secondary schools were therefore divided by fees, selection tests and curriculum. In general the former were more likely to study arithmetic, English, general science, history and geography whereas the latter followed courses in the traditional three sciences, a foreign language, algebra and geometry. Only in the latter were pupils prepared for major national examinations. The majority of children left school at the earliest possible age in elementary schools; at 12 from 1899 onwards and 14 after 1918.[1]

Usually secondary school pupils remained at school until 16. The Liberal Government in 1906 offered secondary schools a higher rate of grant if they would offer up to 25 per cent of their places to pupils from elementary schools who had passed a test usually based upon English and mathematics.

The architects of the 1902 Education Act, Robert Morant (Winchester and Oxford) and Arthur Balfour (Eton and Cambridge), the Prime Minister, imprinted their hierarchical views of society firmly upon the education system. The elementary schools would provide a basic education for the working class, the majority of whom would take their place in the vast army of labour needed to work in British industry and commerce. A minority of working class children who had managed to pass an examination would join a majority of fee-paying middle class pupils from the secondary schools and go on to supply the managerial and professional positions in society. The fee-paying private sector, especially the major public schools catering for the higher social classes and using endowments originally intended for poor scholars would continue to provide a privileged ruling elite. Naturally this was no caste system as it enabled social mobility to take place, for talent was always recognized as worthy of recruitment to the higher reaches of society. At the same time the trend towards meritocracy was held in check by a selective system of education in which parental wealth had considerable influence upon the educational opportunities of children.

A divided local authority education system dominated the inter-war period and the arguments which buttressed and rationalized it were numerous. There were perhaps three major ideas which supported separate types of schooling for children. That most children were incapable of following a secondary grammar school course, that just as the private sector of education was available according to purchasing power of parents so too this should at least be reflected in the local authority secondary schools as well as by the maintenance of fees for the majority of places, and finally that the nation could not afford to provide secondary education for all children.

The idea of a majority of the population being only capable of a limited elementary education was strongly held at the beginning of the century. Many leading members of the Labour Movement used to the grading of jobs into skilled craftsmen and unskilled labourers qualified demands at Labour Party and Trades Union Congress annual meetings for secondary education with such phrases as, 'for all children who would benefit'[2] or 'for all children who pass qualifying examinations'.[3] There was always the difficulty in distinguishing lack of ability with lack of formal schooling and to this extent the early 'intelligence tests' pioneered by Alfred Binet in France were thought to be a scientific means of measuring the innate intelligence of children which would allow accurate predictions to be made as to who would and would not be capable of benefitting from secondary schooling. As time passed the infallibility of the psychometrists became debatable but their views, encouraged by Britain's most famous educational psychologist, Cyril Burt, were not seriously challenged within the educational establishment.

The belief that for most children the education provided should be linked to their social class was not just a reflection of the idea that goods and services should be largely available according to purchasing power but also a part of the outlook which suggested that schooling should be related to the possible future lifestyle of the pupil. Most would follow occupations similar to those of their parents and neighbours and as these would be largely in factories or low prestige service work there was not much point in teaching such children a foreign language or English literature. Indeed it might be harmful because a liberal education might make many dis-contented with the kind of job for which they were destined and which had to be done by someone in society. There were always working class parents who were also dubious about the benefits of secondary education even if their child did win a free place. There was the economic problem of not just finding the money to support a teenager for two more years at least but also of foregoing the money that would come into the family budget if their son or daughter did go out to work. For some there were anxieties lest this better education might lead to estrangement between the working class values of the home and some of the new ideas brought home from the school. There was also the gender dimension whereby some parents would allow a son to take up a secondary school free place because he would get a better job but deny a similar opportunity to a daughter, arguing that in the long run she would 'waste' the education by getting married and staying at home to raise a family.

The economic argument was always in the background, often based upon a political philosophy which did not believe it was the responsibility of society to provide anything beyond the minimum in terms of welfare services including education. Whenever the economy looked like faltering there were always pressure groups at work arguing for cutbacks in public expenditure including education. At local level ratepayers had often tried to cut costs by reducing the salaries of teachers or increasing the numbers of pupils in classes and frequently this had led to long disputes which had resulted in strikes such as those at West Ham (1907), the Rhondda (1919) and Lowestoft (1922).[4] At national level a series of reports aimed at cutting educational expenditure, including reducing teachers' salaries, squeezing the number of free places by use of a means test, and increasing class sizes were put forward by the Geddes Committee (1922), the May Report (1931) and the Ray Report (1932).[5]

The full recommendations were never implemented from any one of these reports but the educational world saw itself as constantly under threat from Conservative Party dominated governments.[6] More teachers moved towards the Labour Party and this in turn was seen by some as a means of potential subversion in the schools. The Special Branch began to report on radical teachers, especially if they were members of the

Teachers' Labour League and proposals were put forward in Parliament for teachers to be required to sign an Oath of Allegiance.[7]

In the Hadow Report (1926) it was accepted that most children would not go to secondary schools but attend a school suited to their 'probable occupation in commerce, industry and agriculture'. By the late 1930s schooling was still being considered in two separate divisions, elementary and secondary, but by now the Spens Report (1938) was willing to consider an expansion of the latter with the addition of a minority of secondary technical schools. Multilateral schools, with various types of secondary schooling on the same site, were rejected. When World War II started in 1939 most of the population, and certainly the overwhelming proportion of working class children, had received only an elementary education in schools which were inferior in buildings and resources, staffed by non-graduate teachers who taught a limited curriculum as compared to the better resourced secondary grammar and fee-paying schools which were dominated by children from middle class backgrounds.[8] By this time, however, the social divisiveness in education was under strong attack from organized Labour which had adopted R.H. Tawney's influential pamphlet 'Secondary Education for All' (1922) as the basis for a programme of extended secondary education. Given the limited education available to the majority of the children in the 1930s it is perhaps surprising that within a generation, there were those on the political Right who were prepared to argue in the 1960s that this period was some Golden Age for schooling which could provide a model for the future.

The 1944 Education Act and Secondary Education for All

Myths rapidly become established and enter into national folklore and the view that the 1944 Education Act was designed as a springboard for future advances in equality of opportunity in education is one such myth. Just as the 1918 Education Act was a product of Edwardian thinking and already obsolete by the time it was enacted in terms of the nation's educational requirements so too the 1944 Act was a product of pre-war thinking. The major step in terms of educational emancipation can be seen as the decision to make secondary education in local authority schools free and to provide some form of secondary education to all children. There was, however, no question of providing a common secondary experience for all children; less still was there any serious move to challenge the socially divisive private sector. Parental affluence was still to be given a prominent part in determining access to educational resources and opportunities.

During both world wars millions of people were called upon to make sacrifices for their country in order to defend a way of life threatened from outside, perhaps more so in 1939 than 1914. Both wars upset the accepted routine of life and 'taken for granted' assumptions began to crumble, especially when the end of the war was in sight. Fundamental questions were raised about the kind of society to be constructued when the war was over. One general answer was that the new society should be fairer than the one that had preceded it and that meant that ideas of privilege, hierarchy and status which seem inevitably anachronistic to those who have faced death, would be seriously challenged. Those in positions of privilege would be forced to make concessions, at least in the short term. With the inter-war memories of widespread unemployment, limited access to medical treatment and educational opportunities some form of welfare state was demanded. This partly explains the scale of the 1945 Labour Party success at the general election and the rejection of a Conservative Party, even one led by the popular war hero Winston Churchill, because both he and his party were strongly linked to a pre-war period of means testing and harsh treatment of working people, as personified in the attitude adopted to the coalminers following the General Strike of 1926.[9]

The 1944 Education Act was the product of earlier reports: the Spens Report of 1938, the Norwood Report of 1943 and the White Paper of the same year. The Spens Report declared, 'all the evidence we have heard on the existing methods of selection for one or other type of school confirms us in our opinions that the line as drawn at present is always artificial and often mistaken ...'[10] but having considered multilateral schools 'reluctantly decided that we could not advocate as a general policy the substitution of such multilateral schools for separate schools of the existing type ... even as the goal of a long range policy'.[11] It is in the Norwood Report that the rationalization for a tripartite system of secondary schooling is to be found. It suggested that three groupings of children could be discerned from past general educational experience, 'and the recognition of such groupings in educational practice has been justified both during the period of education and in the after-careers of the pupils'.[12] Three types of school were duly recommended: secondary grammar, technical and modern, with the majority of children destined for the latter. It was explained that secondary modern schools would cater for the child who, 'Because he is only interested in the moment he may be incapable of a long series of connected steps; relevance to present concerns is the only way of awakening interest, abstractions mean little to him ...'[13] The White Paper of the same year reinforced the view of separate secondary schools even if it did suggest they would be of 'equal standing' and the system designed was strengthened further by a Ministry of Education pamphlet entitled 'The Nation's Schools' published in 1945.

However, it has since been argued that far from R.A. Butler being seen as the architect of a forward-looking education proposal for which he has been given much credit, it appears that the designs for the 1944 Education Act were drafted by influential civil servants and colleagues linked by common public school backgrounds long before Butler was appointed President of the Board of Education by Winston Churchill in

1941.[14] The details of the intrigue by Griffith Williams (Head of the Secondary Branch), William Cleary (Head of the Elementary Branch), Cyril Norwood (President of St. John's, Oxford and ex-Head of Harrow School), Maurice Holmes and Robert Wood, Secretary and Deputy Secretary at the Board of Education respectively, would provide a good script for the television series *Yes, Minister*.

As early as January 1941 Robert Wood provided

> the political context for the discussion. In a remarkably prescient note to the secretary, Holmes, ... he warned that their planning should take account of war-engendered egalitarianism and that if they did not go some way to meet such aspirations, a post-war Labour Government elected with a large majority would reject their advice and seek guidance elsewhere.[15]

They were willing to give way on secondary school fees in order to retain direct grant grammar schools and a selective secondary education system, and here Griffith Williams' influence was strongest:

> He was determined to preserve selective grammar school education, given in institutions separate from the rest of secondary education ... His response to the social upheaval of the War was to argue for the end of patently social selection, fee paying and the admission of wealthy but academically inadequate pupils to grammar schools — as the price to be paid for the retention of the more important principle which was academic selection and segregation. The 1944 Act reflected his goals precisely.[16]

Butler was more radical in his approach but no match for the knowledge, experience and influence of Holmes and his colleagues. Churchill's understandable preoccupation with the War, his experience of the hostility surrounding the 1902 Education Act and his general indifference to education matters enabled Butler to make plans just as Churchill's positive support in 1944 ensured the Bill's success. Alternative radical proposals had been made not just for Tawney's vision of secondary education but also for raising the school leaving age to 16 as recommended by the Spens Report and the development of multilateral schools, the forerunners of comprehensives, which had been favoured by teachers' organizations and the Labour Movement. Butler was able to avoid widespread discussion of these issues as well as references to the private sector, direct grant grammar schools and the religious schools in the time honoured way of setting up a committee of enquiry. Hence whilst some concessions to popular opinion were made, 'The threat of radical change had been held at bay. The "New Order" in English Education, celebrated by Dent (Editor of the *Times Educational Supplement*) and many others, turned out to be the old order in disguise'.[17]

There is, therefore, documentary evidence for political conspiracy aimed at social control behind the 1944 Education Act just as can be found among the leading architects of the 1870 and 1902 Education Acts. It has been shown how radical forces got to work in the School Board era to construct a better quality of education for all children than had been intended by such people as the Revd Fraser[18] and Robert Lowe. It is not so easy to show such comparative progress within the inter-war period, because the struggle here for improved schooling took place for a long time against a background of proposed cutbacks in education, including the suggestion by Lord Eustace Percy that fees be reintroduced into primary schools, in 1925.[19] In the post-war years, once more individuals and groups combined to provide a better system of schooling than that envisaged by the conservative designers of the 1944 Education Act.

Initially free secondary education for all children was welcomed and the idea of access to grammar schools by competitive examination instead of fees seen as a boon.

For some it was not equality but equality of opportunity which was sought and in what may now seem to be a somewhat naive view it was believed that once secondary schools were free and entrance based solely upon competitive examination large numbers of working class children would enter and by their success bring about far reaching social changes. When Middlesex made proposals for comprehensive schools in 1949 George Tomlinson, the Labour Education Minister, rejected them. Having at last won access to grammar schools for more working class children it hardly seemed to be wise to close them. Both Ellen Wilkinson and George Tomlison, Education ministers in 1945–47 and 1947–51 respectively, seemed to be so concerned with the opportunities now offered to intelligent working class children that they appeared to have lost sight of the destination of most children, the secondary modern schools.[20] All the wishful thinking that the different secondary schools would enjoy parity of esteem evaporated when it became apparent that secondary modern schools followed a different curriculum, were staffed largely by non-graduate teachers, and took no major external examinations, so that the career opportunities of the pupils were usually restricted. In a hierarchical society schools were not seen just as different but better and worse.

As early as 1946 the Labour Party conference rejected Wilkinson's aims of a tripartite system[21] and from then onwards both Wilkinson and Tomlinson were to remain out of step with majority opinion in their Party although probably not so much within the country at that time. Hence Tomlinson's rejection of Middlesex's plans to develop three comprehensive schools in 1948 were justified by him educationally because he favoured grammar schools and politically because he thought such action would lose the Labour Party votes.[22] He retained these views in spite of regular defeats at Labour Party conferences right through until the Party left office in 1951. By 1953 the Labour Party had developed a coherent policy on comprehensive schools.

It is sometimes assumed that the Labour Party supported comprehensive education whilst the Conservative Party favoured selection. That this is too simplistic a view has been demonstrated by Tomlinson's policy. It would be more accurate to say that at local and national level the Labour Party was won over to the comprehensive ideal but within the Conservative Party national support for selection was not always supported at local level, for by the 1960s a considerable number of Tory local authorities had established comprehensive systems of schooling, although in general there was always some safeguard made for selective schools. It has to be remembered that between 1951–1964 the Tory Party was in power and as Pedley commented in the mid 1960s:

> If Labour has been timid, Conservative resistance has been stupidly obstructionist ... Conservative ministers made it clear that while they were prepared to sanction the development of comprehensive schools in rural areas and on new housing estates, they would not allow their development if it would mean the abolition of an existing efficient grammar school.[23]

It is now apparent that in the first few years of Tory rule when Florence Horsborough was the Minister for Education, R.A. Butler, now as Chancellor of the Exchequer, constantly demanded cutbacks in educational expenditure in spite of the fact that the post-war baby boom had produced one million more school children and that in the new housing estates there was a desperate need for schools to be built.[24] Butler's aim was to divert resources from education to a massive rearmament programme, a familiar recurring story in British twentieth century educational history.

It is true to say that by the 1970s the only local authorities retaining selective secondary schools were those controlled politically by Conservatives. If Conservative MPs were less committed to comprehensive schools it was partly because large numbers of them had no experience of local authority schools as pupil or parent as they had been educated at fee-paying schools.[25] It is also notable that whilst many leading Conservatives supported the retention of grammar schools they rarely sent their own children to them but preferred to patronize the private sector. There were also some Labour MPs who supported comprehensive schools in principle but sent their own children to fee-paying schools.

Support for comprehensive schools gained ground slowly in the 1950s but increased in the 1960s. The first comprehensive schools were established for geographical rather than ideological reasons; those in the Isle of Man (1946–48) and the Isle of Anglessy (1949–53). Kidbrooke opened in London in 1953 and within three years there were ten more in the capital. Some schools in Birmingham and Coventry became comprehensive in the 1950s and in the next decade Manchester, Liverpool, Lancashire and Sheffield developed such schools. A promise to end secondary school selection by the Labour Party in the 1964 General Election played a major part in their victory.

There were a large number of facts which led to a move away from selective secondary schools and it was a combination of these which finally convinced most people at the time that some form of comprehensive schooling would be better for the majority of children. Among the issues supporting this move were:

(a) Gradual realization that whilst it might be possible to achieve parity of esteem between grammar and modern schools in terms of resources this did not lead to parity of prestige between schools within the community.

(b) Whilst many at first may have genuinely believed that the different curricula offered in grammar and modern schools was of equal value, parents, employers and many of the pupils themselves came to see the latter as second best for those who could not cope with grammar school studies.

(c) Confidence in the validity of the 11+ test as an accurate predictor of academic potential was gradually undermined, largely because secondary modern schools began to develop GCE classes with considerable success thereby invalidating the earlier academic predictions made by selective tests. The fact that some pupils who went to grammar schools left early or did not succeed in GCE examinations received less publicity.

(d) It became increasingly apparent that even for those who believed it was possible to measure 'intelligence' in some manner, social factors were of greater significance in influencing the academic attainment of pupils. A series of studies, of which perhaps the most widely read was Brian Jackson and Denis Marsden's *Education and the Working Class* (1962) began to show with monotonous regularity that explanations for academic achievement and underachievement were linked to a series of social factors relating to various aspects of home background including the occupation and education of parents, the interest taken by parents in the schooling of their children, etc.[26]

(e) More difficult to assess is the pressure generated by middle class parents. The 11+ tests meant that a majority of the children were judged to have 'failed' and whilst most working class parents were likely to accept the decision this was less true of some of the more articulate middle class parents who not only resented the judgment passed upon their child but were unhappy about them going to a secondary modern school in a predominantly working class area, such as a local authority housing estate. However unjustified or irrational such views may have been in many cases they were nevertheless felt and the result was that many vociferous middle class parents began to add their weight to an end to selection, especially if their children did not get a grammar school place.

(f)   There was a growing realization that the selective system whose origins lie in the pre-war period was not suited to the times in which Britain found itself under intense challenge from industrial competitors. The launching of the space age with the first Soviet Sputnik (1957) produced a traumatic shock to the country and the realization that in terms of certain technology the country was falling rapidly behind. It was noticed that neither of the space explorers, the USA and USSR had selective education systems like the British model and that far higher percentages of young people were on undergraduate courses.

A combination of these facts began to discredit the grammar school system. Even the frequently quoted view that they provided an opportunity for intelligent working class children was undermined by the publication of the Early Leaving Report of 1954 which stated that 'of approximately 16,000 children who in 1946 entered grammar schools throughout England from such homes (i.e. children of semi-skilled and unskilled workers), about 9000 failed to get three passes at Ordinary level, and of these about 5000 left school before the end of their fifth year'.[27] The Newsom Report (1963) aptly sub-titled 'Half Our Future' which examined the education of pupils between the ages of 13 and 16 of average and below average ability found that standards had risen but that 'the educational performance of many of the children in the "Newsom" group is held back more by social factors than by genetics'.[28] They regretted the waste of talent and suggested a raising of the school leaving age as one move for they claimed there 'is very little doubt that among our children there are reserves of ability which can be tapped, if the country wills the means'.[29] The Robbins Report (1963) reviewing higher education showed that the provision of such education in the USA, USSR and many other countries far exceeded our own: 'Judged on grounds of opportunity offered for entry, our system is well down the list' of other systems with which it was compared.[30]

When the Labour Party was returned to Government in 1964 it was with an electoral mandate to complete the comprehensive system of secondary schooling which had been making progress but in a piecemeal manner. By this time just over 70 per cent of all authorities had established some form of comprehensive schooling or were at the planning stage. Yet by the end of this decade criticisms were being made about these new schools from various points of view. To begin with the Government did not provide the scale of funding necessary for either the buildings or the new teacher training courses which would be needed in staffing what was in many ways a different approach to education. One result was the amalgamation of schools some distance apart which forced either pupils or staff to travel between the split sites bringing all manner of difficulties. Then there was the constant attempt to compare the new comprehensives with the previous grammar school in terms of results ignoring the fact that one school was academically and consequently socially selective. Comprehensives were forced to concentrate upon examination results and copy the traditions of the grammar schools in terms of uniforms, speech days, houses and prefects just as the grammar schools in turn had copied these from the public schools a generation earlier. Unrealistically some authorities set up comprehensive schools but retained selective secondary schools as well so that the former was in fact a secondary modern school with a different name. It could be argued that a comprehensive secondary system of schooling has never really been established in England and Wales yet in spite of all the difficulties standards in terms of examination successes continued to rise.

With the Conservatives back in power in 1970 Circular 10/64 requesting local authorities to go comprehensive was withdrawn and replaced with Circular 10/70. Local authorities would now decide for themselves, was the newly-declared policy as Margaret Thatcher took over at the DES as Secretary of State for Education and Science. She has often been chided for closing more grammar schools than any other minister but a closer look at her record shows a lack of consistency within her own policy in practice. This was to some extent inevitable because she wished to retain selection in order to preserve parental choice but found this often conflicted with local authority educational planning and the majority of local popular parental opinion as opposed to a smaller group of parents acting as a pressure group for the retention of a grammar school attended by their own children:

> One of the most startling and indicative actions came in September 1970 when the Conservative controlled Barnet Council voted to end selection. In October the Council conducted a referendum of parents and teachers that showed 79.4 per cent in favour of reorganization. Further, the Council's plan, its third, had been worked out over the years in close consultation with the DES. In response, in June 1971, the Secretary of State decided not to allow one of the five grammar schools to merge with two secondary modern schools. This decision, made only a few months before the plan was due to come into operation, enforced the retention of selection and 'threw the borough into confusion'. The Barnet action showed the uncertainty of the local option ... The local option was expendable.[31]

In other words local authority opinion would be allowed to decide, providing the decision coincided with the views of the Minister.

The 1970s turned out to be most fruitful years for the small groups which constantly attacked local authority schools. They were largely right-wing pressure groups campaigning for general changes within society including education, such as the Institute of Economic Affairs, founded in 1957, which aimed to see 'how far market principles and pricing can be introduced into the disposition of goods and services organized by the government', others concentrated solely upon education, such as the Black Paper authors and pressure groups like FEVER campaigning to privatize schooling through a voucher system. Their publications ranged from the scholarly of the IEA to those stronger in rhetoric than serious argument, a common feature of numerous Black Papers.[32] Primary schools which had gained an international reputation for innovative methods were caricatured as places where children played instead of studied, but most venom was concentrated upon the comprehensive schools where isolated examples of poor behaviour or standards were turned into generalizations concerning the whole system. Most of the booklets from these pressure groups were not widely read but their generalizations were widely publicized in the tabloids as well as the quality press. Even the BBC joined in the attack with its *Panorama* programme on Faraday Comprehensive School during 1977, presenting a distorted picture of life in a London school which was uncritically accepted by much of the public. By then the minority Labour Government of James Callaghan was in office (1976–79) and instead of coping with mounting criticism of education was swept up by the tide.[33] Callagan's Ruskin College speech in October 1976 seemed to accept all the arguments of the radical right; the schools were out of touch with industry and commerce, standards were falling, there was a lack of discipline, and so on. This in spite of Government HMIs, reporting improvements in standards.

Discontent and Dissent in the 1980s

In 1979 the first of the three Thatcher administrations was returned to power. Where Mrs Williams may have dithered at the DES the new Tory Government had no such doubts as to the direction schooling should take. Private schools would provide the model and the introduction of the Assisted Places Scheme, which would allow children from homes on below or average incomes to attend such schools and have their fees paid for by the State, was the first indication of the new sense of priorities in education.

This was to be the decade of the enterprise culture when money was to be seen as the measure by which success would be judged. In education, as in many other public sector services, privatization was seen as a way of cutting back on public expenditure. School meals introduced originally to build up a healthy nation were undermined by the removal of statutory duties to maintain nutritional standards and many were forced to become self-financing. The cafeteria system which had developed was welcome in most schools but the demand for junk foods was a worrying trend among many concerned with long-term health patterns. School cleaning was put out to private tender in spite of complaints by teachers about the declining standard of cleanliness which resulted. In some areas pupils were employed at lower rates than adults to help in such work.

The Government claimed that it was spending more money than ever on education even if this was not the impression of the teachers who worked within the system. There were several reasons for this apparent confusion suggesting that the Government was being 'economical with the truth'. The rate of inflation for educational goods was above that of the general rate of inflation so that increased expenditure in line with the latter in fact meant a cutback in finances for schools (precisely the same problem facing the National Health Service during these years.) This was underlined by the evidence of experienced teachers who found that their departmental budgets bought less in terms of books and equipment than they had done in previous years. In addition it could be clearly demonstrated from Government statistics which showed that the percentage of the Gross National Product spent on education fell from 5.5 to 4.8 between 1970/71 and 1985/86.[34] In addition the money provided by central Government to local government, known as the Rate Support Grant, for provision of local services including education, was cut from 60 per cent in 1974/75 to 47 per cent in 1985/86. This meant a loss of millions of pounds in the educational budgets of local authorities. Several reports from the independent HMIs severely criticized the poor state of repairs in school buildings which were a result of this underfunding. In many areas local authorities were so hard stretched that they could only afford to provide the materials for maintenance, leaving groups of teachers and parents to decorate the schools.

That much needed to be done in schools was never denied by most teachers. It was, after all, teacher organizations which campaigned for years to bring in a common examination for 16-year-olds. It was recognized that new curricula initiatives proposed were necessary but the rate at which they were pushed forward made it impossible for them to be implemented as rapidly as might be desired. Hence language across the curriculum, equal opportunities, multicultural awareness, computer awareness, records of achievement, were welcomed by many teachers but rarely funded by the government with the resources necessary to promote them efficiently.

The main criticism of the treatment of education in this period was the failure to realize that simplistic solutions were of little help in dealing with complex problems. There seemed to be a belief that if only the clock could be turned back and some mythical 'golden age' in schooling restored all would be well. Enough has been written about the past selective system to show that the majority of pupils were denied access to the opportunities provided. In any case social changes have been so profound that the approach to education of the 1930s or 1950s is rarely relevant to the teaching situation of today.

It needs to be grasped that pupils stay on at school two years longer than they did a generation ago as the leaving age was raised to 15 in 1957 and 16 in 1972. They are taller and heavier than their parents and grandparents and come to school with different values, many of them shaped by a sophisticated popular culture financed liberally by commercial interests in music, clothing, videos, discos, television and pop concerts. Many of these portray values at odds with those fostered in schools. Like many other authority figures the respect for teachers has been undermined by constant criticism of parents, politicians and the media. This has been reinforced for years by the comparatively low salaries which show little acknowledgment of the value of the college, polytechnic and university education they have undertaken or their role in society. The bitter teacher disputes of 1984–86 were largely a result of the resentment felt by teachers about their treatment by successive governments since the Houghton pay award of 1974.

Alongside this must be seen the changing conditions of the society in which teachers work. The very social fabric has been widely damaged by inner city decay, record levels of unemployment, increased use of drugs, widespread vandalism; much of this, it could be argued, a result of government policies which had contributed directly to these problems.[35] At the same time there have been rising expectations among parents that schools will deliver the examination results which will enable their children is get good jobs. The increasing demands upon time especially with the GCSE exam and the greater stress involved in teaching have only slowly been grasped by a public still clinging to a past image of a '9 am to 4 pm' job with long holidays.

It seems once more that good schooling is to be rationed because it is too expensive to provide on a mass scale. The Inner London Education Authority has been regularly criticized for spending too much money on education when compared with other local authorities. (By contrast one rarely reads of Government ministers criticizing those local authorities who spend too little!) Yet given the situation faced by many London boroughs it is inevitable that they will need to provide greater resources. According to the Hargreaves Report (1984) on London secondary schools 'there is greater deprivation in Inner London than in Birmingham, Liverpool or Manchester ... (and) ... a recent census discovered that 147 languages are spoken in London schools', in some cases as many as fifty in one school.[36] That there have been some mistakes made in some boroughs is true, although sensational tabloid press reports, often completely inaccurate, have exaggerated such incidents. What is clear is that many of the positive policies, such as equal opportunity, have born fruit with, for example, more females appointed to secondary school headships than in any other local authority. Academic standards in recent years have begun to rise. A recent survey showed that most parents were satisfied with schools in London. In 1988 the Government passed a Bill which abolished the Inner London Education Authority. For a Government which has made so much of the need for parents to make decisions about the education of their children it is interesting to note that London parents were not consulted on the abolition of the ILEA, a decision which has little support on educational grounds although one can readily see the political motives. In a ballot organized by the Electoral Reform Society there was a vote in favour of the retention of the ILEA by 19 to 1: (137,021 to 8004 with 234 abstentions, 55.7 per cent of those eligible to vote did so — a far higher turnout than at most local elections.)[37] For the immediate future it looks as if the results of the 1988 Education Act will be a return to selective schooling at the secondary age range.[38] More money will be provided but much of it will come from parents themselves and increasingly it will be spread unevenly. Schools in the more affluent areas will 'opt out' of local authority control convinced that this will increase their prestige. Parents will be told this will give them greater choice but as the most popular schools become over-subscribed so the schools will begin to become the selecting agent and all past experience points to the decision being made along academic and social grounds. The City Technical Colleges will reinforce the views of those on the radical right, that business interests can run schools better than teachers. Those business interests which step forward to finance the new CTCs will appoint the governors of the school and they in turn will decide the curriculum to be followed, choose the headteacher and decide on the methods for selecting the pupils. By offering higher salaries they will be able to attract teachers of art and design technology, subjects in which there are teacher shortages.

The CTCs will enable a minority of children to pursue well financed courses whilst the majority of pupils will have to get along in other schools less well resourced in terms of staffing and equipment. It is a policy which accepts that schooling for the masses will not be adequately funded but with the offer of a lifeline to a few selective 'better schools' for a minority of parents providing their children can pass the appropriate entrance test. Parents opting for oversubscribed schools will be faced with a fee of some kind whether it be as a payment for registration or as a 'donation' to the library or school fund. To make it seem fairer a few scholarships could be on offer for those children who perform exceptionally well in the entrance examination and who might bring academic credit to the school. How long it will take the majority of parents to realize that a form of privatization has been introduced and that selection for the few inevitably means rejection for the many remains to be seen.

N.B. On several occasions writers quoted use language — 'he', 'him', 'man' — which may jar on the reader in times of greater gender awareness. It is not easy to know years later whether the author deliberately or sub-consciously excluded girls/women or whether they were using such terms in the conventional manner of the time to include them.

Notes

1 Most Government reports covering elementary and/or secondary education did so in terms of social class. For example, referring to the 1943 Norwood Report Wolpe (1981) suggests:

> ... their ideology reflected their elitist approach to education in general. Their overriding concern was with those pupils who would comprise the top sectors in the occupational hierarchy. As women were not deemed to comprise any significant element in this group they were not considered at all. Conversely because the bulk of the working population comprised products of what they regarded as the less significant sector of the school population their disregard for both girls and boys in this sector was on a par.

2 GRIGGS, C. (1985) 'Labour and education' in BROWN, K.D. (Ed) *The First Labour Party 1906–1914*, Beckenham, Croom Helm.
3 GRIGGS, C. (1983) *The Trades Union Congress and the Struggle for Education 1868–1925*, Lewes, Falmer Press, chapter 4.
4 For detailed studies of numerous teachers' disputes see LAWN, M. (1987) *Servants of the State: The Contested Control of Teaching 1900–1930*, Lewes, Falmer Press; and SEIFERT, R.V. (1987) *Teacher Militancy: A History of Teacher Strikes 1896–1987*, Lewes, Falmer Press. For a study of one of the longest running strikes in British history see EDWARDS, B. (1974) *The Burston School Strike*, London, Lawrence & Wishart.
5 For full details see SIMON, B. (1974) *The Politics of Educational Reform 1920–1940*, London, Lawrence & Wishart.
6 From 1922 to 1940, with the exception of minority Labour governments in 1924 and 1929, the Conservatives were in power. The Parliament of the National Government of J.R. MacDonald (1929–35) was comprised of 556 MPs of whom 472 were Conservative; as the Liberals sided with the Government the only significant opposition came from the forty-six Labour MPs.
7 LAWN, M. (1987) *op cit*, pp. 118–19.
8 'In 1938, the last full year before the war, 88 per cent of children aged 5 to 14 in England and Wales attended public elementary schools...' RUBINSTEIN, D. and SIMON, B. (1969) *The Evolution of the Comprehensive School 1926–66*, London, Routledge & Kegan Paul, p. 21.
9 See SHINWELL, E. (1963) *The Labour Story*, London, Macdonald; and FARMAN, C. (1974) *The General Strike: May 1926*, London, Panther.
10 MACLURE, J.S. (Ed) (1986) *Educational Documents from 1816 to the Present Day*, London, Methuen, p. 196.
11 *ibid*.
12 *ibid*, p. 201.
13 *ibid*, p. 202.

14 WALLACE, R.G. (1981) 'The origins and authorship of the 1944 Education Act', *History of Education*, **10**, 4.

15 *ibid*.

16 *ibid*.

17 SIMON, B. (1986) 'The 1944 Education Act: A Conservative measure?', *History of Education*, **15**, 1.

18 'Even if it were possible, I doubt whether it would be desirable, with a view to the real interest of the peasant boy, to keep him at school till he was 14 or 15 years of age. But it is not possible. We must make up our minds to see the last of him, as far as the day school is concerned, at 10 or 11' (part of the evidence given by Revd Fraser to the Newcastle Commission of 1858 — MACLURE, J.S. (Ed) (1986) *op cit*, p. 75.

19 DEAN, D.W. (1971) 'Conservatism and the national education system 1922–40', *Journal of Contemporary History*, **6**, 1. R.A. Butler was to suggest a return to fees for secondary schools in 1953 (see MORRIS, M. (1984) 'Built to last', *Times Educational Supplement*, 10 August, p. 4).

20 For a detailed account of the personalities, pressure groups and arguments behind the educational issues of the time see DEAN, D.W. (1986) 'Planning for a post-war generation: Ellen Wilkinson and George Tomlinson at the Ministry of Education 1945–51', *History of Education*, **15**, 2.

21 PARKINSON, M. (1970) *The Labour Party and the Organization of Secondary Education 1918–65*, London, Routledge & Kegan Paul, p. 39.

22 *ibid*, p. 47.

23 PEDLEY, R. (1966) *The Comprehensive School*, London, Penguin, pp. 44–5.

24 SIMON, B. (1985) 'The Tory government and education, 1951–60: Background to breakout', *History of Education*, **14**, 4.

25 GRIGGS, C. (1985) *Private Education in Britain*, Lewes, Falmer Press, pp. 36–43.

26 See SILVER, H. (Ed) (1973) *Equal Opportunity in Education*, London, Methuen. Subsequent writers have stressed more structural reasons for working class underachievement. See, for example, the discussion on Bowles and Gintis in chapter 1.

27 MACLURE, J.S. (Ed) (1986) *op cit*, p. 237.

28 *ibid*, p. 279.

29 *ibid*, p. 281.

30 *ibid*, p. 290.

31 WOODS, R. (1981) 'Margaret Thatcher and secondary reorganisation 1970–74', *Journal of Educational Administration and History*, **XIII**, 2.

32 See MUSGROVE, F. (1987) 'The black paper movement' in LOWE, R. (Ed) *The Changing Primary School*, Lewes, Falmer Press.

33 For the period covering the early 1970s to the late 1980s see MORRIS, M. and GRIGGS, C. (Eds) (1988) *Education: The Wasted Years? 1973–1986*, Lewes, Falmer Press.

34 *Social Trends*, **18** (1988), London, HMSO, p. 64.

35 Unemployment rose from 1.25 million in 1979 to 3.25 million in 1985 and began to decline slowly from 1986 onwards. At all times the figures quoted were an underestimate of the true total as the Government eliminated thousands on several occasions by changing the way in which the calculations were made. Homelessness rose, partly due to the sale of council houses and the refusal by the Government to allow local authorities to spend the receipts so gained in building dwellings to meet demand. Public sector building fell from an average of 140,000 dwellings in the 1970s to 43,000 in 1985. Whilst the highest income earners had their tax rates cut from 85 per cent in 1979 to 45 per cent in 1988, at the other end of the social scale poverty increased: the number of claimants below pensionable age, who had been dependent on supplementary benefits for five years or more rose from 218,000 in

1977 to 659,000 in 1987. Controversy continued over the possible links between unemployment, homelessness, squalid conditions, low income and poor health. See TOWNSEND, P. and DAVIDSON, N. (Eds) (1982) *Inequalities in Health: The Black Report*, London, Penguin.

36 HARGREAVES, D. (Ed) (1984) *Improving Secondary Schools*, London, ILEA, p. 7.

37 SUTCLIFFE, J. and HUGILL, B. (1988) 'Parents endorse ILEA', *Times Educational Supplement*, 15 April.

38 See SIMON, B. (1988) *Bending the Rules*, London, Lawrence & Wishart. Even allowing for real differences in opinion many believed that the 1988 Education Act was rushed through without adequate thought, partly because it was a product of successful right wing pressure groups, such as the Hillgate Group who put forward simplistic ideas to deal with complex problems. One measure of the indecent haste came when 'Ministers moved to squeeze scrutiny of 569 legislative changes agreed by peers, covering bitterly contentious topics from religious education to redrawn plans for schools to opt out of council control, into eleven hours of debate . . .' *The Independent*, 19 July 1988, p. 6.

References

BENN, C. and SIMON, B. (1972) *Half-Way There: Report on the British Comprehensive School Reform*, London, Penguin.

BOWLES, S. and GINTIS, H. (1976) *Schooling in Capitalist America: Educational Reform and the Contradictions of Economic Life*, London, Routledge & Kegan Paul.

DEAN, D.W. (1971) 'Conservatism and the national education system 1922–1940', *Journal of Contemporary History*, **6**, 2.

DEAN, D.W. (1986) 'Planning for a post-war generation: Ellen Wilkinson and George Tomlinson at the Ministry of Education 1945–51', *History of Education*, **15**, 2.

FARMAN, C. (1974) *The General Strike: May 1926*, London, Panther.

GRIGGS, C. (1983) *The Trades Union Congress and the Struggle for Education 1868–1925*, Lewes, Falmer Press.

GRIGGS, C. (1985a) 'Labour and education' in BROWN, K.D. (Ed) *The First Labour Party 1906–1914*, Beckenham, Croom Helm.

GRIGGS, C. (1985b) *Private Education in Britain*, Lewes, Falmer Press.

HARGREAVES, D. (Ed) (1984) *Improving Secondary Schools*, London, ILEA.

JACKSON, B. and MARSDEN, D. (1962) *Education and the Working Class*, London, Routledge & Kegan Paul.

LAWN, M. (1988) *Servants of the State: The Contested Control of Teaching 1900–1930*, Lewes, Falmer Press.

MACLURE, J.S. (Ed) (1986) *Educational Documents 1816 to the Present Day*, London, Methuen.

MORRIS, M. (1984) 'Built to last', *Times Educational Supplement*, 10 August.

MORRIS, M. and GRIGGS, C. (Eds) (1988) *Educaton: The Wasted Years? 1973–86*, Lewes, Falmer Press.

MUSGROVE, F. (1987) 'The black paper movement' in LOWE, R. (Ed) *The Changing Primary School*, Lewes, Falmer Press.

PARKINSON, M. (1970) *The Labour Party and the Organization of Secondary Education 1918–65*, London, Routledge & Kegan Paul.

PEDLEY, R. (1967) *The Comprehensive School*, London, Penguin.

RUBINSTEIN, D. and SIMON, B. (1969) *The Evolution of the Comprehensive School 1926–66*, London, Routledge & Kegan Paul.

SEIFERT, R. (1987) *Teacher Militancy: A History of Teacher Strikes 1896–1987*, Lewes, Falmer Press.

SHINWELL, E. (1963) *The Labour Story*, London, MacDonald.

SIMON, B. (1985) 'The Tory goverment and education, 1951–60: Background to break-out', *History of Education*, **14**, 4.

SIMON, B. (1986) 'The 1944 Education Act: A Conservative measure?', *History of Education*, **15**, 1.

SIMON, B. (1988) *Bending the Rules*, London, Lawrence & Wishart.

Social Trends, 18 (1988), London, HMSO.

WALLACE, R.G. (1981) 'The origins and authorship of the 1944 Education Act', *History of Education*, **10**, 4.

WOLPE, A.M. (1981) 'The official ideology of educaton for girls' in DALE, R. *et al* (Eds) *Education and the State Vol 2: Politics, Patriarchy and Practice*, Lewes, Falmer Press.

WOODS, R. (1981) 'Margaret Thatcher and secondary reorganisation 1970–74', *Journal of Educational Administration and History*, **XIII**, 2.

Part 3
Class, 'Race' and Gender: Britain

Chapter 4

Social Class in Britain*

John Urry

In much popular discussion Britain is said to be a peculiarly class-ridden society. This is because of the importance apparently attached to distinctions based upon accent, dress, manners and schooling. It is maintained that these class distinctions are of especial significance and that they transcend obvious divisions of economic interest. Indeed, it is said that there is a strong cultural bias in British society which de-emphasizes the simple making of money, profit maximization and indeed, in some versions, work itself. It is also part of conventional wisdom that in this sense, class has declined in significance in recent years. Britain, it is said, is now a much less class-ridden society since these sorts of distinctions no longer function to separate off different groups. The growth of the media and mass culture, the expanded entry into higher education, the declining significance for private, family ownership of land and the heightened value placed on work, profit maximization and monetary success, have all weakened the power of these conventional class distinctions.

What should be made of these arguments? First, there is no doubt whatsoever that this view of class is strongly held and that many people do genuinely associate class with these kinds of distinction, what sociologists call 'status'. Furthermore, there is very little doubt that there is something distinctive about class relations in Britain, that they have been particularly mediated by these distinctions of status, by conceptions of snobbery, and by a set of exclusionary social practices revolving around public schools, Oxbridge, London clubs, the London season, country houses, the ownership and pleasurable use of land, the Royal Family, and so on. Indeed, there is much to be said for the view that capitalism was established in Britain in a strangely compromised form. So although there is no doubt about the extraordinary changes brought about by the wide-

* This chapter is a completely revised, shortened and updated version of 'The class structure' in COATES, D., JOHNSTON, G., BUSH, R. (Eds) (1985) *A Socialist Anatomy of Britain*, Cambridge, Polity Press.

spread development of industrial capitalism in Britain (by factories, new massive cities, steam power and so on), the effects of all of these on political and cultural life were rather less marked. Indeed, amongst the industrial capitalists of Britain there has been a process of what Wiener calls 'the gentrification of the industrialists'.[1] He maintains that leaders of industry and commerce in England over the past century have accommodated themselves to an élite culture blended of pre-industrial aristocratic and religious values that inhibited their quest for expansion, productivity and profit. Moreover, a crucial feature of twentieth century British politics has involved the fight against class *in this sense*, against what used to be called the Establishment.[2] In recent years there has been some diminution in the importance of such an Establishment and of the related social practices of snobbery, rank and status evaluation. However, this does not mean that class in a more straightforward 'economic' sense is not of tremendous significance in Britain.

In the following it is class in this economic sense that I shall consider. I shall assess the Marxist argument that Britain remains a fundamentally capitalist society in which the exploitation by capital (the capitalist class) of labour (the working class) is the central social relationship and it is this which shapes other patterns of social inequality and occupational division. It will be seen that there are forms of social inequality and division which are not simply explicable in terms of this capital/labour relationship. I shall begin here with a brief analysis of the distribution of income and wealth in Britain.

Income and Wealth

There are considerable difficulties in measuring wealth held in the form of land, houses, shares, factories and durable possessions. It is almost impossible to conduct a survey, and so the best estimates of its distribution are based on the values of the estates declared for death duty. And even these contain considerable inaccuracies as families try to minimize their declarations and hence their liability for paying such duties. There is also much debate as to what counts as wealth, for example, whether it should be taken to include occupational pension rights or a house bought on a mortgage which many employees now 'own' and which make the distribution of wealth less uneven. A further difficulty is raised by the unit under consideration. Should we consider the individual or the family as the unit of investigation? The former would seem appropriate in relation to the study of income distribution since otherwise we would be adopting sexist assumptions about the organization of families and the role of the family breadwinner. However, in relation to the distribution of wealth families play an absolutely central role, especially through inheritance and the provisions of more diffuse educational, social and cultural attributes in

Table 4.1   Britain's wealthiest families.[3]

Family	No of half-millionaires in last 150 years	Origins of family fortune
Rothschild	21	finance
Wills	21	tobacco
Coats	16	textiles
Colman	10	food
Palmer	10	food
Morrison	9	commerce
Ralli	9	commerce
Gosling	7	banking

the reproduction of the British ruling class. And indeed 'family' here does not mean the 'modern' nuclear family but the much wider 'extended' families which have been able to sustain their extraordinary concentrations of wealth. Table 4.1 presents a list of the wealthiest families in Britain.

There is, however, considerable controversy about the role that inheritance plays in accounting for the distribution of wealth in Britain. The evidence suggests that although there was some increase in the numbers of self-made millionaires during the 1950s and 1960s, it is still true that 'inheritance is the major determinant of wealth inequality'.[4] Harcourt and Hitchens suggest that inheritance accounts for between 60 and 80 per cent of the fortunes of very wealthy men and women. Indeed, while a quarter of such men were in some sense self-made, only about 5 per cent of women were. Women inherited money both from their parents and from their husbands and there were high rates of intermarriage amongst the very rich.

Looking at the distribution of wealth 1923–72, the share held by the top 1 per cent of wealth holders fell from about 60 per cent to 30 per cent.[5] The next 4 per cent increased their share from about one-fifth to one-quarter, while the next 5 per cent doubled their share from about 7 per cent to 14/15 per cent and the next 10 per cent tripled theirs from 5 per cent to 15 per cent. Atkinson maintains that the redistribution of wealth over this century has not been between the rich and the poor but between successive generations of the same family and between husbands and wives.[6] This means that age and gender inequalities of wealth have been reduced within households and the wider families of the rich, but there has been relatively little redistribution from the moderately rich to the average and to the poor. Four-fifths of people share about 15 per cent of total wealth. During the 1980s inequalities of wealth appear to have increased. In 1983 there were 13,000 millionaires in Britain — but by 1986 there were 20,000, owning 4 per cent of all wealth.[7]

It is important to examine the distribution of wealth because it is

Table 4.2   Proportions of households in various combinations of income and wealth.[8]

Wealth	Net Disposable Income			
	Top 5%	*6–10%*	*11–20%*	*Bottom 80%*
Top 5%	2.0	0.6	0.6	1.9
6–10%	0.9	0.8	1.2	1.9
11–20%	1.2	1.6	1.4	7.0
Bottom 80%	1.4	4.0	9.2	64.3

much more unequally allocated than earned income, while for some households it provides extremely significant resources which are or can be realized as income. It should though be noted that top wealth holders are not necessarily top earning income recipients or vice versa. This is shown in table 4.2, although this also demonstrates that the bulk of the population (64 per cent) are in the lower 80 per cent of *both* wealth holding and income.

The unequal distribution of wealth is in general a major source of unequal income. The greater the wealth, the more significant is shareholding, and hence the greater the 'unearned' income that accrues. Most people receive no investment income (except indirectly through pension fund holdings), while 1 per cent receive over a third of all investment income.[9] Such 'unearned' income is very important to the wealthy, providing between a quarter to one-half of their income. This particularly results from the ownership of shares which are very unequally distributed.[10]

Turning to income, the Royal Commission on the Distribution of Income and Wealth estimated that there were about 65,000 very highly paid employees in the mid-1970s.[11] Seventy per cent of these were managers, and the rest consisted of those in legal, financial, medical and academic professions as well as senior civil servants, entertainers and sportsmen. There were approximately similar numbers of high-earning self-employed, mainly in the professions and commerce. The most distinctive feature, however, was the extraordinarily low representation of women amongst these high-earnings groups. Only 2 per cent of the high earners were women.

The most dramatic consequence of these patterns of social inequality is that a considerable proportion of the British population live in a state of poverty, although by no means all of those who are propertyless employees are in fact poor. Nevertheless, according to Townsend's definition, which is based on the absence or inadequacy of those diets, amenities, standards, services and activities which are common or customary in modern Britain, 25 per cent of households and 23 per cent of persons were in poverty.[12] Or, to put it another way, more than half the population in Britain will experience poverty at some point in their lives. Poverty is more likely to be experienced by women than by men, by the old and increasingly by the young, by those with larger families, by those with, or dependent on those with, unskilled manual occupations, by those with no assets or negative assets, by those who have experienced unemployment in the previous year, by immigrants, by those in one-parent families and by those disabled.[13] During the 1980s it has been estimated that 1 million more men, 1 million more women and 1 million more children are living at or below the poverty line.[14]

Nonetheless, there have been some important changes in the structure of earnings *between* different occupational classes. Amongst men there has been a substantial reduction in the relative incomes of 'higher professionals/managers' over the course of the century, although as the Royal Commission pointed out there has also been a sizeable growth of various 'fringe benefits' which partly compensate for this.[15] Also there has been a substantial increase in the number of such professionals and managers, rising from 7.5 per cent of the workforce in 1911 to 26 per cent in 1981.[16] It should also be noted that there has been a convergence between the weekly wage of clerks and of manual workers over the course of the century.[17]

So far I have considered a number of snapshots of British society that reveal, at different points in time, particular patterns of social inequality.[18] However, this does not account for the manner in which classes are formed and reformed over time. It also does not take account of how classes are experienced as such by the members of a class — whether they feel and act as class members, or as members of other social groups (for example, as women, blacks etc), or as separate, relatively isolated individuals. These all involve complex issues which can only be briefly discussed here.

Social and Geographical Mobility

The best-known academic research which relates to the formation of social class is the study of social mobility. The basic idea behind such work is that of 'structuration'.[19] By this is meant that the more that mobility chances are closed off (the greater the structuration) the more that this facilitates the formation of identifiable classes. This is because the lack of intergenerational and intragenerational mobility provides for the continuation of common experience for all members of a given class. Conversely where mobility in and out of a given class is high then that class is relatively weakly formed, people will not feel much class identity, and few effective class organizations are likely to develop. The lower the mobility chances in a society the greater the degree of class structuration.

It was commonly thought in Britain following research just after the

Second World War that social mobility was relatively restricted. This was because although a third of the (male) sample had been mobile out of the class they had begun in, the range of this mobility was fairly limited.[20] There was a buffer zone of lower white-collar and skilled manual occupations beyond which those from the upper class or working class did not pass as they moved downwards or upwards. Overall, this research suggested that the British class structure was fairly well-structurated, that the majority of men would have an occupation which was the same as, or close to, that of their fathers. In particular, there was very little chance whatsoever of a working-class boy (defined in occupational terms) becoming a capitalist employer, a manager, or a 'higher professional'.

Later research has, however, partly modified this analysis. The Nuffield mobility project surveyed 10,309 men aged between 20 and 64 in 1972 and found, *inter alia*, that (a) there was more long-range mobility than had previously been thought; (b) there was little in the way of a buffer zone between the working class and the service class (approximately professionals, managers, employers); (c) there was a fair amount of work-life mobility from the working class into the intermediate class and from the intermediate class into both the service and the working classes; (d) only about 25 per cent of the service class was self-recruited and indeed was recruited from all the other classes in roughly similar proportions; and (e) the working class was largely self-recruited.[21]

Many commentators would argue that the main reason for these changes lay in the expansion of, and improved access to, the education system over the past forty years or so. However, the Nuffield researchers concluded that 'school inequalities of opportunity have been remarkably stable'; they endorsed Tawney's comment, originally made in 1931, that the 'hereditary curse upon English education is its organization upon lines of social class'.[22] Halsey, Heath and Ridge show that the gap in educational opportunity between the service class and the working class is dramatic, so that by the minimum school-leaving age three-quarters of the working class had left school, while three-quarters of the service class stayed on. However, this disparity between the two classes becomes less marked the higher the level of education. Thus, *'for those who survive*, inequalities of opportunity are much reduced'.[23] Yet this applies, of course, to a relatively tiny proportion of working-class boys (less than one in forty passed one 'A' level in the sample). The relative class chances of access to university were more or less constant over the period studied, but the absolute gains for the service class were massive compared with those for the working class.[24]

Overall then educational changes merely facilitated the changing patterns of service-class recruitment in Britain. What explains these patterns is the changing occupational structure as it affected men over the period in question. Goldthorpe maintains that the most significant factor affecting class structure 'has been [the shift] chiefly from manual occupations to those of a higher professional, administrative and managerial character' [the service class].[25] This service class has in a sense been 'forced' to take in some sizeable proportion of men from other classes — its expansion could only be met by a considerable recruitment from below. It is this relatively contingent factor which led to the expansion of what is termed absolute mobility. Relative mobility rates (those rates after abstracting out such occupational changes) remained more or less unaltered. They indicated no substantial increases in the openness of British society.

There are further points to note about the analysis of social mobility in Britain. First, it is necessary to consider in much more detail the very different processes of occupational change which characterise different industries, and the changes in the relative size of such industries.[26] Second attention has to be paid as to how these overall patterns of mobility affect individuals and groups living in particular areas. In the past there were numbers of such areas in which a highly divided local or national class structure generated persistent patterns of trade-union militancy and support for the Labour Party, and in some cases sustained red bases or 'Little Moscows'.[27] These areas were generally ones with a dominance of heavy industry or transportation and where there was a strongly developed and reinforced 'occupational community'. Examples include coalmining, shipbuilding, the railways, automobiles and engineering. Other areas, including some even with concentrations of heavy industry, were much less militant and less structured along lines of class. They, nevertheless, still exhibited other features of 'traditional working-class communities', such as an emphasis upon community and neighbourliness, the importance of kin, the central role of the 'mother', and the importance of ascribed rather than achieved position, and so on.[28]

However, even where traditional working-class communities provided the basis for particular forms of class experience, there have been some important economic and demographic changes in recent years which have partly undermined such communities. These changes include: (a) the rapid decline in employment in manufacturing industry, from 8.5 million in 1961 to 5 million in 1987; (b) the dramatic fall in employment in heavy industry: between 1981 and 1987 the numbers in engineering fell by nearly one-quarter, and those in mining by nearly one-half;[29] (c) a huge reduction in the proportion of manual workers, from 70 per cent in 1951 to less than 50 per cent in 1981;[30] substantial increases in employment in the service industry from 10.5 million in 1961 to 14.3 million in 1987; (d) increases in the heterogeneity of the labour force, with women now constituting 45 per cent of the British labour force;[31] and (e) the decline in the population living in conurbations — the number in the six largest falling by 2 million between 1961 and 1981.[32]

Changes in the Labour Process

In this section I will briefly describe some of the changes that have recently occurred in the workplace in Britain. Broadly speaking the main process can be described as the 'deskilling' of labour. This has been elucidated by Braverman who argues that the organization of the labour process is fundamentally determined by the accumulation of capital.[33] In particular, he suggests that there is in all capitalist societies a tendency for labour to become progressively fragmented and deskilled and for conception (thinking out and planning work) to be separated off from execution (the actual carrying out of the work) and embodied within separate structures of management. These developments occur because of the tremendous savings available in the cost of labour that can be obtained. In particular the fragmentation of work tasks enables capital to obtain *precisely* those quantities and qualities of labour it requires and ensures that more expensive skilled workers do not have to waste their time and their employers' money in doing less skilled work which could be done by cheaper labour. The growth of complex managerial structures both reduces the skill level and hence the relative pay of workers, and undermines the knowledge that workers possess of the labour process, which is one crucially significant source of strength that they previously enjoyed. The effect of these processes is that most manual workers in Britain do jobs in which they have little opportunity to exercise their aptitudes and abilities. Most workers will exercise more skill in driving to and from work than in the actual work they do when they get there.

There are, however, three further points that need to be made here. First, there has not been a simple extension of direct managerial control throughout all British industry during the twentieth century.[35] Rather, there have been two other strategies that employers have used to control labour, those of 'paternalism' and 'responsible autonomy'; the former resulting from the persistence of familial control in much of British industry, the latter involving a reliance upon semi-autonomous but constrained work groups to regulate and police workers. Second, new forms of management and of deskilling in Britain have always lagged behind the USA and, to some extent, West Germany as well. Indeed, in Britain the craft unions at the turn of the century were able to prevent some forms of deskilling and the growth of attempts to develop 'scientific management'.[36] New systems of management only developed in the 1930s with the growth of new industries, particularly those established in the south east with previously non-unionized labour. Some craft unions have been able, even where their work has been technically deskilled, to maintain their skilled status in the face of massive attempts to rationalize and restructure the labour process. Finally, new forms and sources of skill are continuously being created in the economy, the most obvious in recent years being those associated with the electrical, computing, biotechnical and microelectronics industries. And even in cases where deskilling might occur as a result, such as in the use of numerical controlled machines in engineering, this does not occur automatically and universally. The effects on the distribution of skills seem to vary considerably from one enterprise to another.[37]

In recent years deskilling has particularly affected non-manual work, in part because labour costs represent a particularly high proportion of total costs in such work.[38] Thus, for example, in the insurance industry, the issuing of a policy, previously handled by a single 'skilled' under-writer, is now handled by several clerks each working to a closely spe-cified set of separate and divided routines. Specialization and sub-division make it possible to concentrate activities in large pools of labour. While this may at one time have been only true of typing, it is now true of many facets of office work. Furthermore, with the introduction of expensive equipment it becomes necessary to concentrate similar activities in order to make economic use of the machines. A familiar consequence of fragmentation of the labour process is the greater control that accrues to management because each worker has control over a smaller part of the whole. The smaller the task performed, the greater the loss in indepen-dence. This reorganization and rationalization of office work and the reduction of employee autonomy with the growth of managerial control are all related to the increasing mechanization of clerical work. Machines have been introduced into almost all areas. The pace of work is increasing-ly dictated by the machine which also demands very accurate input, particularly where computers are concerned. Deskilled white-collar work-ers become like workers on a production line. Typists working to tele-phone dictation, for example, will move on to the next piece of work as soon as they have finished their current one, since the equipment can store dictations.

Although this is clearly a very important development in the British class structure it does not necessarily follow that the deskilling of white-collar labour will make such employees take up common cause with workers.[39] This is for two main reasons: first, because collectively, white-collar employees organize workers and generally have a better 'work situation'; and second, because three-quarters of such workers are fe-male and hence gender differences may partly undermine common class actions.

Gender, 'Race' and the Class Structure

However, it is important to note in this context that class, gender and 'race' are not to be viewed as dimensions of inequality which are separate and discrete. People experience or live social class through their experi-ence as black or white, male or female. People engage in forms of struggle which are structured by class, but the way those struggles materialize depends upon their relationship to these other structures of gender and racial oppression. Moreover, central to these processes is the working of the British state, which does not just embody some extra aspect of 'political' inequality, but is centrally and systematically involved in the very constitution of the forms and limits of such struggles.

However, these struggles do not simply produce a systematic challenge to the overall class structure and the British state. This can be seen most clearly in the patterns of institutionalized racism or sexism found within the working class, forms which do not merely make working-class struggles difficult, but which actually serve in part to *structure* 'race' and gender relations in Britain. For example, the ways in which certain British trade unions prevented black workers from joining partly forced black workers into less unionized, less skilled jobs often located in inner-city areas. Having established themselves within such areas, black workers have been particularly affected by the dramatic and devastating collapse of especially manufacturing employment in these areas. They have in a sense been left to fight the 'class struggle' but in a situation where they are deprived of the indigenous organizational resources, especially of powerful trade unions, to do so.[40] In the same way skilled workers have partly conducted their struggles against capital through systematically preventing women from joining their unions and by using the state to exclude women from such employment.[41] As a result relations of gender oppression are partly the consequence of trade union practices and policies of a broadly patriarchal kind. Indeed it has been suggested that the relatively high rates of female participation in the labour force in Britain result from the strength of the male-dominated trade unions who have been able, through various exclusionary practices, to crowd women into lower level jobs with poorer wages and conditions than is the case in some other Western European countries.

As a result of such crowding both female and black workers tend to be concentrated within certain occupations which are subordinate to those in which white men operate — there is in other words a high degree of vertical segregation.[42] One very clear area in which this can be seen in relationship to women is in deskilled white-collar work where three-quarters of the workers are female. Male white-collar workers have fairly good opportunities for promotion into 'management' but the female workers concentrated within subordinate positions do not.[43] Thus the class division between male white-collar workers who are being trained for management, and female 'proletarianized' white-collar workers, overlaps with the gender division.

Reorganization of Capital

In the same way that major changes are occurring in various subordinate classes within modern Britain, there are also changes taking place in the organization of capital. Firstly, it is less and less the case that firms are wholly or largely owned by individuals or families; they are increasingly owned, potentially at least, by very many people through share ownership. Modern capitalism is therefore becoming particularly from the viewpoint of wealthy families whose property interests are now spread widely across numbers of enterprises. At the same time ownership is reconcentrated as financial institutions, pension funds, insurance companies and banks come to hold large proportions of company shares.[44] This does not represent any return to personal ownership, since these institutions are similarly owned impersonally or are managed by boards or trustees. Institutional ownership often gives a wide measure of control, and control in an institutionally-owned firm may mean much the same as in a personally-owned firm. The spreading of ownership has also produced a fair degree of mutual ownership between financial and industrial or commercial institutions. Even pension funds, often celebrated as people's capitalism, are essentially financial institutions and, especially where external fund managers are used, they are inserted into a systematic profit-making structure.

What has however changed in the past couple of decades has been the very high rate by which capital has become 'internationalized'. This does not merely mean that companies in the UK own shares overseas — which they do — but that they produce goods and services out of the country, in the Third World and also in Europe and North America. Between 1971 and 1983 the real value of foreign direct assets owned by British companies rose by nearly 45 per cent.[45] At the same time there has been a similar increase in the degree to which the UK is the recipient of capital, from the USA, Japan and Western Europe. The UK has a distinctively internationalized economy. Capital is in effect increasingly international and it becomes more difficult to separate off British capitalists from those based in other countries.

Conclusions

There are a number of points to note:

(i) the 'working class' has shrunk in size as manual work and manufacturing industry have come to involve many fewer workers;

(ii) there are massive social inequalities in Britain — and the 1980s has seen increased differences between the 'have-nots' and the 'have-lots';

(iii) the society is not a closed one — there are chances of upward mobility for white men — but these have not increased recently;

(iv) there are complex differences within the class structure with the growth of various middle class groupings. Although many people may do deskilled work this is not to suggest that they will see themselves as workers;

(v) the capital/labour relationship does not totally generate the complex patterning of occupations in modern Britain;

(vi) capital has become 'institutionalized' and 'internationalized'.

Notes

1 See WIENER, M. (1981) *English Culture and the Decline of the Industrial Spirit*, Cambridge, Cambridge University Press; and SCOTT, J. (1982) *The Upper Classes*, London, Macmillan.
2 See the essays in THOMAS, H. (Ed) (1959) *The Establishment*, London, Anthony Bland, for example.
3 See SCOTT, J. (1982) *op cit*, p. 21, as well as SCOTT, J. (1985) 'The British upper class', in COATES, D., JOHNSTON, G. and BUSH, R. (Eds) *A Socialist Anatomy of Britain*, Cambridge, Polity Press, pp. 29–54.
4 HARCOURT, G.C. and HITCHENS, D. (1979) *Inheritance and Wealth Inequality in Britain*, London, George Allen and Unwin, p. 136; and more generally see RUBENSTEIN, W.D. (1981) *Men of Property*, London, Croom Helm.
5 See ATKINSON, A.B. and HARRISON, A.J. (1978) *The Distribution of Personal Wealth in Britain*, Cambridge, Cambridge University Press, p. 159.
6 See ATKINSON, A.B. (1972) *Unequal Shares*, Harmondsworth, Penguin.
7 See RENTOUL, J. (1987) *The Rich Get Richer*, London, Unwin Paperbacks, p. 43.
8 TOWNSHEND, P. (1979) *Poverty in the United Kingdom*, Harmondsworth, Penguin, table 9.3.
9 See WESTERGAARD, J. and RESLER, H. (1976) *Class in a Capitalist Society*, Harmondsworth, Penguin.
10 See ROUTH, G. (1980) *Occupation and Pay in Great Britain, 1906–1979*, London, Macmillan, pp. 54–7.
11 See ROYAL COMMISSION ON THE DISTRIBUTION OF INCOME AND WEALTH, *Report No. 3, Higher Incomes from Employment*, London, HMSO, p. 10.
12 TOWNSHEND, P. (1979) *op cit*, p. 302.
13 *ibid*, chapters 7 and 26.
14 WALKER, A. and C. (Eds) (1987) *The Growing Divide, A Social Audit 1979–1987*, London, Child Poverty Action Group, p. 23.
15 See ROYAL COMMISSION, *Report No. 7*; ROUTH, G. (1980) *op cit*, chapter 1, as well as KAY, J. and KING M.A. (1983) *The British Tax System*, Oxford, Oxford University Press, p. 48.
16 ABERCROMBIE, N., WARDE, A. with SOOTHILL, K., URRY, J. and WALBY, S. (1988) *Contemporary British Society*, Cambridge, Polity Press, pp. 116 and 171.
17 *ibid*, pp. 149–53.
18 See chapters xx and xxi on social inequalities of gender and race.

19 See GIDDENS, A. (1973) *The Class Structure of the Advanced Societies*, London, Hutchinson, p. 107.
20 See GLASS, D. (Ed) (1954) *Social Mobility in Britain*, London, Routledge & Kegan Paul.
21 See GOLDTHORPE, J.H. (1980) *Social Mobility in Britain*, Oxford, Clarendon Press; HALSEY, A.H., HEATH, A.F. and RIDGE, J.M. (1980) *Origins and Destinations*, London, Fontana.
22 TAWNEY, R. (1931) *Equality*, London, Unwin Books; HALSEY, A.H. *et al* (1980) *op cit*, p. 205.
23 HALSEY, A.H. *et al*. (1980) *op cit*, p. 204.
24 *ibid*, p. 217.
25 GOLDTHORPE, J.H. (1980) *op cit*, p. 59.
26 See PAYNE, G. (1987) *Mobility and Change in Modern Society*, London, Macmillan, especially chapter 7.
27 See MACINTYRE, S. (1980) *Little Moscows*, London, Croom Helm.
28 See the famous YOUNG, M. and WILLMOTT, P. (1962) *Family Life and Kinship in East London*, Harmondsworth, Penguin.
29 DEPARTMENT OF EMPLOYMENT, *Employment Gazette*, various years.
30 ABERCROMBIE, N. *et al* (1988), *op cit*, pp. 118–21.
31 *Employment Gazette*, various years.
32 OPCS (1961 and 1981) *Census of Population*.
33 *See* BRAVERMAN, H. *(1974) Labour and Monopoly Capital*, New York, Monthly Review.
34 See BLACKBURN, R. and MANN, M. (1979) *The Working Class in the Labour Market*, London, Macmillan.
35 See LITTLER, C. (1982) *The Development of the Labour Process in Capitalist Societies*, London, Heinemann.
36 See LASH, S. and URRY, J. (1987) *The End of Organized Capitalism*, Cambridge, Polity Press, chapter 6.
37 See the various chapters in WOOD, S. (Ed) (1982) *The Degradation of Work*, London, Hutchinson.
38 See CROMPTON, R. and JONES, G. (1984) *Whitecollar Proletariat: Deskilling and Gender in Clerical Work*, London, George Allen and Unwin.
39 See the new classic discussion in LOCKWOOD, D. (1958), *The Blackcoated Worker*, London, George Allen and Unwin; and ABERCROMBIE, N. and URRY, J. (1983) *Capital, Labour and the Middle Classes*, London, Allen and Unwin.
40 See *Race and Class*, (1981/82), vol. 23 for a variety of analyses of race.
41 See WALBY, S. (1986) *Patriarchy at Work*, Cambridge, Polity Press.
42 See HAKIM, C. (1979) *Occupational Segregation*, London, Department of Employment Research Papers, No. 9.
43 See STEWART, A., PRANDY, K. and BLACKBURN, R. (1980) *Occupation and Social Stratification*, London, Macmillan, on the class position of male 'clerks'.
44 See for a convenient summary, SCOTT, J. (1982) *op cit*.
45 See STOPFORD, J. and TURNER, L. (1984) *Britain and the Multinationals*, London, John Wiley, p. 49.

Chapter 5

Social Class and Schooling

Jan Lee

The history of mass education in Britain can arguably be viewed as a history of the legitimation and institutionalization of the 'failure' of the working classes. However, the prevailing ideology based on a liberal social democratic assumption, is that education can 'equalize conditions and opportunities and even remove the basis of class'. Despite clamorous evidence to the contrary the myth prevails. Consequently, if the education system is perceived as just and having an equalizing role in an egalitarian democratic society, the continued 'failure' of the working classes has to be explained by natural, individual or familial class factors. Since the 1960s in particular, theories have gained precedence that explain the failure of working class children as the consequence of social factors such as health (Townsend and Davidson, 1982); poverty, housing, family size (Wedge and Essen, 1982; Davies *et al*, 1972); language and socialization (Bereiter and Engelmann, 1966; Friedman, 1967). The school failure of the black middle and working classes has largely been attributed to the same causes (see Taylor, 1981). However, these 'social' explanations of differential success in the schooling system are ideologically, historically and politically expedient and do nothing to alter the inequalities of a hierarchically structured society. Setting education in its wider social context, Bowles and Gintis (1976) claim

> To a major extent the schools did successfully weld together the functions of accumulation (of capital) and reproduction (of the capitalist relations of production). By obscuring the underlying contradictions between accumulation and reproduction, the school system has played an important role in preserving the capitalist order; within that order it has also brought tangible, if limited, benefits to the working people ... (p. 240)

John Urry's chapter examines the economic basis of class. He is concerned to assess whether the exploitation of labour by capital is the 'central social relationship' and one which 'shapes other patterns of social inequality and occupational division' in British society. He is, therefore, primarily concerned with the economic *formation* of social classes. This chapter, as well as examining teachers' own class position, is more concerned with the perpetuation and legitimation of class differences and inequalities. Education can be seen then as what Althusser (1971) would describe as one of the Ideological State Apparatuses (ISAs). It is an agent of class domination which operates ostensibly through consent rather than coercion. The schooling process, therefore, acts as an agent of ideological control largely through intellectual and moral modes and constraints in an attempt to bring about conformity, compliance and hegemony. This is not to imply that this is a straightforward deterministic relationship. There are tensions and contradictions which are endemic to any process which has to appear to be universal, egalitarian and just whilst working within a wider social context which requires divisions, inequality and injustice for its development and smooth functioning. Bowles and Gintis (1976) note that a structural weakness in the schooling system was realized in the late nineteenth century, 'the most striking feature of which was the incompatibility between the democratic ideology of the common school and the social reality of the class structure' (p. 186). There are, and always have been, forms of resistance to the schooling process by certain class/cultural groups. Furthermore ideological forms such as schooling develop and maintain a relative autonomy in relation to other spheres such as the 'economic' and the 'state'. This too provides the basis for conflict and resistance at certain sociohistorical junctures.

The Historical Roots of a Socially Divisive Form of Schooling

Historical accounts of the development of compulsory mass education in the late nineteenth century and early twentieth century have tended towards unilinear accounts or overarching explanations that seldom acknowledge or accommodate the struggles, opposition or forms of resistance that might have affected the outcomes of educational policy or practice or indeed the very form of schooling which emerged. There appears to be an assumption that the accounts of educationists and government policy-makers are an accurate reflection of the schooling process and development. This is to ignore the class divisions in the society and the differing perspectives which they may inform. Uncritical use of mainstream historical accounts aids the unquestioning acceptance of 'commonsense notions' of schooling. One such notion is that schooling is a 'good' in itself and has civilized the 'uncivilized masses' giving them opportunities and benefits previously not available to them. This is comparable to the historical accounts of British colonialism as perceived by white, Western historians. These accounts have become increasingly contested with growing evidence being made more generally available of black resistance to colonial invasion and challenges to the prevailing ideology of the 'savage cultures' that benefitted from the 'civilizing' influence of the Western plunderers (see for example, the video *A History of Racism* by the Association for Curriculum Development, 1987; Fryer, 1985). Unquestioning acceptance of these 'commonsense notions' contributes in itself to a compliance with and perpetuation of the hegemonic order. If the education system is to be perceived for what it is, that is, the site of contradictory pressures or demands especially in relation to class divisions, then there is a need for historical accounts of the non-dominant classes, the oppressed, those for whom education was provided, rather than the providers. Working class consciousness, traditions, culture and resistance to the provision of a mass educational system is ill served by historians and by history itself. It is argued that it is this failure to provide the past actions, arguments and traditions of the working classes in an accessible form, which in part enfeebles and inhibits the development of traditions of working class consciousness. As Lynch (1974) states: 'Thus when the past comes to be conceptualized and made a meaningful source for present action, working class consciousness is handicapped in opposing versions of history that seek to legitimize contemporary ideological conceptions of social and political realities' (p. 148). The recent demands of black groups and women's groups for accounts of their 'hidden history' highlights the ideological function of received historical accounts.

Historians such as B. Simon, H. Silver and R. Johnson have attempted to detail the ways in which working class demands, particularly through the Chartist movement, affected the provision of mass schooling. They identify the earlier part of the nineteenth century as characterized by the 'radical awakening' of the labouring poor who had been so much affected by industrialization. They argue that the working class, as it became conscious of itself as a class, came to see education as one of the means of political and economic emancipation. On the contrary, the desire to develop education for philanthropists such as Kay Shuttleworth was in order to ensure social stability in an era of massive alienation and discontent — of riots and strikes and popular actions which were seen to potentially threaten the social order. The French Revolution (1789) was still regarded as a warning to the ruling powers in Britain and elsewhere. Johnson (1976) in particular regards as immensely significant the transition of the working class movement's opposition (as expressed mainly through the Chartists) to *provided* forms of education, to that of agitation for educational provision through the state. He regards the latter as linked to 'popular liberalism' and an 'anti-Anglican alliance'. He postulates that the basic adaptation and destruction of alternative forms of education was the starting point for the 'long haul up the alternative route' which has provided the modern educational process with all its defining characteristics:

the identification of education with schooling; the radical separation of the learning processes of child and adult; the notion that only sponsored, managed or controlled or 'certificated' forms of education are worth the name; the professionalization of teaching and the making academic of study of education (and of its history); above all the key social-democratic assumption (which no Owenite or Chartist would have endorsed) that education can really equalize conditions or even remove the basis of 'class'. (Johnson, 1976, p. 24).

Small scale studies such as those by Frith (1977) render as problematic the present reified form of schooling by outlining the way in which the rational organization of children in an institution based on teachers and formal curriculum is only one method of education that was potentially available for development. His concern is with how rational schooling developed as a form of socialization, with the problems this created and solved for the relationship between the educators and the educated; the providers and the provided. Frith outlines how between 1800 and 1850 the benevolent middle class had to adjust its notion of education as charity in the face of the working classes' marked 'independence of feeling'. Even at this early stage the tensions and contradictory requirements of the educational process are evident. Thus, at the same time as schools began to justify themselves as efficient means to the secular end of literacy, to stress the efficiency of their pedagogical methods and the superiority of their teachers, the importance of the religious function of education to maintain moral, political and social control of the 'dangerous' lower classes was also promoted. It is this delicate balancing role of education particularly in times of rapid social, political and economic change that potentially provides the site and means of social control or social rebellion.

Frith's study outlines working class resistance to the provided form of schooling before 1870. Working class children did not attend school regularly nor did they take much notice of the rational organization of time in schools which clashed with the 'rhythms' of home and work life. There were conflicts over dividing children into separate classes according to age; the parents wanting the children to stay in family groupings. There were conflicts recorded between parents and school over behaviour, discipline, dress, punishment and the curricula. In short, there were not and still are not shared criteria about the purpose and process of schooling. By utilizing this information about the working class view of education and the process of education, Frith shows that national education was not simply a matter of providing an elementary education to a class that was otherwise intellectually and morally destitute but that: 'It was rather a matter of providing a particular *form* of education to a class which had (however unsystematically) alternative *forms* of learning available' (Frith, 1977, p. 85).

Thus the evolutionary approach to the history of education can obscure quite fundamental changes in opinion and conflicting demands and pressures on governments. Silver (1977), for instance, cites the Newcastle Commission on the state of popular education in 1861 as stating that 'the Englishman (sic) would never permit state compulsion' for it would be 'too great a shock to our educational and social system'. So how did such a major change in popular opinion and social consciousness occur? There appears to have been no historical analysis of this factor even though such an analysis may reveal important information about changes in Victorian perceptions of government, the school, the family, social class, occupational structure and concepts of freedom, childhood, etc. An understanding of such developments in the social and historical context of time may provide different perspectives with which to view the present educational system.

It is clearly crucial to an understanding of the reification of education that the class struggles and contradictions over the form and control of education are made explicit. In many ways these set the wider social parameters and the nature of constraints within which educational developments or potential for change are contained. Furthermore, it needs to be noted that the actual experience of education for some of the working class had been accompanied by significant economic and social gains. It was these largely skilled labour groups who were accommodated by the education system and came to form the backbone of the trade union movement and local labour parties. In the twentieth century the latter groups were instrumental in the development of secondary and comprehensive education. Finn, Grant and Johnson (1977) in their article 'Social democracy, education and the crisis' provide an excellent appraisal of the recent history of the Labour Party's role in the development of secondary and comprehensive schools and the notion of equality of opportunity. So whilst the *content* of education may have been challenged to some limited effect for the working class élite, the *control* of education by the ideological apparatus of the state has not been significantly challenged and this too must set limits for the possibilities of change. There must, however, be a constant problem of legitimating that authority at the classroom level at least. It would appear, therefore, that there are contradictions inherent in the educational process, not only related to relative class positions, but to the realization of education's twin aims — that of developing the intellectual capacity of the child to serve the 'national need' and that of preventing radical change — the maintenance of social hegemony. A sociohistorical analysis can then provide an understanding of how and why the education system embodies the values of the middle classes and ensures that working class 'success' in the schooling process is achieved at the expense of working class consciousness, culture, language and identity. Unless and until the *form* of schooling and accordingly what counts as valid knowledge, learning, i.e. education is radically changed and the *control* of education is therefore not mediated by and through the dominant classes, the pious, social-democratic hopes of an educational system which enables *all* classes to achieve equally cannot be effectively realized.

Social Class and Educational Achievement

In the previous chapter, John Urry reported on the 1970s Nuffield mobility project which concluded that the *inequality* of opportunity provided by schools had been remarkably stable despite some occupational mobility in a period of changing occupational structures. The mobility studies of the early 1930s and late 1970s provide equally damning evidence of the failure of the educational system to provide opportunities for working class boys to achieve educational and social mobility. As Halsey *et al* (1980) demonstrate, three-quarters of working class boys have left school by the minimum school leaving age, whilst three-quarters of the boys from the service or professional classes had stayed on at school. As John Urry states, this endorses Tawney's comments of 1931 that the 'hereditary curse upon English education is its organization upon lines of social class'.

It is essential to note here that these large-scale and nationally influential surveys were concerned with the mobility of only half of the population, i.e. the male population. Furthermore, most research on class issues or research that utilizes class categories, defines a person's class position by the occupation of the man, as does the Registrar General's classification. This largely unquestioned sexist bias in research must inevitably give a distorted picture and disguise important factors particularly in relation to the apparently upwardly mobile working class children. For instance, how many of these children have come from single parent families where the woman is the only parent? What is the mother's occupation? Is the mother from a more professional class background than the father? Given that traditionally for many classes education has been regarded as a female arena, then it could be argued that it is indeed the mother's social class that is of particular significance here. The ILEA Junior School Project (1986) as outlined later made a nominal move towards acknowledging the presence and influence of mothers' occupations and class background on children's educational progress and attainment.

There is considerable quantitative as well as qualitative evidence which demonstrates the unequal outcome and process of the educational system related to the social class of the parents (usually fathers) and the social intake of the school. Early studies such as that of Douglas (1964) found that in a cohort of children born in March 1948, considerable differences in school performance were found by the age of 8 according to the social class of the father. In 1958, the study of a second cohort of children found similar class differences in attainment. The National Child Development study (Davie *et al*, 1972) found that at age 7 years the proportion of children perceived as having reading problems in social class V (unskilled) was more than five times that of class I (professional and managerial).

Astoundingly, whilst acknowledging the weight of evidence related to social class influence on educational achievement, Tizard *et al* (1988) effectively ignore social class in their research into the attainment and progress of infant children in inner-city schools. They return again to 'home' factors as one indicator of differences in attainment and progress. They acknowledge sex and ethnic factors but particularly emphasize 'school' and 'classroom' effect. They acknowledge the low expectations of teachers in working class areas but state: 'If their (teachers') expectations of both parents and children in working-class areas are low, they only reflect widely-held views' (p. 187). By the time these children were 11 years old the difference between the groups had doubled and by 16 years the gap was even wider. So, those people who might postulate that working class children have a generally lower IQ than middle class children, must accept that there is a negative schooling effect on the children of the working classes and furthermore that schooling exacerbates rather than diminishes class differences in achievement. The Junior School Project (1986) was an extensive four-year longitudinal study carried out in the early 1980s in the ILEA. One of its many aims was 'to assess the impact of social class upon children's attainment and progress in the junior years'. To this end information was obtained about both mothers' and fathers' occupations. A variety of analyses were carried out to ascertain any correlation between social class and school attainment. Account was taken of factors such as ethnic family background, fluency in English, family size, eligibility for 'free' school meals, etc. However, even after taking into account the effect of these influences, a gap of nearly ten months in reading age was found between children with fathers in professional or intermediate non-manual work, and those with fathers in unskilled manual work. They also found a similar effect was in evidence for the mother's occupation. As in other studies, the gap between social class and reading attainment increased throughout the four year period of junior education. The study also demonstrated the strong relationship between teachers' assessments of pupils' ability and the pupils' class background.

In Rutter's (1979) study (*Fifteen Thousand Hours*) of twelve London secondary schools, the researchers found that there were highly significant differences between social class groups. They found that children from the families of the professional/managerial classes gained on average twice as many high grades in public examinations as those from skilled and unskilled families. The most recent analyses from the NCDS cohort on public examination results demonstrates that 39 per cent of the children of non-manual families gained five high grades in 'O' level equivalents; whereas only 12 per cent of the children of the manual classes gained the same. Work in the ILEA and the EPA studies also demonstrated a strong relationship between the social class intake of schools and their perform-ance in the public examinations. This is particularly important to note at a time when publication of schools' examination results is being promoted. The HMI Primary Survey (1978) did not specifically examine social-class intake to schools but they did note that 'High and low levels of perform-ance were more strongly associated with the location of the school ... than with either the size of school ... or its age range' (p. 109). One could reasonably surmise that the differing NFER test results they obtained according to 'inner-city', 'other urban' and 'rural' locations would have correlated with differing social-class compositions in the different loca-tions. This is supported by the LEA Junior School Project (1986) where it is noted that 'the majority of children were from working class homes, a reflection of the social class composition of the inner London population' (Part A, p. 39).

The composition of higher education shows even more marked social class differences. Halsey *et al's* (1980) study of the educational mobility of working class boys shows '... how the chances of a boy from a working class background going to university, despite the increases in provision, were virtually the same as had existed for forty years before' (Mortimore and Mortimore, 1986, p. 9). The University Central Council of Admissions (UCCA) (1982) shows that there is an inverse proportion of working class and middle class candidates accepted to university in comparison to their social class composition in society generally. Social classes IV and V form around 24 per cent of the working population but the proportion of accepted candidates to university from these social class backgrounds is around 5 per cent and there has been no significant change in the past decade. Conversely, social classes I and II form around 16 per cent of the working population yet the proportion of accepted candidates to university from these class backgrounds has increased from 62 per cent in 1977 to 70 per cent in 1980. As the ILEA document on *Race, Sex and Class. No. 1* (1983) states:

> When adjustments are made to take account of the larger sizes of the manual working groups the chances of a pupil with a profes-sional or managerial family background going to university are nearly twelve times better than those of a pupil from a family with an unskilled or semi-skilled occupational background. There are ... clear class differences at every stage of education. (p. 9)

Other work by Farrant (1981) showed that between 1962 and 1977 there had been a 7.5 per cent increase in middle class participation in higher education (from 19.5 per cent to 27 per cent) however, there was only a

1.8 per cent increase in working class participation in higher education (from 3.2 per cent to 5 per cent). Farrant also shows that working class students tend to be found in higher proportions on part-time (rather than full-time) courses at polytechnics and on Open University courses. An interesting exercise carried out by Williams and Blackstone (1983) calculated that if the participation of working class students in higher education increased to the level of their middle class peers, a further 140,000 places would be required, i.e. twenty new universities!

The whole special education process, especially since the 1940s, can be seen to be a major agent of social control and to be intimately bound up with issues of class, 'race' and gender. As Tomlinson (1982) states: 'A sociological perspective on the history of special education can show how provision developed to cater for the needs of ordinary schools, the interests of the wider industrial society and the specific interests of professionals' (p. 57). In so doing increasing numbers of black children and white working class children have been disenfranchized by their removal from the mainstream system in order to facilitate the 'smooth functioning' of an education system geared to narrow middle-class norms.

Tomlinson identifies two different categories of special education; the normative and non-normative. Normative categories tend to include those categories of handicap, disabilities 'about which there is some consensus amongst lay people and professionals'. Thus categories such as blind, deaf, epileptic, physical disabilities, etc. can usually be agreed upon by using commonsense but particularly medical criteria and assumptions. However, categories such as feeble-minded, educationally sub-normal, maladjusted, behavioural difficulties, learning difficulties, etc, are socially constructed categories which depend on the values, beliefs and interests of those (usually middle class professionals) making the judgments rather than congenital or intrinsic features of the child. The proportion of children assigned to these non-normative categories has increased enormously since 1945 but in particular since 1974. For example, the number of children categorized as maladjusted (now labelled 'children with emotional and behavioural difficulties') in 1974 was 6000; by 1979 this number had increased to 22,402. An analysis needs to be made of the sociohistorical context in which this change occurred in order to see education's increasing social control function at a time of the beginning of economic recession following the 1960s 'boom'. In 1979 almost three-quarters of children ascertained as requiring special education were in the non-normative categories of ESN and maladjusted. The number of children categorized as ESN-M (now labelled 'children with moderate learning difficulties') has, since 1945, always constituted at least 50 per cent of *all* children classified as 'handicapped'. The normative categories of blind, deaf, etc. contain children from all social classes as one would expect given that these disabilities are the nearest to 'natural' inequalities.

However, the non-normative categories contain almost exclusively children from manual working class backgrounds. Furthermore, black children are assigned in disproportionate numbers to these categories. Coard (1981) drew attention to this latter factor in his research concerned with the disproportionate number of black children of Caribbean origin in special schools. The NCDS study found class differences in recommendations for special educational help; 4 per cent of social class I were recommended for special help but 25 per cent of social class V. The numbers recommended as suitable for transfer to special school were less than 0.5 per cent for social class I and over 6 per cent for class V. It should also be noted that boys outnumber girls by three to one in the crucial non-normative categories of behavioural difficulties and learning difficulties. The issue of 'disruptive' behaviour and social class is examined in greater detail by Mortimore *et al* (1984). Additionally in the ILEA project, Mortimore *et al* (1988) note that: 'Overall, it appears that the main differences in teachers' classroom contact with girls and boys was in the greater number of negative comments, referring to their behaviour, made to boys' (p. 67). However, they also note that: 'Boys also received more communication in general, and work feedback in particular, from their teachers. *Given their poorer performance in cognitive areas this is perhaps not suprising.*' (my emphasis). However, the work of Spender (1982) details the normative expectations and demands of boys for teacher attention as a function of their gender rather than the level of their performance. Even more importantly, this latter research details the *lack* of attention and teacher-time that girls receive (but see also Wolpe (1988) for a Marxist-feminist analysis of teacher attention and gender).

As Tomlinson (1982) states: 'From a conflict perspective much of special education can be regarded as a form of social control over a part of what used to be termed the "social problem classes"' (p. 69). The unproblematic acceptance of the concept of special needs can in part be attributed to some misguided assumption that there is an objective, 'fair' assessment procedure which can accurately define children's needs. But educational assessment is not unproblematic and is one of the major means of justifying and reifying inequalities in society. (This issue is examined further in chapter 11 by Brian Matthews). So, as Barton and Tomlinson (1981) state:

'Special needs' have become the rationalization by which people who have the power to define and shape the special education system, and who have vested interests in the assessment of and provision for more and more children as 'special', maintain their powers. The rhetoric of needs is humanitarian, the practice is control and vested interests. (p. 24)

Considerable time and money has been spent trying to ascertain the possible reasons for the persistent 'failure' of the working class in the schooling system. The genetic deficiency theories and the sociobiological theories are no longer the orthodox explanation of failure but these theories and their supporting philosophies still form the bases and limits of later 'social' explanations and theories. Issues such as health, poverty, housing, and size of family, have been found to be clearly linked with the educational failure of the working classes. However, no *causal* link has been proven, nor is it likely to be. First, an objective way of measuring intelligence or manifestations of cognition would need to be devised. IQ tests have been discredited, although frequently still used, due to the questionable processes by which they were devised and their intrinsic cultural bias. It is questionable whether a culture-fair test for *all* groups of people is possible or desirable. It is perfectly conceivable that a test could be devised on which working class pupils scored very high and middle class pupils very low. Thus, there is no objective way of defining what intelligence is; it is a socially constructed concept that embodies the values, attributes and manifested cognition of the middle and upper classes. Secondly, even if an objective test were possible, it would be difficult to prove the exact process whereby poor housing affected the intellectual development of a person. Those studies which identified housing, health, etc. as influential factors in a child's ability to achieve at school, are merely identifying the structural, social, economic and political features of working class life. Their effect, if any, is to negatively affect middle class teachers' attitudes towards children from such backgrounds and to position the child in a culturally disadvantaged way in a schooling process that demands a cultural competence possessed by the minority. Bourdieu and Passeron (1977) are concerned with the function of education in legitimating and perpetuating a given social order, by making social hierarchies appear to be based on gifts or equally obtainable merits. They argue that while educational achievement is purportedly based on ostensibly fair testing, the system actually demands a 'cultural competence' which is mediated through the hidden curriculum and enshrined in the overt curriculum.

In the 1960s, especially after the publication of the Plowden Report, cultural factors became the predominant explanation of working class failure and middle class success in the schooling system. Language, socialization, parental attitudes are the kind of factors identified as being influential. The issue of language is particularly crucial in the labelling and stratification process that occurs at the very earliest stages of the schooling process. Evidence of difference in working class language was perceived as a deficiency of language which in turn would affect the working class child's ability to develop abstract or generalized concepts. In 1975 a small-scale study of West German and English primary schools found that in both countries over 90 per cent of teachers involved in the study 'perceived the language of children coming from working class homes as being deficient in some way' (Schafer and Schafer, 1975). The work of Brice Heath (1983) in the USA identifies the different child rearing and literacy practices of different class and cultural communities. She demonstrates substantively the way in which these differing practices are reflected or not in the expectations and values of the school. For middle class children there is a high degree of match between home and school, whereas for the black and white working class children the implicit and explicit principles and practice of school are frequently alien. The work of Bernstein and Henderson (1969) and Holland (1981) defines some of this mismatch as class differences in orientation to meaning i.e. 'the selection and organization of meaning, of what is seen as relevant and taken as the focus of attention in any situation, and the way in which these meanings are organized in practical discourse' (Holland, 1981, p. 1) Recent research notably by Wells and Nicholls (1985) and Wells (1987) has irrevocably questioned the myth of deficient language in the homes of working class children. However, within a short time of being in school, class differences are apparent in the children's literacy development. This 'proof' of the negative schooling effect on working class children is nevertheless still interpreted by Wells as largely a deficiency in the homes of the children. This time the deficiency is insufficient access to stories which purportedly inhibits working class children's ability to develop higher cognitive forms and symbolic language. Alternatively Brice Heath's work highlights the way in which the implicit assumptions, expectations and ideology of the schooling process deny, militate against and in many instances denigrate the culture, knowledge, procedural rules and learning processes, etc. of the working classes and thus prevent educational 'success' when measured by narrow, white middle class norms. The ILEA Junior School Project's (1986) findings on the association between reading achievement and oracy indicated that the oral skills of children from working class homes is relatively more developed than their reading and writing skills. It is stated that: 'It will be important, therefore, to consider ways in which cognitive assessments can incorporate oral elements, so that children's achievements in verbal communications are taken into account in teachers' assessments of ability' (Part A, p. 47). The work of Brice Heath and others, therefore, even if it is not their explicit intention, give evidence which supports the view that it is not that the middle class knowledge, discourse, understanding, meaning, etc. are cognitively and intellectually superior to that of the working classes but that the middle class have the power to legitimate their versions of the 'stories'. As Brice Heath (1983) states:

> We have even less information about the variety of ways children from non-mainstream homes learn about reading, writing and using oral language to display knowledge in their pre-school

environment. The general view has been that whatever it is mainstream school-oriented homes have, these other homes do not have it: thus these children are not from literate traditions and are not likely to succeed in school. (p. 50)

The research by Ashendon *et al* (1987) into the issue of class and the schooling process in Australia calls attention to the particular mechanisms which they argue need to be understood as the operation of class practices and institutional constraints within the education system. Their theory is particularly pertinent to the secondary sector of education. The two mechanisms are the 'institutional control of schooling' and the 'hegemony of the competitive academic curriculum'. One of the most striking contrasts they found between the working class and ruling class schools was in the forms of control and the organizational forms thereby generated. They claim that: 'Ruling class schools are connected to their clientele principally by a market; working class schools principally by a bureaucracy'. These very different organizational forms are bound up with very different educational practices. '. . . Within limits, these different mechanisms permit the ruling class school to be organic to its class, and make the working class school as an institution a form of cultural disruption and domination' (p. 257). They argue, as has been argued earlier in this chapter, that the curriculum serves the purposes of the 'ruling' classes in the education system. They regard the 'individualist' ethos as a disadvantaging factor in the schooling process. This has been argued in more detail in Lee (1984). Ashendon *et al* (1987) claim that '. . . the practices of individual "achievement" through academic competition are in tension with most working class families and communities and the academic origin of knowledge that is institutionalized in the hegemonic curriculum is very much at odds with the way knowledge is organized, used and passed on in working class people's jobs' (p. 258).

The only way in which the children of the working classes can then succeed in the present schooling system is to acquire the language, procedures, rules, expectations, etc. of the middle classes. They must do this not because these forms are in any way inherently superior but because they are perceived as natural or universal by middle class teachers who, in general, have not acquired the intellectual attributes of critical consciousness which most working class children appear to have acquired at a very early age. This may well be due to the lack of disjunture, contradiction and conflict experienced by the middle classes particularly in relation to home and school environments. Their 'weltanschauung' or world-view has never been seriously jolted, whereas on transition to school, if not before, many working class children will experience severe discontinuities and conflicts. Many children who are capable of taking on these forms recognize the schooling process for what it is, a middle class institution where working class values and skills are unwelcome. Consequently they resist the schooling process and are then either syphoned off into some form of 'special schooling' (for example, remedial classes; ESL classes; sin-bins, sanctuaries; or special schools) or they are afforded little chance of succeeding academically within the mainstream system (see, for example, Willis, 1977; Corrigan, 1979; Ball, 1981). Either way the children of the black and white working class are systematically disenfranchised.

Teachers and Class

It can be seen from accounts in the two preceding sections that teachers are, therefore, crucially positioned as mediators between the wider structural inequalities of society and a universal schooling process. Teachers are, therefore, in *potentially* powerful positions to resist or relay the prevailing ideological consensus. Teachers' own class positions and professional socialization are therefore of fundamental importance in maintaining the present form of schooling and its ideological purpose. Teaching is an example of what in chapter 4 Urry calls 'vertical segregation' where women workers are concentrated in particular occupations which are subordinate to those in which white men of the same class might operate. In the early nineteenth century the majority of teachers were male but by 1914 women constituted around 70 per cent of the teaching force. This change was in part an economic response to the cost of recruiting the large numbers of teachers required by the introduction of compulsory state education — women always being a cheap source of labour. McCann and Young (1982) also suggest that in the early nineteenth century overt reasons for selecting men as instructors of infant children were related to assumptions about the ordering and disciplining of families. With the inclusion of large numbers of young children from all classes into a compulsory form of schooling, it could be argued that the concept of childhood and mothering changed (see Bernstein, 1975, p. 132; Steedman, 1987). These changes, however, need to be set in the wider socio-economic context of rapid expansion in industrial capitalism and urban trade. As Nava (1984) argues '. . . in this context both the "urban" and the "domestic" took on an unprecedented symbolic resonance, particularly among the middle classes' (pp. 161–2). The early nineteenth century saw considerable change in the organization of domestic life with the increasing separation of the workplace from the home. Notions of separate spheres of life for men and women along domestic/work divisions led to both a changing idea of family life and its moral influence. Since by the second half of the nineteenth century women had been firmly established as providers of the 'domestic' arena, then their incorporation into the schooling process as teachers clearly denotes both the status and purpose of mass education from its earliest days. Consequently, schooling for this and other sociopolitical reasons became concerned with the developmental and moral as well as the custodial and instructional. The 'moral' purpose of schooling is a particularly persistent and pervasive one (see Lee, 1980) as befits its role as an agent of ideological social control through consensus.

Some educationists, like David (1985) and King (1978) would appear to be claiming that it is this gender and therefore status aspect of teaching that marks out the defining features of the teaching process. However, many would argue that it is the *class* dimension of the teaching profession which is crucial in understanding and explaining the unequal process of schooling in society. It is primarily the teacher's class position in society and vis à vis the pupils' rather than their gender which enables the operation of a divisive schooling system. There are two main factors in relation to the teacher's role in facilitating — albeit unconsciously — the social stratification and social control purpose of the schooling system. One is their own class position and professional status in the wider society; the other is their educational and professional philosophy and practice which denies the existence of structural inequalities and therefore of social class. Teachers have traditionally been drawn from the lower middle classes and from the skilled working classes. Teachers, then as now, had to be trained in a way which facilitated the dominant role and purpose of schooling at that time. The desire to control the mass of people, especially the urban working classes, was an overriding aim of the development of state elementary schools. The historian Johnson (1976) states that 'the early Victorian obsession with the education of the poor is best understood as a concern about authority, about power, about the assertion (or the reassertion) of control' (p. 119). The way in which this control was to be asserted was through

> an enormously ambitious attempt to determine, through the capture of educational means, the patterns of thought, sentiments and behaviour of the working class. Supervised by its trusty teacher, surrounded by its playground wall, the school was to raise a new race of working class people — respectful, cheerful, hard working, loyal, pacific and religious.

There is much evidence (see, for example, King, 1978; Hartley, 1985; Sharp and Green, 1975; Pollard, 1985; Grace, 1978; Lee, 1984 and 1987) to suggest that little has changed in the role and purpose of education or the majority of teachers' uncritical compliance with the process. One of the potential problems in the late nineteenth century was the need to draw on women from the skilled working classes to be teachers. Since they were close to the social origins of many of the children they were teaching and 'civilizing' it was clearly important that they acquired the values and attitudes of the middle classes. Hence the purpose of teacher training colleges. As Roberts (1971) describes: 'sons and daughters from top working class families felt the need to conform as closely as possible to what they knew of middle class standards'.

Teachers were to become what Grace (1978) calls 'social and cultural missionaries — a kind of secular priesthood dedicated to the work of "civilisation"' (p. 11). Kay Shuttleworth, a leading educationist, set up a scheme of organized training for teachers in 1840 at Battersea. It was an explicit aim of the college that the 'human agents of control should themselves be controlled'. Cook (1984) outlines the content and purpose of early teacher training and in doing so demonstrates the remarkable similarity with present institutions. Grace's work on urban secondary schools (1978) reveals the mismatch between teachers' values, attitudes and experiences and that of their working class pupils. He describes the teachers as historically (1850) and presently suffering from a 'sense of shock at a cultural reality never previously encountered, and a sense of revulsion from the values of language and behaviour of the members of that world. This is shown in the typification of pupils as "utterly destitute of feeling or propriety" as "lazy and degraded"' (p. 32). Startlingly similar views were expressed by teachers of the urban working class in an infant school in 1980 (see Lee, 1980). Today, it is necessary for prospective teachers to have achieved quite significantly in the schooling system. For working class and black pupils this achievement can only be acquired, as was done historically, by taking on middle class language, values, attitudes, etc. at the expense of their own cultural identity and intellect. Achievement in the schooling process is significantly related to social and affective factors but which are deemed to have cognitive and intellectual significance (see Rist, 1970). So, whilst the feminization of the teaching profession is crucial to an understanding of the professional status and the moral control function of the schooling process, an analysis of the *social class* perspectives of the teachers is essential to an understanding of the legitimation of the socially divisive nature of the educational system.

Another significant contributory factor to continuity in teacher training is the development of a missionary ideology. Grace (1978) details the way in which teachers were (and still are) presented with a view of demoralized and disorganized working class life which is seen to be the consequence of *personal* failings rather than structural inequalities. Teachers then become concerned with ameliorating these personal conditions, compensating the working class children. This social pathology view of the working classes prevents serious analysis of the structural conditions which promote these differences or any critique of the ideological purpose of perceiving working class values, behaviour, etc. as deficient rather than different. The evidence of this process operating at the classroom level is substantiated in Lee (1984 and 1987). King's book *All Things Bright and Beautiful* (1978) also provides classroom evidence of this process although his interpretation of the data is singularly lacking a class analysis. Grace (1978) sums up the important role of the missionary ideology which more recently has perhaps become translated into the notion of 'professionalism':

> A missionary ideology for teaching in the popular system could then serve a number of social functions. It could help to sustain teachers in the face of considerable pedagogical and other difficulties which they faced in the large classes of urban elementary schools; it would preoccupy them with a Christian and humanitarian concern for amelioration and rescue; and it would serve as a powerful means of occupational control through its associations with notions of vocation and humility and relative unconcern for political, economic and social status questions. (p. 13)

Much of the writing about schools ignores the fundamental social class process and purpose of schooling (see, for example, Bennett *et al*, 1984; Alexander, 1984). Research evidence shows that teachers generally profess a 'classless' view of society. They deny their own social class origins and, overtly, that of their pupils. Students at teacher training colleges express similar views on the issue of class (see Lee, 1987). Many students and teachers appear to believe that they have achieved educationally because of their own individual ability and choice in a just competitive system. They appear to be relatively unaware and unconcerned that they are predominantly white, middle class women. The 'success' of these particular categories of people does not even appear to raise questions about whether this might mean that the schooling system is biased towards these groups even though this may mean the marginalisation of women in the process (see an earlier section in this chapter on the historical roots of the schooling system). More commonly, one finds, any pursuance of this issue either raises the social pathology view of the working classes (i.e. linguistic deficit; cultural deprivation) or indicates an underlying assumption that hereditary factors operate, i.e. the genetic inferiority theory. The cult of 'individual liberalism' fostered by training colleges militates against a structural or class analysis of the schooling process. There is considerable evidence, however, to demonstrate that teachers continuously make implicit class distinctions in their perceptions of, and response to, the parents and children, and that much of the teachers' ideology is based on implicit class assumptions (see Rist, 1970; Keddie, 1971; Grace, 1978; Lee, 1980 and 1987). Research in Australia into teachers and working class schooling (Ashendon *et al*, 1987) also highlights the way in which teachers 'categorise' children but make little reflection on what might produce these differences. The 'explanations' of the teachers are strikingly similar to those of Lee's research. For example one teacher in the Australian study explains differences as follows:

I think it is the parents' attitudes, the academic ability of the child, the set of friends he or she mixes with, the personality of the child. (Ashendon *et al*, 1987, p. 251)

As Ashendon *et al* state: 'This illustrates the characteristic mixture of psychologism, biological determination and simplistic sociology'. It also, as in Lee's study, highlights the predominance of individualistic rather than social explanations. Ashendon *et al* conclude that, 'In general teachers' images of their (working class) clients do not provide a good basis for mutual respect'. A crucial factor in all this is that teachers' middle class perspectives are not perceived as emanating from a specific class base but as being related to universal laws of 'nature' and 'reason'. The professed universal nature and interpretation of certain values and attitudes such as 'respect for persons', 'equality of opportunity' are central constructs in the philosophy of schooling and are either explicitly, or implicitly through the hidden curriculum, promulgated in teacher training institutions.

This therefore helps to perpetuate a consistent, coherent and uncritical view of middle class values and dominant ideologies. If the values etc. of one class are ideologically constituted as 'normal' and 'natural' then anything that differs from this or questions it is perceived as deficient or deviant. In this way the social construction of the 'failure' of the black and white working classes is effected and perpetuated by apparent consent through the schooling process.

Mardle and Walker (1980) found in their research into teacher training as a process of socializaion that even though teaching styles and strategies might change and develop over time 'they develop from within a pre-existing material and social context. Conceptions of alternatives will always be framed in this way'. Teachers' responses to contradictions and conflicts *within* the schooling systems and *between* schooling and society are resolved in varying ways. In the past few decades the development of the 'cult of individualism' and the social pathology model have served to explain these contradictions. The emphasis on individualism is a pervasive social norm but its acceptance at the classroom level not only militates against greater social consciousness but also ignores the nature of institutional schooling which at all levels is essentially a *social* process. The social pathology perspective facilitates the emphasis on individual developmentalism whilst in some part it also provides a rationalization of low academic standards and the typification of children (see Lee 1980 and 1984). At a general level this can perhaps be seen as a consequence of what Holly (1975) terms 'the contradiction of a unitary social organization of learning in a class divided society'. The overall role of teachers in the socially divisive process of schooling is cogently articulated by Sharp and Green (1975):

... ideological development should rather be seen as the result of the interplay between the forces of material and organizational constraints on the one hand and the problems of a middle class teacher confronting a working class clientele in a context of material scarcity on the other ... social deprivation models can function as ideological mediators between a societal context, where at the macro level, there is structured inequality of material conditions and rewards which work against the working class, and a micro situation where a middle class teacher, socialized into the ideology of equality of opportunity, tries to educate and maintain social control when confronted by large numbers of working class pupils with cultural experiences which, from the educator's point of view, are viewed as alien and inappropriate. (p. 195)

Class and the Schooling Process

The majority of children who have been the recipients of schooling since the mid-nineteenth century have been working class children. However, the understanding of childhood that permeates and underpins the schooling process is based on the experience of a limited number of middle and upper class children (for example, Froebel's and Piaget's work). The linguistic and psychological theories that have developed from these roots are the bed-rock of nursery and first school education and have produced a notion of the ideal child which operates frequently implicitly and unquestioningly at all levels of the schooling process. The disjuncture between how children 'ought to be' and how working class children actually are has been noted since the 1880s (Steedman *et al*, 1985).

King's study of three infant schools with differing social class intake notes teachers' definitions of the children from the professional upper middle classes as being implicitly 'normal' children and consequently the children from the working classes are seen as not 'normal' or 'real children'. King's study (1978) demonstrates a clear correlation between the social class of the pupil and what he defines as the 'family-home background' theory i.e. the social pathology view. He claims that the 'consequences of defining the children in this school (Burnley Road — working class intake) as slow in their progress and poor in their behaviour were seen in the organisation of the school and in the actions of the teachers in the classrooms' (p. 96). In contrast, the teachers at Langley School (75 per cent professional families) said little about the children's home and families unless asked and were not heard to be having general discussions about home backgrounds in the staffroom. Since there was little discrepancy between the definition of what children *ought* to be like and what they *are* like at Langley Road, no general explanation was felt to be needed. In particular, King notes that 'the mothers among them did compare the children in the school favourably with their own and talked about their own children in the classroom. Something much less common in the other schools' (p. 121). The children in Burnley Road School were described as 'below average', 'not too bright' and 'you can't afford to take your eyes off them', 'quite a handful', 'not house trained'. The teachers observed the children's behaviour, judged it and distanced themselves from it. Those who were mothers compared them unfavourably to their own children; their own education − 'They never told us children would be like this at college'; their own childhood − 'I never behaved like that when I was their age'. King's study produces evidence of the operation of teachers' class positions and implicit perspectives on the schooling of working class and middle class children. However, King is at pains to deny this class dimension. Astoundingly, he advocates the perpetuation of this elitist process by claiming that:

> Value-judgments are the essence of education. The cultural elements of knowledge, beliefs and behaviour are selected for transmission because *they are considered better or more important than others* ... The analysis of the existing system of infant education cannot ignore its relation to the social and economic structure but this relationship is not a sufficient criterion for its evaluation, which depends principally upon the acceptability of the value-judgements upon which it is based. (my emphasis) (pp. 148−9)

Steedman (1985) in her article 'The mother made conscious: The historical development of a primary school pedagogy' argues that 'The understanding of childhood that we now operate with is based on the experience of a limited number of middle and upper class children ...' This identifies two issues which are influential in the schooling process: (i) the notion of teaching (particularly pre-school and primary) as being premissed on some idealized notion of a middle class mother; (ii) the construct of the 'normal' or ideal pupil based on middle class attributes and values. As King's work exemplifies, it is not merely the gender of teachers but their class perspective and position as middle class 'mothers' that facilitates the social structuring of children's identities. Bernstein (1975) in an article 'Class and pedagogies: visible and invisible' critically theorizes the development of the 'progressive' pedagogy as the domain of the 'new' middle classes. He argues that while the traditional middle class own the physical means of production or control, the new middle class control the symbolic areas of communication. Thus the new middle class are seen as providing for themselves a new form of reproduction at the primary school level which does not, however, fundamentally challenge the structure of class relationships in which they are located. Many aspects of the 'progressive or invisible' pedagogy of the new middle class crucially disadvantage the working classes; in particular the *implicit* nature of the hierarchical sequencing and assessment rules. The implicit hierarchical rules which govern the interrelationships between teacher and learner mask the power relationship. The sequencing rules which govern the progression of how knowledge is to be acquired over time, by being implicit, are only known to the teacher and those of her social class and again mask the power relationships. Implicit criteria of assessment again give the *appearance* of the child being the source of the criteria. The inclusion of working class culture and everyday experience is theoretically possible within the 'invisible' pedagogical form. However, Bernstein argues that this potential may not be actualized 'because the form ... has its origins in a fraction of the middle class'. He points out the difficulty working class parents might have in understanding the hidden and ambiguous value system underlying the invisible pedagogy. Also, in respect of the multiple and diffuse evaluation procedures that are operated through this form, the working class parent is likely to be further disadvantaged in evaluating the child's progress or may disagree with the teacher's evaluation and use of these criteria but will be forced to accept what the teacher counts as progress. This process has been substantiated by classroom research (see Lee, 1980). Frequently, values and attributes such as 'independence' or 'play' that teachers expect even overtly of children in school are class-culturally specific. Children displaying different cultural manifestations of what it means to be independent or to 'play' are very likely to be negatively assessed (see Lee, 1987).

The middle classes' understanding of the practice and ideal of 'mothering' then crucially constrains the perception of childhood in the schooling process. It is possible then, as Steedman (1985) state, that working class childhood comes to be understood as

> an inadequacy, a fall-short of some measure of real and normal childhood which can provide a special vehicle of resistance for teachers implicitly asked to become mothers to working class children. Specifically, the real mothers of the children they taught were not able to provide models for their practice. The history of pedagogy in a class society, in which mothers of children in classrooms cannot provide a model for educational practice, and where it is equally difficult to make an act of identification with their children, may go some way towards explaining the position of working class children in school, and the theories that have evolved to explain their inadequacies. (p. 160)

The construct of the ideal pupil, underlying, usually unconsciously, the practice and process of much of schooling, is highlighted by Sharp and Green (1975) and by Lee (1984). In the latter, the research clearly evidenced that certain 'social' or 'affective' characteristics of the children were the effective basis of the teachers' typification. The teachers regarded the strong peer group interaction of the working class children as a 'problem'. They felt that this was particularly problematic because 'one of the problems in a school like this is the absence of normative models. We seem to have so few natural straightforward children that there are very few models for the children to use'. The teachers were critical of the children being so obsessed with '. . . personalities and people and other children'. This attitude of the teachers denies the social and cultural bases of these children's lives where communality and social interaction are fundamental values and status markers. There is also a clear notion of an 'ideal pupil', a model of childhood that the teachers are wanting the children to develop into and that the children are seen to be lacking.

As Keddie (1971) points out, Becker (1952) developed the concept of the ideal pupil to refer to 'that set of teacher expectations which constitute a taken for granted notion of appropriate pupil behaviour'. Keddie's research with secondary school pupils and teachers demonstrated that teachers' perceived 'knowledge' of a pupil is related to the organisation of curriculum knowledge in the classroom. The curriculum can be seen as what counts as valid knowledge. This can be seen as a contested area given different class-cultural perspectives. However, part of the process of schooling is to render this contentious area unproblematic and unquestionable. Grace (1978) for example, found some secondary school teachers who perceived that the

> traditional curriculum enshrined 'the best that has been thought and known', that it made available to the pupils a richness and width of cultural experience which would not otherwise be available to them; that its essential disciplines were concerned with the inculcation of rationality, order and precision . . . (p. 192)

Keddie (1971) concludes that one use of 'knowledge' in the school is 'to establish that subjects represent the way about which the world is normally known in an 'expert' as opposed to a 'commonsense' mode of knowing (p. 156). These elitist notions of knowledge enshrined in the school curriculum further support the concept of social hierarchies of knowledge and their appropriate manifestation, all of which disadvantageously place the working class hierarchies and products of knowledge in the schooling process.

Keddie also demonstrates that the teachers' categorization of pupils' ability derived mainly from social class judgments of pupils' social, moral and intellectual behaviour. She concludes that

> It seems likely that the hierarchical categories of ability and knowledge may well persist in unstreamed classrooms and lead to the differentiation of an undifferentiated curricula, because teachers differentiate in selection of content and in pedagogy between pupils perceived as of high and low ability. The origins of these categories are likely to lie outside the school and within the structure of the society itself in its wider distribution of power. It

seems likely, therefore, that innovation in schools will not be of a very radical kind unless the categories teachers use to organize what they know about pupils and to determine what counts as knowledge undergo a fundamental change. (*ibid*, p. 156)

Conclusion

On 20 May 1986, Sir Keith Joseph issued a parting statement from the DES on the theme of 'Education for an ethnically mixed society.' In that statement he claimed:

> British history and cultural traditions are, or will become, at least part of the common heritage of all who live in this country, whatever their family origin. Education must ensure that all children have full and equal access to that heritage, so that they can understand the society in which we all live. *Schools should be responsible for trying to transmit British culture, enriched as it has been by so many traditions.* (my emphasis)

This is the voice of ideological consensus and hegemonic order. The schools' role in this process is clearly articulated. This chapter has outlined the ways in which 'British history' is not the history of the white working classes and even more certainly not the history of black people in Britain or of women. Equally, this chapter has shown that British culture is not a homogeneous, unproblematic notion, even though one of the implicit functions of schooling is to render it so.

Sir Keith's ideals have been set in concrete in the *GERBIL* — the Education Reform Bill which became the Education Act in July 1988. Clause 1 (chapter 1, part 1) states that the school curriculum should promote the 'spiritual, moral, cultural, mental and physical development of pupils at the school *and* of *society*' (my emphasis). 'Cultural' in the context of 'society' is the same animal as Sir Keith's 'British culture'. As the NUT (1987, p. 5) response to this clause states:

> There can be no doubt that the purpose of education is being differently perceived from its traditional purpose in England and Wales and the emphasis has swung very much to society's needs. Moreover that society is perceived as significantly unitary in nature. The implications for the teaching of, for example, history are immense. The language of Clause 1 is the language of conformism and authority.

Since the 1960s in particular, there has been well-orchestrated criticism by right-wing educationalists and politicians of the schooling system. The main thrust of the criticism has been that education is failing in its ideological and legitimating function. It could be argued that the role of organized religion, historically, was to operate as the major agent of social control by consensus. In the twentieth century education has largely taken its place. However, in the past thirty years there have been significant 'law and order' crises, especially in the inner cities, which, in the main, can be seen as responses to an unequal and unjust society. This has entailed the coercive agents of control, such as the police, taking a higher profile. The GERBIL ideologically and forcefully reasserts education's place at the crux of the social control process. The Home Secretary, Mr. Douglas Hurd, detailed the role of education in the 'new' Victorian society in the Tamworth manifesto (see *The Guardian*, 5 February 1988). He claimed that a 'good Victorian' would be 'surprised and disturbed' by the 'decline in religion, in discipline and in respect for the law' despite 'the rise in our general standard of living'. Mr. Hurd significantly blamed teachers, parents and the churches in allowing 'social cohesion to break down'. So the wagons of ideological consensus are set to roll once again in a social and economic climate of increased and blatant inequalities (viz. long-term unemployment, etc.).

Bernstein (1985) conceives of the 'pedagogic device' as a 'symbolic ruler for consciousness in its selective creation, positioning and oppositioning of pedagogic subjects. *It is the condition for the production, reproduction, transformation of culture — the question is whose rules, what consciousness?*' (my emphasis) (p. 22). The GERBIL, especially through the medium of the National Curriculum, provides clear and unquestioning statements as to whose rules and whose consciousness and whose culture is to be reproduced in the near future. Through a centrally devised and controlled system of attainment targets, programmes of study, assessment and examinations, the National Curriculum aims to raise educational standards. The contentious, conflictual nature of what counts as educational standards and for whom and the value laden nature of assessment, measures of attainment, etc. are unacknowledged. In particular, the laying down of 'universal' norms or standards makes no cognisance of alternative forms of knowledge and understanding such as that exemplified by the working classes. Given the arguments made in this chapter regarding the process of schooling and the hierarchically divided society, it may well be that the National Curriculum is, at one level, merely making explicit and legitimating that which has operated as the 'hidden curriculum' previously. One might argue then that a centralist, elitist and consensual notion of culture is to be made explicit, legitimated and rendered part of the commonsense assumptions of 'proper' schooling by the National Curriculum and the GERBIL. Inevitably, given the arguments regarding the working classes and schooling made in this chapter, the working classes will continue to 'fail'. However, their failure will be even more unquestioningly legitimated through the proclaimed 'neutral' and 'fair' assessment systems being proposed.

Teachers, in general, have been seen to take a professed 'apolitical' stance. This is a crucial characteristic in a Western 'democracy' where conservatism parades as the 'rational' and the 'norm' and where the ends of capitalism are served by the ideological and hegemonic conception of 'political neutrality'. Surely, however, it is long past the time when educationists can shelter behind the shutters of 'professionalism' or political neutrality. Teachers, in particular teachers of the urban working classes both black and white, will continually and insistently have to try and accommodate the increasingly problematic consequences of the wider social structure, until or unless they are prepared to take action to challenge them and attempt with others to change them. As Benton (1974) claims:

> Educational practice and the decisions which affect it, belong to the field of political debate and political struggle; they cannot logically be taken out of it. Instead of pretending that this is not so, we should declare our interests and take sides. (p. 16)

References

ALEXANDER, R. (1984) *Primary Teaching*, London, Holt Education.

ALTHUSSER, L. (1971) 'Ideology and the ideological state apparatuses', *Lenin and Philosophy*, New Left Books.

ASHENDON, D., CONNELL, B., DOWSETT, G. and KESSLER, S. (1987) 'Teachers and working class schooling' in LIVINGSTONE, D. *et al* (Eds) *Critical Pedagogy and Cultural Power*, London, Macmillan.

BALL, S. (1981) *Beachside Comprehensive*, Cambridge, Cambridge University.

BARTON, L. and TOMLINSON, S. (1981) *Special Education: Policy, Practices and Social Issues*, London, Harper & Row.

BECKER, H.S. (1952) 'Social class variations in the teacher-pupil relationship', *Journal of Educational Sociology*, **25**, April.

BENNETT, N., DESFORGES, C., COCKBURN, A. and WILKINSON, B. (1984) *The Quality of Pupil Learning Experiences*, London, Lawrence Erlbaum.

BENTON, T. (1974) 'Education and politics' in HOLLY, D. (Ed.) *Education or Domination?* London, Arrow Books.

BEREITER, C. and ENGELMANN, S. (1966) *Teaching Disadvantaged Children in the Pre-School*, Hemel Hempstead, Prentice Hall.

BERNSTEIN, B. (1975) *Class, Codes and Control, Vol. 3; Towards a Theory of Educational Transmissions* (2nd edn) London, Routledge & Kegan Paul.

BERNSTEIN, B. (1985) 'On pedagogic discourse', in RICHARDSON, J. (Ed) *Handbook of Theory and Research in Sociology of Education*, New York, Greenwood Press.

BERNSTEIN, B. and HENDERSON, D. (1969) 'Social class differences in the relevance of language to socialization', *Sociology*, 3, 1.

BOURDIEU, P. and PASSERON, J.C. (1977) *Reproduction in Education, Society and Culture*, London, Sage.

BOWLES, S. and GINTIS, H. (1976) *Schooling in Capitalist America: Educational Reform and the Contradictions of Economic Life*, London, Routledge & Kegan Paul.

BRICE HEATH, S. (1983) *Ways with Words*, Cambridge, Cambridge University Press.

COARD, B. (1981) 'What the British school system does to the black child' in JAMES, A.

and JEFFCOATE, R. (Eds) *The School in the Multicultural Society*, London, Harper & Row.

COOK, C. (1984) 'Teachers for the inner city: change and continuity' in GRACE, G. (Ed) *Education and the City*, London, Routledge & Kegan Paul.

CORRIGAN, P. (1979) *Schooling the Smash Street Kids*, London, Macmillan.

DAVID, M. (1985) Review article of 'Education and the city', *Critical Social Policy*, 12, 4, 3.

DAVIE, R., BUTLER, N. and GOLDSTEIN, H. (1972) *From Birth to Seven*, London, Longman.

DEPARTMENT of EDUCATION AND SCIENCE (1978) *Primary Education in England*, London, HMSO.

DOUGLAS, J.W.B. (1964) *The Home and the School*, London, MacGibbon & Kee.

FARRANT, J. (1981) 'Trends in admissions' in FULTON, O. (Ed) *Access to Higher Education*, Guildford, SRHE.

FINN, D.J., GRANT, N. and JOHNSON, R. (1977) 'Social democracy — Education and the crisis' in CCCS (Ed) *On Ideology*, London, Hutchinson.

FRIEDMAN, N. (1967) 'Cultural deprivation: A commentary in the sociology of knowledge' *Journal of Educational Thought*, 1, 2.

FRITH, S. (1977) 'Socialization and rational schooling: Elementary education in Leeds before 1870' in McCANN, P. (Ed) *Popular Education and Socialisation in the 19th Century*, London, Methuen and Co. Ltd.

FRYER, P. (1985) *Staying Power*, London, Pluto Press.

GRACE, G. (1978) *Teachers, Ideology and Control*, London, Routledge & Kegan Paul.

GRACE, G. (Ed) (1984) *Education and the City*, London, Routledge & Kegan Paul.

HALSEY, A., HEATH, A. and RIDGE, J. (1980) *Origins and Destinations*, Oxford, Clarendon, Press.

HARTLEY, D. (1985) *Understanding the Primary School*, Beckenham, Croom Helm.

HOLLAND, J. (1981) 'Social class and changes in orientation to meaning', *Sociology*, 15, 1.

HOLLY, D. (1975) 'Education and the social relations of a capitalist society', paper presented at the annual conference of the British Sociological Association.

ILEA (1983) *Race, Sex and Class 1–6*, London, ILEA.

ILEA (1986) *The Junior School Project*, London, ILEA.

JOHNSON, R. (1976) 'Notes on the schooling of the English working class' in DALE, R. *et al* (Eds) *Schooling and Capitalism*, London, Routledge & Kegan Paul.

KEDDIE, N. (1971) 'Classroom knowledge' in YOUNG, M.F.D. (Ed) *Knowledge and Control*, London, Collier-Macmillan.

KING, R. (1978) *All Things Bright and Beautiful?*, London, Wiley.

LAWN, M. and GRACE, G. (Eds) (1987) *Teachers: The Culture and Politics of Work*, Lewes, Falmer Press.

LEE, J. (1980) 'Teacher ideology and the realization of pedagogy: A study in a progressive inner-city infant school', MA dissertation, London, King's College.

LEE, J. (1984) 'Contradictions and constraints in an inner city infant school' in GRACE, G. (Ed) *Education and the City*, London, Routledge & Kegan Paul.

LEE, J. (1987) 'Pride and prejudice: Teachers, class and an inner city infants school' in LAWN, M. and GRACE, G. (Eds) *Teachers: The Culture and Politics of Work*, Lewes, Falmer Press.

LYNCH, G. (1974) 'Ideology and the social organisation of educational knowledge in England and Scotland, 1840–1920', MA dissertation, Institute of Education, University of London.

McCANN, P. (Ed) (1977) *Popular Education and Socialization in the 19th Century*, London, Methuen and Co.

MCCANN, P. and YOUNG, F. (1982) *Samuel Wilderspin and the Infant School Movement*, Beckenham, Croom Helm.

MARDLE, G. and WALKER, M. (1980) 'Strategies and structure: Some critical notes on teacher socialization' in WOODS, P. (Ed) *Teacher Strategies: Explorations in the Sociology of the School*, Beckenham, Croom Helm.

MORTIMORE, P. *et al* (1984) *Behaviour Problems in Schools: An Evaluation of Support Centres*, Beckenham, Croom Helm.

MORTIMORE, P. *et al* (1988) *School Matters. The Junior Years*, Open Books.

MORTIMORE, F. and MORTIMORE, J. (1986) 'Education and social class' in ROGERS, R. (Ed) *Education and Social Class*, Lewes, Falmer Press.

NAVA, M. (1984) 'The urban, the domestic and education for girls' in GRACE, G. (Ed) *Education and the City*, London, Routledge & Kegan Paul.

NUT (1987) *The Education Reform Bill: A Union Commentary*, London, NUT.

POLLARD, A. (1985) *The Social World of the Primary School*, London, Holt Education.

RIST, R. (1970) 'Student social class and teacher expectations: The self-fulfilling prophecy in ghetto education', *Harvard Education Review*, **40**.

ROBERTS, R. (1971) *The Classic Slum*, Manchester, Manchester University Press.

RUTTER, M., MAUGHAM, J., MORTIMORE, P. and OUSTEN, J. (1979) *Fifteen Thousand Hours*, London, Open Books

SCHAFER, R. and SCHAFER, S. (1975) 'Teacher attitudes towards children's language in West Germany and England', *Comparative Education*, **11**, 1.

SHARP, R. and GREEN, A. (1975) *Education and Social Control*, London, Routledge & Kegan Paul.

SILVER, H. (1977) 'Aspects of neglect: The strange case of Victorian popular education', *Oxford Review of Education*, 3 1.

SIMON, B. (1960) *Studies in the History of Education 1780–1870*, London, Lawrence and Wishart.

SPENDER, D. (1982) *Invisible Women: The Schooling Scandal*, Writers and Readers Publishing Cooperative

STEEDMAN, C. (1985) 'The mother made conscious: The historical development of a primary school pedagogy', *History Workshop Journal*, **20**, autumn.

STEEDMAN, C. (1987) 'Prisonhouses' in LAWN, M. and GRACE, G. (Eds) *Teachers: The Culture and Politics of Work*, Lewes, Falmer Press.

TAYLOR, M. (1981) *Caught Between*, Slough, NFER.

TIZARD, B., BLATCHFORD, P., BURKE, J., FARQUHAR, C. and PLEWIS, I. (1988) *Young Children at School in the Inner City*, London, ILEA.

TOMLINSON, S. (1982) *A Sociology of Special Education*, London, Routledge & Kegan Paul.

TOWNSEND, P. and DAVIDSON, N. (1982) *Inequalities in Health: The Black Report*, London, Pelican.

WEDGE, P. and ESSEN, J. (1982) *Children in Adversity*, London, Pan Books.

WELLS, G. (1987) *The Meaning Makers*, London, Hodder & Stoughton.

WELLS, G. and NICHOLLS, J. (Eds) (1985) *Language and Learning: An International Perspective*, Lewes, Falmer Press.

WILLIAMS, G. and BLACKSTONE, T. (1983) *Response to Adversity*, London, SRHE.

WOLPE, A-M. (1988) '"Experience" as analytical framework: Does it account for girls' education?' in COLE, M. (Ed) *Bowles and Gintis Revisited: Correspondence and Contradiction in Education Theory*, Lewes, Falmer Press.

WOODS, P. (Ed) (1980) *Teacher Strategies: Explorations in the Sociology of the School*, Beckenham, Croom Helm.

Chapter 6

The Causes and Effects of Racism in Britain Today

Barbara McKellar

This chapter will begin with a brief discussion on whether there is any scientific basis for using the term 'race'. I will then go on to explore some of the reasons why racism came to Britain in the twentieth century in its current form. I will then examine some of the ideological means of maintaining racism. Thereafter, I shall try to see modern racism in the context of class relations before finally discussing some of the ensuing structures and identifying the changes in both majority and minority communities.

Racism is a topic which has recently been exposed to much debate and analysis. The term is one which is widely used and very often misused. Issues of 'race' are at times confused with those of cultural differences and ethnic backgrounds. It will be necessary to define 'race', cultural group, racial group and ethnic background before discussing issues related to racism in Britain today. Racism has been shaped by economic and political relations over a number of centuries, such that power relations are the main determinants of how racism is manifested. I shall therefore define my terms of reference and give an account of racial inequalities; examine cultural hierarchies; explore the ways in which direct discrimination occurs and review the structures which attempt to alleviate the effects of racism.

Finally, I will look at the ways in which responses to racism by the victims have created structures and systems of operations within their communities.

In recent times, there has been an increasing awareness that particular cultural group membership acts as an indicator of one's social, political and economic life chances. Analyses of inequalities have focussed on the differences of various income groups and their lifestyles and the outcomes, for example, Newson (1965). Since the development of the women's movement it has also become clear that the careers of women are structured heavily by a gender role which is a subservient one. Parallel to ascriptions of gender and the class relations which a person experiences is the 'race' to which a person belongs. Before discussing the impact which 'race' may have in structuring the socioeconomic positions of people in society, it is necessary to define 'race' and some of the terms which are used interchangeably with it, viz, ethnicity and cultural group.

'Race'

'Race' has been defined as a term to describe members of the human species who bear significantly different physical features. The term has been discussed in recent years with regard to its validity, owing to scientific inconsistencies. Were there to be actual racial divisions, then interbreeding would either be impossible or the offspring would display abnormal qualities. The classic example from the animal kingdom is that of the horse which when bred with a donkey produces a mule, an infertile offspring. When this test of cross-breeding is applied to 'racial' sub-groups of the human species, there is no significant deviation from the parent populations in any measurable qualities or aptitudes (Rose, 1969). In fact, it is impossible to measure genetic potential or aptitude. It is the environment and its related social conditions which act as a determiner, for instance, in varying the scores achieved in I.Q. tests. Another reason for the limitation in using the term 'race' is the fact that most other sub-species are the result of geographical isolation, for example, plants, flightless birds. In the case of human beings, there has always been a tendency amongst all groups to migrate, travel, explore, which has resulted in limiting isolation. The development of qualities distinct from other sub-groups of the human race has not occurred. Human beings of one 'race' do not show qualities distinct from another. People often cite dispositions towards particular pursuits as being typical of racial groups but this is not to say that such skills or strengths are immutable, for example, black sprinters may be the best but this does not prevent there being first class white sprinters who could oust them. Many such phenomena may be socially constructed, via sponsorship and training opportunities.

Despite this, the term 'race' is used as a social and political description for different groups of people and as a shortened term to denote members of different geographic origins of location. It would be fair to say that there are visual (phenotypical) differences between, say for example, an Innuit person and an English person, or between a native American and a native Australian, but where the concept of 'race' becomes significant is not in the visually physical differences, but in the differentials which exist between different racial groups in terms of power over their natural resources and the opportunity to self-determine the future of the nation states to which they belong. The 'race' which occupies a given geographical territory does not by itself offer explanations of how and why some peoples of the world have progressed and been able to sustain their populations whilst others have not. It is for this reason that the term 'race' has the significance it does.

Racial Groups

This term is used to describe people who share the same phenotypical appearance, for example, hair type, skin colour. The association of racial group with geographic location is no longer a meaningful one. It is not a matter for surprise to find members of most racial groups working in various institutions in Britain. It is in the political relationship between groups from overseas origins that issues of 'race' and racial groups assume immense significance. It is not uncommon to find that racial groups have been the basis for the formation of cultural groups within minority communities in Britain in order to confront issues of mutual concern.

Ethnicity

There are ties which exist between people which relate to customs, traditions and the material base which they share:

> Ethnicity is an attribute of membership in a group in which members continue to identify themselves with the nation from which they or their ancestors came. (Gollnick and Chinn, 1986)

This definition highlights one of the central causes of cultural clashes which may occur within an ethnically diverse society. There is a possibility that the maintenance of ethnic ties and the consolidation of ethnic association may challenge national cohesiveness as ethnicity includes adopting values and beliefs common to other countries. The term 'ethnic group' has been used synonomously with 'racial' group, perhaps because some of the many ethnic groups now represented in Britain are close knit groups with non-European customs. However, the Scottish have customs, traditions, dress and language, which would be ethnically different from the English or Welsh but would not be a separate 'racial' group. This confusion of terms has led to inaccuracies when analyzing racism, as not all ethnic groups have experienced racism in the same way, for example the existence of anti-Scottish jokes does not mean that Scottish people experience the same lack of social opportunities as the Irish or Italian resident in Britain. The nomination of an ethnic group does not give clear indications of factors related to group characteristics.

Afro-Caribbean is regarded as an ethnic group but this does not mean that it is ethnically homogeneous. There are many cultures which are subsumed under this heading in that there will be different national, religious and linguistic groups represented. What is closely denoted by

the term Afro-Caribbean is that the membership of this group is Caribbean in origin and that the prevailing culture includes traditions and
influences from Africa, Europe and Asia, as these were the continents
from which people were drawn and whose leaders were responsible for
the manufacture of Caribbean societies as we now know them. It does not
offer any other specific clues about the membership, as included in the
group are religious groups such as Islamic, Hindu, Christian (of a wide
variety, viz Catholic, Seventh Day Adventist, etc). In terms of language
there is a variety of creoles, English, French and Dutch. With regard to
descent, people are African, Asian or European, or indeed a mixture of
these.

Cultural Group

Culture is a system of shared values which is held by those who have
interests in common. This loose definition applies to many forms of group
association. Where one has a national culture, there are within this many
other smaller cultural groups which reflect a diversity of interests, beliefs
and customs, for example, women's groups, ethnic associations, political
interest groups. Gender, class, age, nationality and political belief can all
be microcultures which give shape to the overall culture of a society. The
above considerations suggest that 'race' can now be seen to be a term
which locates only one aspect of a person's overall identity.

Racism

Definitions of racism vary and have included dimensions of discrimination
which often bear no relationship to the reality of victims of racism. It is a
form of oppression in much the same way as sexism. I would define it as
an important aspect of the relations which exist between groups whereby
the same positional inequalities of opportunity, common to class and
gender, are structured around myths of superiority but in this instance
along racial lines. Here one finds the power that some groups hold is often
intangibly used to maintain unequal relations. I would suggest that stratification along lines of colour and power coincide to produce a dominant
group and an ideology which maintains the interests of that group whilst
drawing on the sympathetic support of other groups. An example of this
would be the way in which immigration policies which limit entry are and
have been used as a vote puller in working class districts. In this instance,
the power group is making a statement about the desirability of black and
ethnic minority people as citizens and, by limiting the number, is assisting
in marginalizing their position within society. The existence of minority

groups allows for fluctuations in the labour market to be absorbed by that group in that they are less likely to be able to compete or bargain for changes as newcomers. This is illustrated by the report in the official Labour Force survey:

> The unemployment rate among ethnic minorities is twice as high as that for the white population. (quoted in *The Guardian*, January 1987)

Whilst this phenomenon occurs, the interests of large companies and capital are maintained. The working class voter is made to feel that this situation with regard to employment is in his/her interest because the presence of black minorities has often been identified with employment crises. It could more logically be argued that the presence of black people would in fact act as a lever for social change from which all working class people would benefit. There are those who would say that in the case of education this has in fact occurred. (Dhondy, 1978) (see chapter 8 for a discussion on racism and education). It is racism that has enabled one group to see black people as a political scapegoat and another as a social, economic and personal threat.

What can be discerned from the analysis above is that it is power and discrimination combined across class lines to produce sets of social relations which then generate their own force. What is meant by this is that ideological positions are taken up by those who share different group memberships which respond and react to the presence of non-indigenous minorities.

It is in this way racism quickly enters the belief system of national culture, and because of this, opposition to racism has to be structural opposition. It is not the case that remedies can be found by purely learning to say the right words. It is not uncommon to find people who have been on 'race' awareness courses and have tackled their own personal racism at the level of attitudes but suddenly find themselves feeling uncomfortable when they realize that a black person may hold a structural position in society which is equal to theirs. This realization has resulted from my experience in conversational readjustments to minimize the effect of assumptions based on experience. Until black and ethnic minority people move to higher positions within the power pyramid and this kind of readjustment becomes unnecessary, then racism will constantly be regenerated.

Finally, if one finds a swift remedy to racism, for instance, the elimination of culturally 'normal' words from one's vocabulary, then the problem was not racism but racialism (that is to say non-power related personal abuse, for example). The ability to accept black people on an equal footing would be a more accurate reflection of an anti-racist perspective.

Structural Racism

This is the strongest type of racism. If one examines the figures and statistics for recruitment to positions of power and decision making or those related to income and wealth, what we will find is that with notable exceptions there are very few black and ethnic minorities represented in prestigious positions or in the higher income groups. This is because normal entry to such positions is usually achieved via educational success or by inheritance. The implications of this are that firstly the education system selects knowledge and constructs assessment patterns which operate against the success of both girls and racial minorities. Secondly, there is less likelihood of racial minorities having a high level of social status. Clearly, this is the case in the most part for historical reasons. The effect of blockages to the advancement of black and ethnic minority groups is felt on all fronts but the causes are due to class related ideologies.

Access is also closed because of trade union 'closed shop' practices. These are not intended to keep out black and ethnic minority people specifically, but the result is the same. For example, for entry to the Association of Cinematographic and Television Technicians (ACTT), one has to have experience of the field and yet one cannot usually work without trade union membership. This is in effect a vicious circle. Alternatively, a limited number of trade union memberships are allotted at the end of certain courses but places on such courses are limited and competition is high as a consequence. Those who do successfully get a place at film school are those with either the highest forms of educational qualification, for example, Oxbridge, or those with influential connections. The result is that very few black and ethnic minorities work with the film and TV industries. It is only by structural means that this can be overcome. In this example it was by the creation of black media workshops and enfranchizing them to the ACTT that this was in part resolved giving black media workers an opportunity for employment as well as validating their self-organized training initiatives.

Institutional Racism

Principles and procedures employed within the education service; in its administration as well as in its institutions, may, however well intended or rooted in custom, have the effect of reducing the opportunities open to members of minority ethnic groups and therefore be de facto discriminatory. (ILEA, 1983, p. 4.)

Changes in institutional practices are inevitably slow due to the bureaucratic structures under which they operate. Many institutions have policies which may, in fact, have been developed before the presence of sizeable numbers of black and ethnic minorities. This has meant that institutional arrangements may not have catered to the needs of all. This can be illustrated by educational entry procedures for schools whereby at one stage children of overseas origin were being asked to bring in both a passport and a birth certificate where generally a birth certificate alone would have been adequate.

Personal Racism

Individuals of all 'races' will at times demonstrate a preference for their racial group. To merely do this is not in itself racist as power is not involved. To exclude others from a social group on the grounds of race is a reflection of personal racism. However, to respond to situations and people in such a way as to reflect prejudgments based on racial stereotyping, when involved in interracial contexts, would be a reflection of personal racism, for example, it is often regarded as the most severe form of racism because it affects interpersonal relationships between peoples of different 'racial' groups and then subsequently shapes the nature of future personal interactions. However, confronting this is more possible for the individual than institutional and structural racism, in that others do not need to be involved and the effect is to swiftly alter relations. An example may show how the three aforementioned forms of racism can be interrelated. If we take the way in which house prices are set in certain geographical regions, often very close to each other, one finds that only those who are either wealthy or in stable professional income groups are able to afford them. The differential rewards for employment which are a part of the way in which British society is structured is harnessed to the sorts of privilege a person can enjoy. This is not in itself racist but as there is a strong likelihood that many black people are working class, 'race' compounds the effect. If you are black and go to an estate agent in such an area, the manner in which you are received is due to the visual signal which your colour triggers off. Even before your income group is known, it is possible to be told that the house in the window is sold. This example thus may in fact include all three varieties of racism: *structural*, in that the reality may be that you cannot afford it and will never have the opportunity to earn the required salary; *institutional*, in that there may be a 'white area' policy in operation; *personal*, because there is no way of knowing that you are not a highly salaried employee.

Having defined the terms of reference, I shall now examine the way in which racism has operated in Britain in the past and how this has developed to produce current forms of racism.

Barbara McKellar

Class Structures and Racism

It was previously stated that racism is vertically distributed, in that the ideologies underpinning it are reflected in the development of government policies, like immigration control, as well as in reactions to employment-related recruitment practices and by people in the workforce at grass roots level. It is my belief that the bases for current forms of racism are laid on colonial foundations of exploitation of economically dependent groups. This hypothesis may lend an explanation to how different groups have experienced racism in Britain over a number of years.

Anti-Irish Racism

During the period of colonial rule starting with overseas colonies, Britain has held economic leadership over a number of states. The addition of Ireland to the British Isles to form the United Kingdom is one such example of an economic dependence, in much the same way as Hong Kong or other states further afield. The case of Northern Ireland, in particular, indicates the British attitude to those whom they govern. The arrogance has been described by a soldier in the North of Ireland:

> In the days when we had a proper Empire, the army saw to it that when the lesser breeds were revolting they were summarily dealt with. The world has changed them. And yet after all these years of colonial withdrawal, we don't seem to have learnt anything from the recent past. (England, 1982).

The result is that, nationally, the Irish are viewed both in terms of their economic activities and the economic contribution made to Britain. This type of evaluation which ignores the historical and political background that has accepted Irish people into lower paid, unattractive, menial jobs has resulted in stereotypes of Irish people as less intelligent and also of a lower cultural group. Having suggested previously that there is no evidence which permits thesis of genetic superiority between racism, then it is impossible to substantiate any such ideas with regard to Irish people as an inferior ethnic group.

Based purely on the take up of the jobs which nobody else wants to do, the image of Irish people has become ossified as one of navvies and cleaners who have no intellectual potential. The culturally specific uses of language which in fact highlight differences of social experience have been used to suggest intellectual inferiority. The way in which this group fits into the class structure reveals exploitation and discrimination. The migratory movement to the British mainland is caused by ineffective employment policies and results in Irish people forming part of the reserve army of labour which is needed by the British economy; this applies to the young in particular. The housing and employment experiences are made less discernible by the invisibility of the group. This means that this group visually integrates into the population. There may be centres and social clubs but generally speaking the fact that those from the North are defined as British and there is free entry from the South (and thereby not technically immigrants) means that it is difficult to know where they live, how long they have lived here or whether they go back to Ireland in times of crisis. Recent research conducted by the Irish unit in North London suggests that, in particular, Irish youth are not catered for adequately in terms of welfare provision (*Irish Post*, 2 August 1985).

In summary, if one were to examine an area of social policy such as education, in order to discover the extent of responsiveness to this group, one would find that there was no real special provision. There is no acknowledgement of cultural nor social experiences of Irish people. The likelihood of a mismatch between the culture of the school and the home is high and is ignored in much the same way as for other members of the working class.

The importance of this link between home and school has been documented in the Plowden report as a reason for educational failure amongst working class pupils (CACE, 1963).

The European Context

Having located the most likely victims of racism as the economically dependent, it is necessary to put British racism in a wider context. The reasons for economic dependence on Britain have varied from group to group. Some have been put in this position by religious persecution, for example, the Jewish community, others by political persecution, for example, East African Asians. The appearance of such groups of people in Britain has been responded to via the limitations of class structure, so that if a particular group has financial wealth, then their ability to overcome the obstacles often presented by 'race' and class is likely to be increased. If one examines the case of the East African Asian who may have lived in Kenya for a number of years before coming to Britain, one finds that for reasons of history it was normal to assume British nationality and to bank financial assets here. Time and space do not permit a deeper analysis of the pattern of migration of Asian peoples throughout colonial rule but it is clear that such experiences may have had an accelerating influence in terms of their settlement in Britain. Additionally, this accumulation of wealth has also automatically eroded the class differentials between such a group and the majority community as well as altering the nature of experience of racism faced by that group. The economic position held by this group has altered the power relations which in turn are structured around a secure economic base and positively valued contributions to society as well as economic activities which carry a high status. This ability to alleviate the effect of the existing power relations echoes the experience of the Jewish community in Britain. The initial location of this group was in the lower working class, both in terms of economic activity and geographic location, for example, lower paid craftspeople and the East End of London. This has been improved by tremendous efforts of self-help which have provided the economic base which in turn has developed community cohesiveness, as well as increased the status of the group.

The vast majority of groups who are likely to experience racism as a part of their daily existence are those who came primarily for reasons of employment. It is the case that there are settlements of European ethnic minority groups throughout Britain.

> By 1861 there were approximately 2000 Italians living in London in the Clerkenwell area which came to be known as 'Little Italy' and there have long been small groups of schools, musicians, craftsmen (sic) and merchants living in various parts of the capital. There was also seasonal migration: peasant farmers, who took on subsidiary trades during the long Alpine winters. (Linguistics Minorities Project, 1985).

This early trend has been maintained throughout this century with official recruitment practices being instigated between Britain and Italy, before and after the war, to fill labour shortages. Current figures from the 1981 census reveal a population of 89,000 Italian-born residents (*ibid*). This portrays a pattern of European settlement which is mirrored by other nationalities from Southern Europe, for example, Turkey, Portugal, Greece, Cyprus and Malta, as well as Eastern Europe, Poland. The experience of battling for a secure place in the labour market is a universal feature of immigration and for this group the linguistic divisions which exist between them and the host community together with a strong trend towards linguistic prejudice expounded their experience of racism. The overriding attitude towards languages other than English is that such languages are regarded as inferior. The high status which English has always commanded, due to the influence held as an international world power, acted to devalue the linguistic heritage of the European migrant who subsequently came here to settle.

The Wider Context

The presence of black and other ethnic minorities from a wider international background has its roots in the days of the British Empire. The many European powers, for example, France and Britain, have had at some stage colonies which have supplied the raw material and labour for the development of what are now technologically advanced nations. The result of colonial exploitation has been the unequal development of the world's nations. The ideology which underpins this form of domination was very much based on superiority of one 'race' and its religion which was seen as being a valued motive in travelling and 'civilizing' other peoples. The effective way in which this was done has been a contributor to the notion that Western Europe culture and values are in fact superior. This is judged on the ability of European countries to develop their own nations which is seen as being an indicator of innate abilities, as opposed to being manufactured via favourable economic relations. The transverse of this has been to relegate nations who have not been successful in doing this as inferior in language and culture, and solely responsible for this inability. This perception of issues with regard to development and under-development assumed a greater significance when the period of post-World War II reconstruction started. It was to the very people whose land and resources had previously been exploited — the citizens of the colonies and ex-colonies — that Britain turned to provide the labour for rebuilding Britain. This now means that for historical, political and economic reasons, there is a culturally, racially and linguistically diverse population which makes up British society. This population, for the most part, experiences racism that is built into the means of entry, means of economic activity, as well as into the social interactions. There is an expectation which has been endorsed by previous historical encounters that such people are less equal and it has needed legislation to minimize the effect of such expectations.

The Ideological Effects of Racism

The ideology which informs British racism is based on ideas about how hierarchies of power and prestige are structured and this ideology maps onto the social structures within society. The result is that there is no real definition of racist ideology to which everybody subscribes but more a commonsense logic which is applied to the situations in which people find themselves.

The transmission of the ideology which legitimizes racism is best illustrated by the way in which the mass media are operated as well as how the agenda is constructed. Where relevant, comparisons will be made with regard to other dominant cultural institutions, for example, schools and the education system. The role of the mass media has been to communicate messages, as well as to form a part of the State's machinery. It is in industrial and complex societies that there needs to be constant renewal of consensus, as well as a legitimizing agency for the activities of both state and capital. There is a constant need to relay messages with regard to conflicts of values, both national and international. This is not a value free operation; there is encoded in pictures and texts significant clues as to what is regarded as 'normal', rational and desirable. The context as well as the form is indicative of what is perceived as being in the national interest. In the case of TV/film, both factual and fictional programmes complement one another in consolidating a British view of the world. The 'official line' on the role of the welfare state is endorsed with the content and perspectives of the entertainment programmes, for example, soap operas and sit-coms. The social issues which are seen as prominent, for example, current reforms in the abortion law, are resolved along official lines in weekly episodes of *EastEnders* (BBC, 31 January 1988). This means that when there is a change in ideological stance the media is actively used to gain consensual support. This has been neatly summarized by Ralph Miliband (1969):

> . . . the mass media in advanced capitalist societies are intended to inform a highly functional role; they too are both the expression of a system of domination and a means of reinforcing it.

Black Representation in TV/Film

The geographical distribution of black and ethnic minority groups is structured by the availability of housing and employment. This has meant that there are distinct communities in a variety of inner city locations throughout Britain, whilst in other areas such populations are numerically insignificant. The result means that there is a substantial proportion of the white population whose experience of multiracial Britain is limited to what is portrayed in TV/film as well as to various forms of news coverage. The absence from the screen of any real input with regard to the lives of black people has been an indirect statement with reference to the marginal position held by this group in society. The battles for integrated casting which were fought in the late 1960s and 70s (by the Coloured[1] Artists Movement) have been lost and what occurs now is the dangerous mix of documentaries about famine in Ethiopia (Thames TV, 21 December 1987) and news coverage of South Africa (1985 onwards). This is exacerbated by the stereotypic portrayal of black people in soap operas, for example, *Brookside* on Channel 4. This does not summarize the total media portrayal which is continually changing but poorly reflects the position which Black and ethnic minority groups have or could hope to have in society. This endorses the perspective that Black people should be seen and not heard. The voice through which important concerns are articulated does not speak on racial matters unless it is a matter of crisis.

Patriarchy[2] and Racism

As well as class, another significant feature of British society in terms of how the socially stratified groups relate to one another is that of patriarchy. This is the term used to describe the way in which gender divisions are maintained. Patriarchy has been described as the oppression of women by men (Banks, 1981). It is a concept with which many feminists have been grappling. It is fair to say that within the feminist movement there are differing perspectives with regard to analyzing how this oppression works. Three such perspectives have been identified by Banks (*ibid*) as being the Marxist, intellectual and radical feminists. The Marxist feminists have a socialist tradition where greater emphasis is put on class than on sexism in analyzing women's oppression. The intellectual feminists have placed greater emphasis on theorizing and trying to ascertain how domination takes place. Here the varying aspects of oppressing structures, procedures and institutions are the focus. The radical feminists have identified the most central source of oppression as sex itself. The social and domestic aspects of reproduction and the sexual subordination which accompany it are central to their analysis of feminist issues. It is my contention that the structures which are in place and which operate or have operated in the past to maintain women's roles as subservient have served a multiple function with regard to minorities.

In terms of patriarchy and 'race' all these three perspectives have a relevant bearing. Firstly, there are class-related factors associated with the employment of black and ethnic minority women. Secondly, structural and ideological sexism compound the oppression of black and ethnic minority women despite the Sex Discrimination Act of 1975. Finally, the experiences related to reproduction, namely gynaecological and paediatric care, reflect differential treatment in that services do not necessarily meet the needs of black and ethnic minority women. Invariably, translation services are not available and certain medical conditions have not always been given the financial priority which would enable the improvement in health of black women. A good case in point is that of sickle cell anaemia — an hereditary anaemia mainly affecting Afro-Caribbean people and causing abdominal pain, jaundice and recurrent short periods of fever. It took vigorous and frequent political campaigning to bring the plight of many families to the attention of the appropriate authorities before screening for the sickle cell took place.

The presence of black people here in Britain is fundamentally employment-related. What have been described as the 'pull' factors in Britain and the 'push' factors in New Commonwealth countries are primarily economic. The roles occupied by black women on arrival were predominantly related to the service industries. Reference to the post-war immigration recruitment speeches and adverts has shown that many black and ethnic minority groups were invited for the purposes of post war urban reconstruction (IRR, 1986).

The National Health Service is one area of post-war development for which there was a shortage of labour. A closer scrutiny of the recruitment policies with regard to nursing in particular offers an opportunity to further consider the implications of the feminist theories briefly outlined above. The fact that nursing itself is regarded as women's work, whilst medicine is more often regarded as men's work, demonstrates how a sexual divide can occur within what could be regarded as one profession. The account of how the professionalization of medicine was accompanied by the emergence of the male doctor is best described by Ehrenreich and English (1979). Whilst it is clear that a two-tier system of power and control exists within the service provided to treat the sick, with men very much in positions of influence, it has been asserted that black women are treated even less favourably than their white counterparts:

> The deliberate policy of recruiting Black women as State Enrolled rather than State Registered Nurses effectively limited ... career prospects and ... chances of returning home. (Bryan *et al*, 1985, p. 40).

The policy described above has had the effect of ensuring that there has been racial stratification within the nursing profession, with black and ethnic minority women in the lower strata. The importance of equal access to education and training cannot be overstressed. Success in any field of employment is dependent on educational attainment and to start off with lower qualifications as cited by Bryan *et al* can only guarantee a limited career. With regard to black British women the position in terms of education and access is one of overall underachievement which is less marked than for other groups, i.e. black girls do better than black boys and white working class girls. The overall effect of this is to restrict upward social mobility. The consequence is that first generation immigrants have found that their children have inherited the low social status which they have enjoyed with reference to employment (Taylor, 1981).

In terms of non-professional paid work black and ethnic minority women have had to undergo hardship with regard to employment rights. The overall economic framework within which companies operate is one which encourages the pursuit of maximum profit. Recent Government legislation which has effectively limited the range of trades union activity has also sought to protect the employer from disruption to production. Even before such laws were introduced there have been many struggles during the 1960s and 1970s which reveal the extent to which women in general and black and ethnic minority women are seen as dispensable workers:

In 1971, night agency cleaners employed to clean large office blocks came out on strike for the first time ever ... for more money, better working conditions and the right to belong to a union. (Bryan *et al*, 1985, p. 36)

The exclusion from trades unions is an experience which the workers mentioned above have shared with many others at that time and since. The campaigns which involved the Chix factory and the Grunswick workers received considerable media coverage. That women find themselves in such employment situations owes much to the way in which selection processes are structured and to the way that opportunities occur on the labour market. The ideology which underpins industrial and monopoly capital is one which reflects the need to have a stratified workforce whose members are easily mobilized and able to withstand bouts of redundancy. The threat of unemployment and the fierce competition for paid work is a reality that black and ethnic minority women have had to face for some time. It has been essential to assist family stability.

Many women are mindful of being able to perform their childcare duties. Take, for example, the opportunity to work on the nightshift; this may be unsocial working hours but it has allowed the possibility of taking children to school and collecting them whilst also being available during the daytime. Added to these advantages are the possibilities of also being able to meet hospital, clinic and dental appointments should the need arise. An ability to meet such obligations is essential as failure in this area can prompt the involvement of various agencies of the state. For biographical accounts of how 'race' and gender have shaped the lives of black women see Bryan *et al* (1985). For an attempt to theoretically incorporate gender and 'community' in a class analysis of post-war employment prospects for black people see Cole (1989).

Racial Discrimination

It is perhaps an inevitable consequence of the intrusion and settlement of outsiders that hosts will express doubts and dislikes, will reveal objections towards the newcomers. (Walvin, 1984)

The evidence of discrimination is widespread and although it occurs at different levels of social interaction, it may be that the documented cases are only the most severe and the tip of the iceberg. Even as I write, three white men have been sentenced for a racially motivated murder in the North of England. It would not be unrealistic to say that most victims of racial discrimination experience and, more importantly, expect to experience different treatment and would only refer an insuperable case to the proper authorities. Having said that it would be necessary to exemplify this. The use of abusive language or threatening behaviour is not expected but within minority group cultures there would be preparation for its members to make adjustments to hostility from outside. What one finds, however, is that if a job or similarly significant opportunity has been offered to a less experienced, lower qualified person, then this is more likely to produce a recorded form of opposition. This does not suggest that people who experience discrimination are passive receivers of all the treatment that is meted out to them. In fact, the constant expression of doubts and dislikes by the hosts may produce a personality which reflects resilience and an ability to cope with stress as well as to develop cultural forms of resistance. However, the work on the psychological damage caused by severe racism is worthy of note (Husband, 1982).

Evidence of Discrimination

There has been evidence of racial discrimination of a serious nature over a number of decades but this area is in general terms hard to define. It is often the case that the discrimination is indirect and racist in effect, rather than in intention.

The law on racial discrimination states:

Direct discrimination (Section 1 (1) (a)):
'consists of treating a person less favourably than others on racial grounds'
Indirect discrimination (Section 1 (1) (b)):
'occurs when a condition or requirement applied to all irregardless of race is such that a considerably smaller proportion of persons of a particular racial group can comply with it than others, the requirement cannot be shown to be justifiable on non-racial grounds and inability to comply with it is to that person's detriment'.

It is the former of these I would like to illustrate. A recent case of direct discrimination has been investigated by the Commission for Racial Equality (CRE) at a London teaching hospital. This revealed that the computer programme which was used to select the applicants for an interview was biased against both female and ethnic minority applicants. The questions fed into the programme included reference to the racial group and gender and allocated scores to each of these characteristics. Caucasian scored less than non-Caucasian and for gender, males scored less than females. The lower the score, the more likely a candidate was to be called for interview. It was normal only for candidates with less than 40 points to be interviewed in the first wave of interviewing. A female candidate's score would be multiplied by 1.05 thus increasing her personal score:

> since 'non-Caucasian' had had their scores depressed by the racial (and gender) weightings in the computer programme, they were

likely to be considered for interview later than they should have been and when they already held offers from other universities. The estimated number who might have been affected in this way in 1985/86 is 15 (CRE, 1988, p. 10).

It is worthy of note that the term Caucasian is not unproblematic in that this group includes people from both Europe and Asia and colour is not a significant attribute for categorizing somebody as 'Caucasian'. Also, it would seem that the information used to discern whether somebody was 'Caucasian' or not, was based on their name, place of birth or 'other indications'. There were also questions based on educational background, parental occupation, type of school and connections with the hospital. This in itself is not directly discriminatory but indirectly. This is an area in which many ethnic minority candidates are less likely to be impressive especially in the light of fierce competition. The chances are that they would not be as able to satisfy these criteria in the same way as their white counterparts. Prospective candidates who are not able to demonstrate qualities which are 'class' specific were penalised, for example, evidence of social and community work. The existence of many overseas professionals from the Asian continent would seem to mask the fact that there is any discrimination. The reality is that for those seeking entry from the British born market, the class relations which they enjoy act as a barrier to entry (*ibid*). This is clearly indicative of direct and indirect discrimination. The location of the majority of black and ethnic minority school leavers for reasons outlined earlier is more likely to be in 'class' terms at the bottom of the social strata. This means that the normal routes to high status professions is more likely to be state education; current statistics reveal that pupils from an Asian background are more likely to stay on at school or go to further education in order to reach 'O' and 'A' level standard (ILEA, Research and Statistics 1985/86). This survey would seem to indicate that schools are not assisting pupils to reach their full potential in the normal period of schooling. Therefore, the privileges which are enjoyed by those coming from a more affluent background, especially with reference to use of spare time, are less likely to be shared in common with pupils from ethnic minority backgrounds. The case cited here illustrates the subtle way in which institutional values and procedures operate against those who have a different culture and history.

The operation of entry procedures has been investigated in this instance by the CRE but I would suggest that this area of entry to higher education and the professions is one where there still needs to be much campaigning and vigilance to eliminate racist practices and procedures. The case cited to illustrate the way in which discrimination is legally defined and dealt with also reveals how ingrained and sub-conscious racism is in that the procedures assumed different values in terms of two social groups and this judgment was institutionalized, via computer programmes. There has been an increased growth in industries related to the 'race relations' legislation, not least due to the need for more preventative measures which, in theory, would tackle problems at the roots. Although there may be cynical opposition to the development of 'race relations' agencies, it is the first step in recognizing that there is a need to deconstruct the systems which oppress members of minority racial groups. It is the opinion of the writer that much of the development of the anti-racist lobby has been as a direct result of the resistance of 'racial' minority groups and that although the solutions found as a response, for example, CRE, may not be ideal, it reflects the power of opposition born from oppression. Recent and tangible illustrations of the responses to oppression can be seen in the actions of inner city youth by their involvement in civil disturbances nationally. Although they were not all racial minorities, it was possible whether by fair means or foul, to refocus political attention on the plight of such minorities.

The Effects of Racism on both Majority and Minority Racial Communities

The result of 'racial' segmentation both within and across class, gender, employment, income and power groups is that language is structured as are expectations of both minority racial groups and their counterparts in the society at large. The attachment of values both positive and negative to minority racial groups is fed via language into the cultural norms of the society which in turn is reflected in how such groups are treated and as a consequence of that in how they respond and develop. It is not by accident that some settlers from the Asian sub-continent of India and Pakistan, etc., are successful in terms of economic activity and also bear positive stereotypes. This observation, although a generalization, has been shaped by the colonial experience of such migrants and by the space allotted to them in the employment sector. However, it should be stressed that 85 per cent of Asians are employees rather than employers (Curran and Burrows, 1988). This assertion can be made more credible by the obstacles faced by Afro-Caribbean business people who have not had the same success in establishing a base in the entrepreneurial side of the employment market. A specific case whih exemplifies this is that of a millionnaire black businessperson who did not receive any financial support from the High Street banks, despite numerous attempts to secure a loan. This reveals a lack of confidence in what was seen as a commercial venture linked directly to the needs of the Afro-Caribbean community. This existence of differential expectations and treatment yields its own results and a cycle of perpetuation begins. Those who are seen to prosper reap positive rewards in terms of acceptance and status. The converse of this is also true and, to those who fall into this category, many actions of resistance are needed. Thus the 'racial' experiences of different groups have consequences for their development and interrelationships both with the majority community and with each other.

If one takes the case of the Afro-Caribbean community, the sequence of responses to racial inequality have been distinctive and can allow the development of insight into the cases of other groups. The early immigrant settlers were able to resist the effects of racism by settling in enclaves related to the specific forms of employment. This provided not only protection but also allowed the development of kinship networks within the community. The next stage was not to remain, however, in this tightly bound group but to seek the advancements for which they had originally migrated. This initially involved formulating pressure groups around the issues of education. So where the period immediately post-war (i.e. the late 1940s and 1950s) was characterized by first generation responses to racism in housing and employment, the 1960s became the period of lobbying on behalf of the second generation. This in itself may sound quite tame but when one considers the permanent black enclaves, for example, Liverpool, Cardiff, where little structural change had taken place for a number of decades, this politicization of the more recent immigrant groups is a major achievement.

Those who had settled early bought homes and housed the newcomer and fought actively for an improvement in the future prospects for their children. The next stage was that related to the assertion of cultural status. This was achieved primarily in the fields of music and fashion influenced not least by the revolution in black consciousness which swept the black diaspora in the late 1960s and early 1970s. The period which followed and up until the present time is one which has been dominated by mainstream political activity in both trade unions and party political groups. The focus is now much more on representation in all major spheres of public life as well as on penetrating influential bodies which have the task of allocating (scarce) resources and affecting the quality of life chances.

This brief summary of events has occurred in a rapidly changing Britain. It has been the case that the decline in the British economy and the erosion of the values implicit in the slogan 'British is best' has revealed that the value of 'best' is not immutable. In other words Japanese and German cultural norms can produce economic supremacy in much the same way as any other nation. Potential in any area is now no longer related to a given nationality or continent. The illogic of superiority has not disappeared (and, in fact, has been given a boost by Thatcherism) but it is being eroded as the size and power of Britain assume a more logical proportion. This does not mean that scapegoating does not occur. The shake-up in values has not yet permeated all spheres of thought. The class structure, as previously mentioned, which reserves a place for black people at the bottom allows members of that group to be the centre of focus in exhorting the values which are seen as important. It is for that reason that campaigns against crime are associated with black people. Mugging and burglaries are located as black crime along with fiddling social security and when the point is made that this is undesirable (which it is) then the logical conclusion is that the groups who are identified with causing it are also undesirable. If one were to examine the cases of stock market insider-dealing, one would find that this is predominantly, if not exclusively a white (male) crime, but the same conclusions are rarely drawn. These two examples reveal that racism has its own logic and generates an impetus of its own by appearing and structuring perceptions and actions.

The effect of 'racially' structured experiences in British society cannot be summarized readily because as it was stated earlier there is not one common exprience for all groups although there are generalized similarities. At a personal level, members of ethnic minority groups are less inclined to think of their position here as a transitional one as was first previously thought. In recent times what has occurred is the evolution of a new black identity for Asian, Afro-Caribbean and other peoples which has developed out of the new experiences which people have had. In the case of the Afro-Caribbean community, of which I am a member, the mixture of ethnic backgrounds has resulted in a fusion of diverse groups which have been able to unite around issues of how to cope, sustain and advance. The way in which the newer more subtle forms of racism operate has challenged the individualistic attitudes and the fragmented styles typical of earlier periods. So, for example, social societies which were previously based on specific islands of the Caribbean, for example, Dominican or Barbadian cultural society have given way to a more corporate Afro-Caribbean style of naming coupled with a specific reference to location, for example, Hackney or East London's Black youth/women's project etc. Collectively, a redefinition of aims has been engineered by the new economic oppression and the Thatcherite restructuring of society. The lessons of the early period of settlement, viz 1950s and 1960s, were that individuals cannot break down structures but that groups are forces to be reckoned with. If racism is to be minimized or hopefully eradicated, then reconstruction will need the full force of groups who believe that changes can be achieved.

Notes

1 This term is no longer used and indeed is now considered offensive. The preferred term is black or Afro-Caribbean or Asian, depending on context.
2 See also chapter 8 for a discussion of patriarchy.

References

BANKS, O. (1981) *Faces of Feminism*, Oxford, Martin Robertson.

BRYAN, B., DADZIE, S. and SCAFE, S. (1985) *Heart of the Race — Black Women's Lives in Britain*, London, Virago Press.

CENTRAL ADIVSORY COUNCIL FOR EDUCATION (1963) *Half Our Future*, London, HMSO.

COLE, M. (1989) '"Race" and class or 'race', class, gender and community?: A critical appraisal of the racialised faction of the working class thesis', *British Journal of Sociology*, March.

COMMISSION FOR RACIAL EQUALITY (1988) *Medical School Admission*, London, CRE.

CURRAN, J. and BURROWS, R. (1988) *Enterprise in Britain: A National Profile of Small Business Owners and the Self-employed*, available from the Business Research Trust, Francis House, Francis Street, London, SW1 IDE.

DHONDY, F. (1978) in DHONDY, F., BESSE, B. and HASSAN, L. (Eds) *Black Explosion in British Schools*, London, Race Today.

EHRENREICH, B. and ENGLISH, D. (1979) *For Her Own Good*, London, Pluto Press.

ENGLAND, J. (1982) *British Soldiers Speak Out in Ireland*, London, Information on Ireland (1).

GOLLNICK, D. and CHINN, P.C. (1986) *Multicultural Education in a Pluralistic Society*, London, Merrill.

HUSBAND, C. (1982) *Race in Britain*, London, Hutchinson.

ILEA (1983) *Race, Sex and Class 05: Multiethnic Education in Further, Higher and Community Education*, London, ILEA.

ILEA (1987) *Ethnic Background and Examination Results, 1985 and 1986*, London, ILEA.

INSTITUTE of RACE RELATIONS (1986) *The Fight Against Racism*, London, IRR.

LINGUISTIC MINORITIES PROJECT (1985) *The Other Languages of England*, London, Routledge & Kegan Paul.

MILIBAND, R. (1969) *The State in Capitalist Society*, London, Weidenfeld and Nicolson.

NEWSON (1963) *Half Our Future*, London, The Minister of Education's Central Advisory Council.

ROSE, E.J.B. (1969) *Colour and Citizenship*, Milton Keynes, Open University Press for the Institute of Race Relations.

TAYLOR, M.J. (1981) *Caught Between*, Slough, NFER.

WALVIN, J. (1984) *Passage to Britain*, London, Penguin.

Chapter 7

Monocultural, Multicultural and Anti-racist Education

Mike Cole

Britain is a multicultural society and always has been. This is witnessed in part by the separate existences of England, Scotland and Wales. It is also evidenced by settlement from Ireland and elsewhere in Europe, both in the past and more recently (see chapter 6 of this volume). With particular reference to this chapter, it is indicated by a continuous settlement pattern from outside Europe, specifically from Africa, Asia and the Caribbean.[1] At this stage, it is worth stressing the point of *continuous* settlement. It is not generally known that there were black people in Britain before the Anglo-Saxons ('the English') arrived.[2]

I have dealt elsewhere with the racist origins of the Welfare State and with the continuity of racism and education from the 1870 Act up to the period of mass immigration starting in the 1950s.[3] Here I will concentrate on education in a multicultural society in the 1980s and beyond.

There are three broadly identifiable approaches to education in a multicultural society: monocultural, multicultural and anti-racist education.

Monocultural education has the aim of propagating and implementing the values of the British male white ruling class. Multicultural educators set out to teach children about other cultures, other people's ways of life, thereby hoping to instill respect for black culture and improving black people's self-image. Anti-racist education starts from the premise that Britain is an institutionally racist society, that racism cannot be understood without reference to economic, political and ideological factors, without reference to class and gender, and that educators should aim to dismantle racism.

The underlying ideologies behind these approaches has been well summarized by Richardson[4] (see table 7.1).

Table 7.1   Three approaches to education in a multicultural society

A — 'conforming'	B — 'reforming'	C — 'transforming'
Immigrants came to Britain in the 1950s and 1960s because the laws on immigration were not strict enough.	Ethnic minorities came to Britain because they had a right to and because they wanted a better life.	Black people came to Britian, as to other countries, because their labour was required by the economy.
Immigrants should integrate as quickly as possible with the British way of life.	Ethnic minorities should be able to maintain their language and cultural heritage.	Black people have to defend themselves against racist laws and practices, and to struggle for racial justice.
There is some racial prejudice in Britain but it's only human nature, and Britain is a much more tolerant place than most other countries.	There are some misguided individuals and extremist groups in Britain, but basically our society is just and democratic, and provides equality.	Britain is a racist society, and has been for several centuries. Racism is to do with power structures more than with the attitudes of individuals.
It is counterproductive to try to remove prejudice — you can't force people to like each other by bringing in laws and regulations.	Prejudice is based on ignorance and misunderstanding. It can be removed by personal contacts and the provision of information.	'Prejudice' is caused by, it is not the cause of, unjust structures and procedures. It can be removed only by dismantling these.
There should be provision of English as a Second Language in schools, but otherwise 'children are all children, we should treat all children exactly the same' — it is wrong to notice or emphasize cultural or racial differences. Low achievement in immigrant pupils is caused by factors within immigrant families and cultures.	Schools should recognize and affirm ethnic minority children's background, culture and language . . . celebrate festivals, organize international evenings, use and teach mother tongues, community languages, teach about ethnic minority history, art, music, religion, literature.	Priorities in education are for there to be more black people in positions of power and influence — as heads, senior teachers, governors, education officers, elected members, and to remove discrimination in the curriculum, classroom methods and school organization, and to teach directly about equality and justice and against racism.

Monocultural Education

The Monday Club, the largest pressure group in the Conservative Party, believes that:

> The Government should stimulate both research and discussions on the role of education in creating a tolerant, harmonious multiracial society based on British values and traditions.[5]

Whereas fascist parties like the National Front, for example, see the solution to what they see as a 'problem' simply as 'repatriation', The Monday Club, while favouring voluntary repatriation, accepts (at least publicly) that the 'problem' is likely to remain. If it must remain, then its culture must be destroyed:[6]

It has been Monday Club policy that there should be a ban on all further permanent immigration but it has always accepted that notwithstanding further controls and generous resettlement provisions (for any who wish to take advantage of them) a substantial number of such citizens will remain permanently in the United Kingdom ... we believe that many of the 'problems' of race are created by the continuing growth in the size of the immigrant derived community and by the real cultural differences that exist ... An integrated nation, rather than a 'multicultural' society, is the best way to reduce racial tension on the one hand and guarantee racial tolerance on the other ... The alternative proposed is that the Government should recognize in enshrining fully the human rights of every citizen permanently and legally settled in the United Kingdom, that these rights are best protected where *all* citizens are encouraged to regard themselves as socially and culturally British.[7]

This assertion is, of course, premised on the belief that there is such a thing as 'British culture'. There are two problems with such a claim. Firstly, it renders the term 'British' unproblematic. As Thomas has argued, in another context:

While there is some community of interest called Britain, and common institutions and historical experiences called British, and indeed a nationality on a passport called British, it is not an identity which is self-contained. ... Britain is a state, rather than a nation. The British state imposed upon the English, Scottish, Welsh and part of the Irish people, and then imposed worldwide, is an inherently imperial and colonial concept, at home and abroad.[8]

Secondly, as far as 'culture' is concerned it becomes immediately obvious that working class culture is different from middle class culture which, in turn, is different from upper class culture. There are certain cultural activities which are predominantly male, others predominantly female (owing to choices and restrictions). Some cultural activity is more associated with the young, other activity with the old. Moreover, there are a number of permutations within these identities, for example, young male working class cultural activity versus old female upper class cultural activity, old male middle class cultural activity versus young working class female cultural activity and so on and so on. What the Monday Club is referring to are the dominant ruling class white male values. For the Monday Club these values are inspirational and unifying. As they put it:

> Black and white children need to learn, and they can, of the nation in which they live and the forces that have shaped it. Britain has a great and inspiring heritage. Our children need to be fed on it, to be encouraged to make its values their own. Such an approach to education will unify, not divide; nurture shared pride and common loyalties, not cynicism and racial hatred.[9]

To the Monday Club, the urban uprisings in Britain were not about racism, urban deprivation, high unemployment but rather 'the consequences of attempting to create an unnatural "multiracial society"'. For them the idea that Britain is a racist society is a myth perpetuated by 'politically motivated groups':

> The vast majority of immigrants go about their daily business like everybody else but they are confronted with endless newspaper and television reports telling them that they are 'discriminated against'. They are so bombarded with literature from race relations groups, telling them how deprived they are, that they may be forgiven if they come to believe that they are deprived even if they are not.[10]

From this perspective, the educator's job is clear: *propagate the values of the British white male ruling class, devalue and destroy 'alien' cultures.* This is what I mean by monocultural education.

This perspective has been the dominant one in Britain despite the aforementioned continuous settlement. In the 1960s, the Assimilationist Phase, it was particularly elevated as *the* approach since there was a culture deficit ideology in operation which was predicated by a liberal racism which implied that though black people were not yet equal to whites, they could be if they adopted so-called British culture.[11]

After the Assimilationist Phase, there was a move towards integrationism which replaced the call for black people to 'get lost in the social fabric or perish' with a call for the black community to make an effort to integrate. Their culture was to be tolerated as long as *they* did the integrating.[12]

The third phase was that of multicultural education, based on the premise that social relations can be wholly explained through culture. This is discussed in detail below. It should be pointed out that none of these phases were merely *imposed* by governments with varying degrees of social awareness (many LEAs and schools steadfastly maintained a monocultural approach anyway) but occurred as a result of demands and responses by black communities, teachers and respective governments. The point that needs to be made is that none of them have actually challenged institutionalized racism (or sexism or classism) and, as such, they are fundamentally different from anti-racist education, which although 'always present as a form, [has] only recently [been] expressed as a specific educational ideology and kind of educational politics [which] reflects a truly alternative and oppositional expression'.[13]

The policy favoured by the present Government is, as substantiated by recent written and spoken pronouncements, and, of course, by their policies, clearly monocultural. However, as Hatcher argues, there was a time when anti-racist education (or 'education for racial equality' as he puts it) was tolerated. Such tolerance for anti-racist initiatives demanded by dissatisfied parents and school students was the result, he suggests, of three conjunctural factors: (i) the uprisings in the inner cities of 1980 and 1981 which 'gave credence to more radical indictments of racism, from the Rampton Report onwards, and demanded a more urgent response'; (ii) the coming to power of a number of left Labour councils, strongly influenced by the socialist current within the Labour movement and committed to policies for racial equality; and (iii) what Hatcher describes as a 'vacuum in Tory policy' in the early 1980s. The Tories, he argues, had still to win those decisive political victories — in particular over the miners and local governments. This weakness, he goes on, allowed space for local authorities to introduce education for racial equality policies which even sucked in local Tory councillors who had no operable alternative.[14] Times have now changed. The left wing Labour councils have either been defeated, are under threat or have given in and Tory councillors and MPs (and their academic supporters)[15] are actively opposed to anti-racist practices both for ideological reasons (the province of 'the loony left') and for possible electoral mileage.

Hatcher suggests that the Scarman Report, following the uprisings of 1980/81, is the last concession to the politics of liberal consensus. The uprisings of 1985, he reminds us, led not to more Scarmans but to more policing. In education, he concludes, the Conservatives' real solution is not education for racial equality but for projects like City Technology Colleges (CTCs) which offer a privileged ladder up for a few and which are targeted mainly in inner city areas where black people live.[16] Hatcher's analysis was reinforced at the 1987 Conservative Party conference when Kenneth Baker, the Secretary of State for Education and Science, challenged those who 'simply refuse to believe that the pursuit of egalitarianism [in education] is over'.[17] The Education Reform Act will accelerate the trend towards racist and monocultural education by increasing the likelihood of schools separated on 'racial' lines (since parents can choose their schools and schools can choose their intake) and by a National Curriculum tested at ages 7, 11 and 14 which will leave harrassed teachers little space for implementing an anti-racist curriculum. The Commission for Racial Equality (CRE) has suggested additional dangers:

— Grant maintained schools might, once they were established, introduce discriminatory admissions criteria that excluded ethnic minority pupils.
— Financial delegation to schools might result in a neglect of the particular needs of ethnic minority pupils, such as English as a second language.
— LEA equal opportunity and multiracial education policies would no longer apply to schools that opt out nor to polytechnics and colleges that transfer from LEA control.
— The proposals for the National Curriculum take no account of the Swann Committee's recommendations, there appears to be no place for community languages in the curriculum and the introduction of standardized testing and assessment may be culturally biased against ethnic minority pupils and disadvantage those for whom English is a second language.[18]

National control of in-service training and the National Curriculum will mean less guidelines and projects incorporating concerns for equality. The National Curriculum is an attempt to transmit Conservative values throughout the system. As Minhas has reminded us, it is no secret that the National Curriculum and other proposed educational changes have been the creation of an all white, middle class extreme right wing group known as the Hillgate Group, prominent members of which are Roger Scruton and Baroness Cox.[19] It is hardly surprising, therefore, given the political philosophies of such people, that the 1988 Act contains no reference to anti-racism (or anti-sexism). There is no acknowledgement either in the Act or the consultation document on the *National Curriculum 5–16* (1987)[20] of the Swann Report (1985)[21] or the DES-funded Eggleston Report,[22] let alone a recognition of racism[23] or sexism as issues to be considered in education, nor an understanding of the way in which class inequalities in general are reproduced through schooling. Again, this is to be expected given the class allegiances and consequent self-interests of those concerned.

Traditional Multicultural Education

Multicultural education, unlike monocultural education, aims to celebrate cultural differences in schools. The approach sees the school (and the classroom) as a neutral arena and all that remains is for teachers to provide the right materials.[24] In fact, all education is political. To do nothing about the activities of international capitalism is just as profoundly political as attempting to represent the interests of the powerless. For example, it is surely in the interest of the multinational mining companies for there to be no publicity about Aboriginal resistance to their activities in Australia. Hence, if a geography project or lesson on mining in Australia ignores the Aboriginal struggle for Land Rights either deliberately or not this *is* political. Most people would recognize a discussion of struggles over Land Rights as political, but how many would view ignoring them as equally political?

The traditional multicultural approach requires the teacher to 'teach' a list of unchanging attributes. This is in itself problematic. As discussed above, 'culture' is heterogeneous and differentiated according to factors such as class, gender and age. It is also, of course, dynamic rather than static. Curriculum materials have tended to limit black culture, to reduce it to the artefacts produced within a specified number of safe 'cultural' sites — the arts, religion [food].[25]

This approach aims not only to increase respect for minority cultures but also to 'improve self-concept' as a result of the content of the teaching. Self-concept is also to be enhanced by the general attitude of teachers. The belief that teachers are morally equipped to enhance black self-concept means that dangerous assumptions have been made about the capacity of white middle class teachers to 'do good' to young blacks. Such an approach is patronizing and allows the teacher to avoid examining her/his own racism. It encourages an aura of cultural superiority. Moreover, Stone has questioned the whole notion that black children need their self-concepts raised.[26]

As Bhavnani and Bhavnani explain:

> multiculturalism and a 'tolerance' approach are felt by many black people to be patronizing and offensive. It is also felt that such approaches do not confront the basic power relationships which perpetuate racism: racism is economic, social and political institutions.
>
> The attitude behind much of this work in schools is that if there are maps of Jamaica on the wall, or pictures of Bangladesh, with photos of yams or mangoes and projects in progress on saris, all will be well. This type of work is often referred to as the 'steel-bands, saris and samosas' approach. The racist education system, the racialism of schoolteachers and white students can be safely ignored within such an approach.[27]

Radical Multicultural Education

More recently, attempts have been made to conflate multicultural education and anti-racist education — to bridge the gulf.[28] In her article, written in part in response to Grinter's piece, Leicester goes even further and tries to argue that no gulf exists.[29] She begins by counter-posing structure and content, referring to the view, attributed to Mullard, that structure should get high priority and is equated with anti-racist education while multicultural education is to do with content. Agreeing with the necessity of a high priority for structure, she also demands a serious concern with content. Accordingly, she attempts to develop her ideas for an anti-racist form of multicultural education.[30] Before moving on to how she envisages this approach which she later terms radical multi-cultural education, I would like to argue that counterposing structure and content is unnecessary. My view is that there is a need to undermine *structures* which uphold racism and that this must include an anti-racist *content* within the teaching/learning situation. Once one dispenses with the notion that structure needs an anti-racist approach and content needs a multicultural approach, and continues to work for anti-racist structure and content, her distinction between alternative forms of multicultural education — racist (R) and anti-racist (AR)[31] becomes redundant as does her claim that 'anti-racist education must be ... "multicultural"'.[32]

What then is the content of Leicester's 'radical multicultural educa-tion'? It amounts to little more than an extension and a revamping of traditional multicultural education. She argues for a thematic approach at both primary and secondary schools. This means, for example, in the former level 'looking at "families across cultures"' instead of doing 'a project on India' (the traditional approach) and, in the latter 'developing our pupils' understanding of the internal logic of both Islam and Chris-tianity'.[33] I have argued elsewhere about the dangers of the traditional multicultural approach to the family — a session on the West Indian family, a session or two on 'the Asians', a session on 'the Greek Cypriots' inevit-ably leads to racist, sexist, classist and heterosexist stereotypes whether in the classroom or the teacher education seminar room.[34] Leicester admits that project approaches which are unrelated to the rest of the school curriculum tend to encourage the idea that minority cultures are 'exotic' and 'strange' but fails to convince how stereotypes would not still abound, even given a teacher committed to cultural relativism and who would look at families from a variety of conceptions of 'family' and from a variety of conceptions of what constitutes the norm even when there was an emph-asis on assumed universal features or a set of features to be discovered in all families.[35] As far as the internal logics of major world relations are concerned — and to be truly multicultural she would logically have to advocate many more than Islam and Christianity — I am left wondering just who is to undertake this massive task. Again stereotypes, misinfor-mation and confusion would surely abound. As Gus John argued recently, it is probably a better idea for religious education to take place after school.[36] He described a Moslem project for Moslem children, but there is no reason why different religious groups couldn't provide opportunities for anyone to attend. In the multicultural classroom envisaged by Leicester 'other cultures are surveyed' by 'teachers who are on the inside of various cultural modes of thought'.[37] 'Are these white (middle class) teachers?' the reader wonders. The answer is revealed in the next paragraph which refers to the 'relatively homogeneous teaching force that we actually have' who shouldn't assume that 'other ways of life' are '"exotic", "strange", "deviant" or "inferior"'.[38]

This has an additional flaw of the old multicultural approach — white middle class teachers teaching about people from other cultures' 'ways of life'. This I would submit, they can never be equipped to do. That it has been felt possible for (white) teachers and (white) teacher educators to undertake a feat of such towering proportions as acquainting themselves with a number of cultures to such an extent that they can 'teach' those cultures even to *members* of such cultures is quite staggering. Even if 'cultures' were totally static and homogeneous (which, of course, they are not) this would still present enormous problems.[39] Let me point out at this stage that I am not against the sharing of cultural experience in schools per se. Many black and other minority community and white children may often wish to do so. I am also positively *in favour*, as I will argue later, of the black community defining and prioritizing current and future needs. The result may well be, as it was in my experience of teaching black children in inner London, that issues at stake will be racist abuse and attacks, conflicts with the police, bad housing and, of course, unemployment rather than the 3Ss ('steelbands, saris and samosas'). Nor am I arguing against the passing on of information: religious festivals, proscribed foods, etc. However, as I shortly argue, I believe that anti-racism must be the guiding principle in the realm of education and in this paradigm white middle class teachers teaching about the lifestyles of other people from other cultures has no place.

Leicester goes on to reiterate her plea for relativism, the equal validity of all norms and perspectives, and her rejection of absolutism which assumes that 'there *must* be some overarching culturally transcendent principles of thought and value judgments'.[40] She attributes absolutism to the '"conservative" wing' of multiculturalists.[41] It would also apply to the right wing Conservatives as this chapter has shown. However, I think Leicester is wrong in denying absolutism any progressive potential. Anti-racists do respect cultural diversity but they also subscribe to 'culturally transcendent principles' — the principles of equality and the right for power over our own destiny. According to Leicester 'the "radical" wing [of the multiculturalists] concentrate on changing the structures of the educational system to provide equality (of outcome) for all children, regardless of race, class or gender'[42] but her article does not demonstrate this.

Leicester concludes:

Like Grinter, I believe that the liberal voice of genuine multiculturalism, working (albeit slowly) from within the curriculum, should not be stifled. However, there are important lessons to learn from the radical voice in the debate. The wider anti-racist emphasis is crucial. A multicultural curriculum must be developed within an anti-racist perspective, and we must never forget that multicultural education, even this anti-racist multicultural education, is not IN ITSELF sufficient, it is, after all, still located only in *education*, so it leaves institutional (structural) racism intact.[43]

While I would agree that we must dismantle the structures of racism inside and outside of education (strategies for which Leicester says very little) it seems to me that the 'anti-racist' multicultural education as outlined by Leicester, totally contrary to her wishes, could actually work to maintain racism intact by reinforcing platitudes and stereotypes.

Multicultural education, then, in both its traditional mode and in its new more radical mode, is essentially a white approach to education in a multicultural society. Its apparently innocent evolutionism (everything will eventually turn out all right) and its hostility to black struggle flow from its fundamental belief in the status quo. The protagonists of MCE aim 'to reform the system rather than to change it'. Thus, for leading multiculturalist James Lynch, the central issue which ethnic minorities have highlighted is the 'contrast between the ideals proclaimed in Western democratic societies, such as equality of educational opportunity, and the reality of the treatment — economic, social and educational — of minorities, particularly visible minorities'.[44] Rex, another avid contributor to theoretical perspectives, goes as far as to proclaim that he is not talking about equality of outcome: 'We should be concerned to ensure that all children have an equal chance of unequal rewards', since we can't wish the present system away.[45]

The minimum demand of black children, he informs us, 'would be that they be allowed the same opportunities as [white] working class children'.[46] Anti-racist education is based on a fundamentally different set of premises and it is to such education that I now turn.

Anti-racist Education[47]

The differences between multicultural education (MCE) and anti-racist education (ARE), as outlined by Mullard, have been well summarized by Troyna and I will quote him in full.

> [Mullard] characterizes MCE as *microscopic* in that its advocates tend to focus narrowly and intently on issues relating to culture. They are concerned with formulating policies to eradicate ignorance of other cultures, undermine the prejudice and discrimination which stems from ignorance, and develop greater under-

standing and tolerance of members of minority ethnic and cultural groups. The site of change is the school: the nature of change concerns the removal of ethnocentric material from the curriculum and teaching materials and their replacement by more culturally sensitive and appropriate educational aids and stimuli. Most recently, pedagogical considerations have been identified as important to the MCE model and the 'prejudice reduction' movement.

In contrast, ARE had been defined by Mullard as *periscopic*; that is to say it deliberately seeks to make 'a connection between *institutional* discriminations and inequalities of race, class and gender'. Here it is possible to see a link between Mullard's depiction of ARE and Stuart Hall's prescriptions for teaching 'race' which he outlined in his article for 'Multiracial education' in 1980. Both imply that ARE is intended to probe the manner in which racism rationalizes and helps perpetuate injustice and the differential power accorded to groups in society. Both also suggest that for the aims of ARE to be realized the issues of 'race' and racism cannot be abstracted from the broader political, historical and social processes of society which have institutionalized unequal power. In specific terms, this calls for the development of general theories of oppression and inequality within which the specificity of racism is not obscured. What is more, it implies the forging of alliances between groups both within and beyond the school gates and the identification of school staff and students as responsible for combatting manifest forms of racial, class and gender inequalities. In sum, then, and going further than Mullard, I would suggest that MCE focusses mainly on individual conversion. Moreover, when multiculturalists do take on board the notion of institutional racism, they propose reforms in cultural pluralist terms. ARE, on the other hand, prioritizes collective action and conceives strategies for change in explicitly political terms which lead to challenges of existing power relations.[48]

Elsewhere Troyna has suggested that the work of the black anti-racists like Stuart Hall, Prathiba Parmar, Hazel Carby, Gus John and Chris Mullard both informs and reflects the struggles against racism which the black community are engaged in.[49] In the educational context, the history of the struggle is marked by campaigns by black parents, teachers and students to improve the delivery of education to the black community — the bussing protests of the late 1960s against black children being bussed out to white schools, the 1970s campaigns against the substantial misplacement of black children in schools for the educationally sub-normal (ESN schools) and disruptive units ('sin bins'), the pressure groups to improve examination results and the development over several decades of strong supplementary schools.[50]

The work of the black anti-racists:

> is easily distinguishable from the multicultural education model, which continues to draw its rationale, inspiration and support from white, middle class, professional understandings of how the education system might best respond to the 'needs' and 'interests' of black students and their parents.[51]

In a similar way Hatcher has argued that the project of newer multi-cultural approaches is still not to see what role schools can play in strengthening black resistance by opposing racism, but rather to incor-porate a selectively expanded (and I would add, from their perspective, improved) cultural programme in schools. This is indeed implicit in Leicester's aims. As she puts it:

> A teacher with a relativist conception of multicultural education accepts that there are alternative and equally valid modes of thought and ways of life and incorporates multiculturalism not just in terms of lesson content and materials, but at the deeper pro-cedural level, at the level of the logic of the various forms of knowledge and their alternative key concepts, methods of investi-gation, truth criteria and so on.[52]

While making pupils/students aware that there exist various forms of knowledge that can be used to outline the essential mutuality of human-kind,[53] there are dangers, *if opposing racism is not central*, of institu-tionalizing difference. As Mullard (1986) argues:

> As the cultural representation of the ideological form of racism, ethnicism then constitutes a set of representations of *ethnic* differ-ences, peculiarities, cultural biographies, histories and practices, which are used to justify specific courses of action that possess the effect of institutionalizing ethnic/cultural differences. In doing this ethnicist policies and practices also tend to obfuscate the common experiences, histories and social political conditions of black and (ethnic) minority groups and hence the degree of communality of experience that might exist between these and certain white class groups in society. (p. 11)[54]

An anti-racist approach[55] starts from the premise that the society is institutionally racist — that there exists a complex 'race'/sex class hier-archy located within an exploitative white male power structure and that part of the role of education in *all* educational institutions is to attempt to dismantle that structure both through the hidden curriculum and the actual curriculum. It is absolutely essential, therefore, that all institutions draw up and implement an anti-racist policy.[56] This should cover such aspects as the recruitment of all staff and pupils/students, including advertising in areas where black people live and in publications read by black people, as well as the use of informal networks. It should entail fair interviewing procedures and the recognition of overseas qualifications and Access qualifications, etc. Any required qualifications should be examined to establish that they do not exclude black people disproportionately. If they are unjustified, such requirements are likely to be unlawful. In addition, the policy should include the monitoring of all practices within the institution, including the grading of pupils/students and the promotion of staff. In the teacher education context close scrutiny should be kept on teaching practice and school experience. For racism to be undermined in educational institutions it is crucial that the anti-racist policy *works*. All racist practices should be declared against the interests of the institution and therefore 'unlawful'. Appropriate sanctions and/or disciplinary action should be available for proved intentional racist conduct or practices. Such action should also be available for proved unintentional racist conduct or practices if warnings are not heeded. Finally, in terms of personal relationships, just as all women have a fundamental right to be protected from sexual harrassment, so do black women and men, girls and boys, have a fundamental right to be protected from racial harrassment whatever form it may take. Thus procedures should be available to prevent racist gestures, graffitti, remarks, insinuations or suggestions. Equal attention should also be paid to the written word both in school documents and text books.

The Monday Club advocates the repeal of race relations legislation and the abolition of the Commission for Racial Equality. I would consider the freedom of black people *not* to be discriminated against on grounds of 'race' to be much more important than the 'rights' of racists to hurl abuse at and discriminate in other ways against black people and would therefore welcome truly effective and seriously enforced race relations legislation both inside and outside of educational institutions.

As far as content is concerned, this will, of course, depend on the ages of the pupils/students and on available resources. Suffice it to say that there are good arguments for beginning anti-racist education at the pre-school stage and continuing through schooling into further and higher education.[57]

With both monocultural and multicultural approaches, it is likely that economic, political and gender-based relations of domination are ignored, possibly also along with racism itself. Anti-racists insist that these issues be central and that it is up to the black and other minority communities to define and prioritize their current and future needs with respect to combatting racism.

Such changes would clearly entail a fair share of resources in educational establishments where there are black and other minority community pupils/students and a major recruitment drive for teachers and other workers from those communities to work in all state institutions.[58] It is crucial too that such teachers are not marginalized. As Johnson *et al* have pointed out, even when black teachers are recruited 'they are often peripheral, or the ESL teacher working outside the classroom, or the mother-tongue teacher working as a part-timer in a hut in the playground and, as a consequence, underpaid'.[59]

It is essential that anti-racist initiatives be taken in full consultation with, and with the support of, the *white* working class community. The tragedy of Burnage High School, where an Asian boy was stabbed to death, has reinforced the idea that anti-racism cannot be forced on people; rather it must be linked with broader issues of class and gender.[60] This is no easy task. This history of white working class support for anti-racism has been contradictory.

Racism is a social product and is not 'biologically inherent'. There have been significant examples in Britain's colonial history where a minority stance has been taken against racism because of its inhumanity. We need to draw on this minority tradition.

As Hatcher has put it, in a good analysis, marred by its marginalization of gender,

> In Britain the Anti-Nazi League and Rock Against Racism represented a massive popular movement against racism in the late 1970s, and the 1985 miners' strike demonstrated the mutual solidarity of the black communities and the bastions of the traditional white working class, symbolized by the NUM's support at the 1985 Labour Party conference for the right of black people to organize within the Labour Party.
>
> In other words, the white working class contains two contradictory responses to 'race'. For specific historical reasons the anti-racist response has been a minority one, but, nevertheless, it represents a real current within working class politics and culture, including that of its youth. Its existence today is of crucial importance for anti-racist education, for two reasons. First, because it provides the potential basis for alliances with wider forces outside education to press for anti-racist reforms within education. Secondly, because it provides the potential basis within the cultural of white youth in schools for anti-racist teaching.[61]

As with class and gender, both short and long-term strategies are required. We must rid the classroom and the school of insidious and not so insidious forms of racism while at the same time not losing sight of the structural dimensions of racial inequality in the institutions of the wider society. Our immediate task must be to debunk the myths of anti-racist education popularized by sections of the press and to mobilize a concerted opposition to the anti-democratic direction in education, symbolized by the 1988 Education Act. There are several national organizations in existence dedicated to changing power relations, such as NAME (the National Anti-racist Movement in Education)[62] and ARTEN (the Anti-racist Teacher Education Network).[63] At the time of writing CARE (the Campaign for Anti-racist Education)[64] has been set up, in its own words, to

> mount opposition to and continue the fight back against central Government attacks on education and, in particular, anti-racist education, by forming broad-based alliances with the organized labour movement, communities and community groups, existing anti-racist campaigning bodies, voluntary sector groups, churches, charitable groups and others who wish to ensure that we all live in a just and humane society.

Quoting its aims and objectives will serve as a fitting way to end this chapter:

1 To mobilize a concerted opposition to the current anti-democratic direction in education, and challenge the new structures which undermine 'race' equality in education.
2 To bring together teachers, parents, pupils, working class black and white communities and other oppressed minorities to exercise greater control over the education system.
3 To redefine terms and regain the ideological and political ground which has been lost.
4 To present a vision/model of education which challenges the anti-democratic view and encompasses the rights of community groups through collective action.
5 To re-establish/expand the network of groups involved in furthering anti-racism and in particular anti-racist education.
6 To forge links between groups and individuals who are the targets of racist attacks and racist propaganda.
7 To present an accessible 'popular' critique of the current political, economic and ideological trends to be used by communities to protect and fight for anti-racist education.
8 To reclaim anti-racist education as good education.

Acknowledgements

I would like to thank Jane Lane, Barbara McKellar, Rehana Minhas and Madan Sarup for their very helpful comments on earlier drafts of this chapter. Responsibility for any inadequacies in the final version remains mine.

Notes

1 This is not to say that the concerns of multicultural and anti-racist education should not or do not apply to Europeans and others (see McKellar's discussion in chapter 6, for example). However, current practice and debate around that practice arose mainly as a result of the immigration of black people into Britain in the post-war period (black is used throughout the chapter in its contemporary political sense to include people of both the Asian and African Diaspora who, along with certain other groups, experience racism in their daily lives).

2 As Godfrey Brandt explains, following Fryer, some black people were part of the Roman army which occupied the Southern part of England for three-and-a-half centuries; others were slaves. Among the troops defending Hadrian's Wall in the third century AD was a division of 'Moors'. Not only were there soldiers and slaves, but officers (praefecti) from North Africa. Fryer cites evidence of a large percentage of skeletons of black Africans found among the 350 excavated in 1951, dating back to Roman times. From the evidence, Brandt concludes that there has been a continuous black presence in Britain. However, it is from the sixteenth century onwards that this presence has been most notable. (See BRANDT, G. (1986) *The Realization of Anti-racist Teaching*, Lewes, Falmer Press, pp. 6–7.) For further documentation of the presence of black people in Britain see FRYER, P. (1984) *Staying Power: The History of Black People in Britain*, London, Pluto Press, and conference papers 'History of blacks in Britain' and 'History of blacks in London', London, Centre for Multicultural Education, University of London Institute of Education.

3 COLE, M. (Forthcoming) *Racism and Schooling: From the Origins of the Welfare State to the Rise of the New Right*, London, Routledge.

4 RICHARDSON, R. (1989) 'Material, resources and methods' in COLE, M. (Ed) *Education for Equality: Some Guidelines for Good Practice*, London, Routledge.

5 PEARCE, S. (1985) 'Education and the multiracial society', policy paper no IR4, The Monday Club, May.

6 COLE, M. (1986a) 'Multicultural education and the politics of racism in Britain', *multicultural teaching*, autumn, p. 20.

7 LAUD, D. (1984) 'The law, order and race relations', policy paper no IR3, The Monday Club, October.

8 *The Guardian*, 14 April 1986.

9 PEARCE, S. (1985) *op cit*.

10 LAUD, D. (1984) *op cit*.

11 BRANDT, G. (1986) *op cit*, p. 13.

12 *ibid*.

13 MULLARD, C. (1986) quoted in BRANDT, G. *op cit*, p. 16.

14 HATCHER, R. (1987) 'Education for racial equality under attack', *multicultural teaching*, V, 3, summer, p. 5.

15 See, for example, PALMER, F. (Ed) (1986) *Anti-racism: An Assault on Education and Value*, London, Sherwood Press.

16 HATCHER, R. (1987) *op cit*, pp. 5–6.

17 Speech to the Conservative Party conference, 1987.

18 COMMISSION FOR RACIAL EQUALITY (1987) *Press Release*, no. 264, p. 1.

19 MINHAS, R. (1988) 'The politics behind the National Curriculum', *multicultural teaching*, 6, 2, spring, p. 9.

20 DES (1987) *The National Curriculum 5–16: A Consultative Document*, London, HMSO.

21 DES (1985) *Education for All* (The Swann Report), London, HMSO.

22 EGGLESTON, J., DUNN, D. and ANJALI, M. (1986) *Education for Some: The Educa-*

tional and Vocational Experiences of 15–18 Year Old Members of Minority Ethnic Groups: A Report on a Research Project for the Department of Education and Science, Stoke-on-Trent, Trentham.

23 This is pointed out in CROZIER, G. and MENTER, I. (1988) 'Anti-racism and the National Curriculum: The gerbil's tail — initial teacher education', *multicultural teaching*, **6**, 2, spring, p. 31.

24 CARBY, H. (1980) 'Multi-culture', *Screen Education*, **34**, spring.

25 *ibid*.

26 COLE, M. (1986a) *op cit*, p. 22. The reference to Maureen Stone is STONE, M. (1981) *The Education of the Black Child in Britain: The Myth of Multiracial Education*, London, Fontana.

27 BHAVNANI, K.K. and R. (1985) 'Racism and resistance in Britain' in COATES, D. *et al* (Eds) *A Socialist Anatomy of Britain*, Oxford, Polity Press, p. 148.

28 GRINTER, R. (1985) 'Bridging the gulf: The need for anti-racist multicultural teaching', *multicultural teaching*, spring.

29 LEICESTER, M. (1986) 'Multicultural curriculum or anti-racist education: Denying the gulf', *multicultural teaching*, spring.

30 *ibid*, p. 4.

31 *ibid*.

32 *ibid*, p. 4.

33 *ibid*, p. 5.

34 COLE, M. (1986b) 'Teaching and learning about racism: A critique of multicultural education in Britain' in MODGIL, S. *et al* (Eds) *Multicultural Education: The Interminable Debate*, Lewes, Falmer Press.

35 LEICESTER, M. (1986) *op cit*, p. 5.

36 Gus John, *Split Screen*, BBC 2, June 1988.

37 LEICESTER, M. (1986) *op cit*, p. 5.

38 *ibid*.

39 I am aware that this has general implications for current modes of teaching. Is the logical extension of the argument that primary teachers, in particular, in needing to cover such a wide range of knowledge can *never* be sufficiently au fait in order to teach? I think it depends on one's perspective on the role of the teacher. If the teacher is perceived as 'expert', then the answer is 'yes'. If, however, the teacher is thought of as a 'facilitator', then she or he does not need and, in fact, *should not* have all the answers. Her or his role is of guiding and enabling so that pupils/ students can learn for themselves from those, who, in our case, are *really* 'on the inside', but on the inside of complex, multifarious cultural formations.

40 LEICESTER, M. (1986) *op cit*, p. 5.

41 *ibid*, p. 6.

42 *ibid*.

43 *ibid*, p. 7.

44 LYNCH, J. (1987) *Prejudice Reduction and the Schools*, London, Cassell, quoted in PILKINGTON, A. (1988) 'Anti-racist versus multicultural education', *New Community*, spring, p. 489.

45 REX, J. (1987) 'Multiculturalism, anti-racism and equality of opportunities in the Swann Report' in CHIVERS, T.S. (Ed) *Race and Culture in Education: Issues Arising From the Swann Committee Report*, Slough, NFER-Nelson, p. 4.

46 *ibid*, p. 5.

47 The following discussion is essentially theoretical. For practical guidelines on implementing education for equality see COLE, M. (Ed) (1989) *op cit*.

48 TROYNA, B. (1987) 'Beyond multiculturalism: Towards the enactment of anti-racist education in policy, provision and pedagogy', *Oxford Review of Education*, **13**, 3, pp. 311–12.

49 TROYNA, B. (Ed) (1987) *Racial Inequality in Education*, London, Tavistock, p. 7.

50 BRYAN, B. (1989) 'The FE experience' in COLE, M. (Ed) *op cit.*
51 TROYNA, B. (Ed) (1987) *op cit,* p. 7.
52 LEICESTER, M. (1986) *op cit,* p. 5.
53 GURNAH, A. (1989) 'After bilingual support' in COLE, M. (Ed) *op cit.* Gurnah argues for a new discipline — multilingual studies — to run throughout the whole range of the education system.
54 MULLARD, C. (1986) *Pluralism, Ethnicism and Ideology: Implications for A Transformative Pedagogy,* working paper 2, Amsterdam, Centre for Race and Ethnic Studies, University of Amsterdam.
55 The following analysis is based on COLE, M. (1989) 'Class gender and "race": From theory to practice' in COLE, M. (Ed) *op cit.*
56 For some practical advice see GAINE, C. (1989) 'On getting equal opportunities policies and keeping them' and LYSEIGHT-JONES, P. (1989) 'A management of change perspective: Turning the whole school around', both in COLE M. (Ed) *op cit.*
57 For some guidelines on how this might be attempted see COLE, M. (Ed) (1989) *op cit.*
58 One of the difficulties inherent in this is that if the school experience of black people has been of harassment, stereotyping, low expectations and racial discrimination and if they have seen black teachers and other workers suffering in the same way, they will not want to work in schools. This reiterates the need for effective anti-racist practices and policies at *all* levels of the education system — pre-school to higher educaton.
59 GRANADOS JOHNSON, J. *et al* (1989) 'The infant years' in COLE, M. (Ed) *op cit.*
60 Whereas sections of the media have used this incident to devalue anti-racism itself, the intention of the McDonald Report (not publicly available at the time of writing) was to criticize the way the policies were implemented in that school, particularly the way in which they were imposed from above without substantial input from black and other ethnic minority communities and the fact that they failed to involve and get the support of the white working class community. The Report was certainly in favour of anti-racism as a guiding principle, but as something which should be implemented with intelligence and sensitivity.
61 HATCHER, R. (1987) '"Race" and education: Two perspectives for change' in TROYNA, B. (Ed) *op cit,* pp. 187–8.
62 Details of publications and membership are available from NAME, PO Box 9, Walsall, West Midlands, W1 35F.
63 Details of publications and membership are available from ARTEN, Jordanhill College of Education, 76 Southbrae Drive, Glasgow, G13 1PP.
64 Details of membership of this new organization are available from CARE, PO Box 681, London, SW8 1SX.

Chapter 8

What is Gender: Gender in Britain Today

Janet Holland

Introduction

A succinct statement by the UN in 1980 drew attention to the extent of inequalities between women and men: 'women constitute half the world's population, perform nearly two-thirds of its work hours, receive one-tenth of the world's income and own less than one-hundredth of the world's property' (UN, 1980). Apart from the rather startling informational content of the statement, it is interesting in drawing attention to women as a group, despite clear differences in ethnic origin, social class and other categories to which these women must belong which render much of their experience quite different. Perhaps such gross differences only appear as a result of aggregating the experience of women, where the vast proportion living in harsh and hazardous conditions in the third world will produce a general picture which does not reflect the conditions of life in industrialized societies. But one constant does seem to underlie the organization of social relations across widely differing social, cultural and geographical settings, and that is sexual hierarchy, an unequal distribution of power between women and men, with women subordinated to male power, authority and control. Patriarchy is the term used to describe this distribution of power in society.

One major and straightforward explanation offered for the observed social differences between women and men is that it can be traced back to biology. Observed behaviour, character traits readily identified as female or male, are seen as stemming from biological differences between the sexes elaborated in various ways[1], but clearly therefore natural and ineradicable. If such differences were shown to be securely grounded in biology and 'natural' there would be little that could or should be done to change them. It was partly as a defence against recurring biologistic arguments in support of existing differences between the sexes that a distinction was made between sex and gender (Stoller, 1968; Oakley, 1972). Sex is defined as referring to biological differences between females and males, 'the visible differences in genitalia, the related difference in procreative function';[2] gender is defined as 'a matter of culture' and refers to the social classification into feminine and masculine. Despite problems in maintaining the division between the innate and the socially ascribed,[3] this distinction between sex and gender is in current use, and points up the fact that the content of femininity and masculinity are socially and culturally defined, subject to change, and indeed malleable.

Cross-cultural and anthropological studies provide us with examples of the different content that socially defined femininity and masculinity can have. Some societies do not have such strongly differentiated stereotypes of femininity and masculinity as we do ourselves.[4] History too provides examples of changes in what has been considered appropriate and acceptable masculine or feminine behaviour or appearance. An historical analysis also demonstrates that gender differences and inequalities cannot be viewed independently of other forms of inequality such as those based on class and 'race'. Appropriate and acceptable versions of feminine or masculine behaviour vary in relation to social class and ethnic or cultural background. Gender, class and 'race' inequalities intersect and interact, and the precise ways in which this happens is the subject of considerable theoretical debate within feminism, and a matter of considerable practical importance in the effort to improve the lives of women.

Gender Inequalities

A useful place to start looking at gender inequality is in relation to poverty. As we can see from the UN quote which opened this discussion, women are more likely than men to be living in poverty in general, and this is also true of Britain today. It has recently been argued that poverty is becoming 'feminized' in industrial societies (Scott, 1984; Weitzman, 1985), that women are becoming the new poor. For example, 60 per cent of adults for whom supplementary benefit is paid in Britain are women. But Lewis and Piachaud (1987) point out that at the start of the century 61 per cent of adults on all forms of poor relief were women (GB, 1909), and that it is simply the case that throughout the last century women have always been much poorer than men. Despite the difficulties of defining poverty, magnified by attempting to take an historical perspective, one thing which stood out in their study, regardless of the definitions employed, was 'the continuity of women experiencing an inferior economic position to men'. What appears to be happening currently is that the poverty of women is becoming more visible.

Women's poverty was rendered invisible in many classic and conventional studies of poverty by virtue of the focus being on collective units — households, families or tax units — which ignored variations within those units. Women would be counted amongst the poor only if the household unit of which they were part fell below the poverty line, whilst they might in fact experience substantial poverty and deprivation in households which would not be classified in that way (Pahl, 1983; Land, 1983). Efforts to minimize the burden of poverty for the rest of the family by careful management and self-sacrifice fall mainly on women (Wilson, 1987), and the fact that some women are dependent upon men (rather than on their own low income) for their overall standard of living has been used to justify ignoring the lower resources of most women. Millar and Glendinning (1987) argue that a mere 18 per cent of adult women in Britain are wholly dependent financially on a male breadwinner, but the assumption that most women are dependent is a contributory factor in their poverty. It structures their access to resources in the family (Graham, 1984; Brannen and Wilson, 1987), in the labour market and in the welfare state.

There are two major demographic reasons for women becoming more visible when amongst the poor: increasing numbers of them have become heads of households due (i) to the population explosion amongst the old, of which women form a much higher proportion and are more likely not to be married than men; and (ii) to the increase in lone parent families, 91 per cent of which are headed by women, and more than half of which are living in poverty (Millar, 1987).[5] But these are not the only reasons for women's poverty, other contributory factors are redundancy and unemployment, the latter being particularly significant for young women (Griffin, 1985; Wallace, 1986; Buswell, 1987 and 1988), and becoming a parent, lone or accompanied by a partner. Joshi (1987) points out that 'The price a man pays for parenthood is generally being expected to support his children and their mother. The price a woman pays is that of continuing economic handicap and an increased risk of poverty' (p. 130). The mother of very young children typically withdraws from the labour market and undertakes full-time childcare and domestic labour,[6] her main source of income being the earnings of a partner or social security. She foregoes current earnings, and her future earning capacity is affected by this withdrawal. Women's unpaid work in the home, domestic labour and caring, contribute to their relative poverty in relation to men, by rendering their own participation in the labour market problematic, and enabling that of their partner. A major contributory factor in women's potential poverty is their disadvantaged labour market position.

Clearly there are variations within the overall patterns described in these general statements. The risk for working class women, and particularly black women of living in poverty is greatest (Cook and Watt, 1987; Thorogood, 1987). The contribution of the state to changing or maintaining the position of women is thrown into relief in relation to poverty, since employment, pensions, immigration and social security policies are deeply implicated in women finding themselves and remaining in poverty. The role of ideology, of stereotypes of appropriate feminine behaviour in relation to caring and to women's work form a crucial part of the overall picture which will be discussed further below. But what is also thrown into relief by taking a starting point in women's relative poverty, is the relationship between women's position in the home, as performers of unpaid caring and domestic labour, and their position in the market place as workers. It is this relationship which is central to an understanding of gender inequality.

Production and Reproduction

Women and Paid Work

Work is a crucial part of women's lives. Women's economic activity rates[7] range from 70 per cent at ages 20–24, to 21 per cent at ages 60–64 (1983 figures). Child bearing and full-time rearing take up a tiny proportion of the average female lifespan. Joshi and Owen (1981) estimate that women are likely to be out of employment for about seven years as a result of these activities. The proportion of married women entering the labour market has risen from under 10 per cent in 1901 to over 50 per cent in the 1980s, with variations according to age and level of domestic responsibility, particularly age of children.

Numerous studies have shown that without the woman's wage a large number of families would fall below the poverty line (Land, 1976; Royal Commission, 1978). Women's labour is then a major component of the formal as it is of the informal and the household economies.

Most women do work which is done mainly by women. The deeply ideological, commonsense category 'women's work' refers to two types of sexual division. A division in the home, in which most of the work is in fact seen as women's work, and a division in the labour market in which most of the work is seen as men's work. This is not to deny that more than 40 per cent of the workforce are women, but to point out that the range of jobs they can be found in is radically limited. The labour market in the UK is horizontally and vertically sex segregated. Horizontal occupational segregation means that men and women work in different types of occupation. The vast proportion of both manual and non-manual women workers are each concentrated in only three occupational categories.[8] Vertical segregation means that men are more usually found working in higher grade occupations, and women in lower grades (Hakim, 1979). This hierarchical principle with men at the top operates within occupations when women are present. School teaching at both primary level, where women predominate, and secondary level, where there are almost equal numbers of women and men, provides a typical example.

Most professions are male-dominated and women work in a 'discriminatory environment' within them (Bourne and Wikler, 1978). The introduction to a collection of essays describing the situation of women in a range of professions, argues that 'In the legal profession women are still very much in a minority and are channelled into certain types of work and pushed to the margins of the profession by a variety of mechanisms. The other contributors to this volume identify similar dynamics of exclusion and marginalization of women across a number of male-dominated professions.' (Spencer and Podmore, 1987.) A casual inspection of any area of high status, high paid work will reveal a distinct paucity of women.[9] Few women are in positions which give them the power to make decisions which radically affect people's lives and work, and more than half of the people about whom such decisions are made are women. Again education, this time higher education, provides a graphic example of gender hierarchy and exclusion. The proportion of women who are professors is 2 per cent, senior lecturers and readers 6 per cent, and lecturers and assistant lecturers 14 per cent. Women figure disproportionately in part-time and temporary posts, particularly in research.

But, some might argue, the universities are equal opportunities employers, women are either just not coming forward with the right qualifications, or are not putting themselves forward for employment and promotion. The first kicks responsibility for inequality back down the line, and draws attention to gender differences in experiences within the educational system as a whole for pupils and students, resulting in different outcomes in terms of qualifications and expectations, discussed in detail in the next chapter. The second is a classic attempt to blame the victim, but implicitly draws attention to broader issues relating to women's position in society as an explanation for women's disadvantaged position in this particular sphere (Williams *et al*, 1974).

And the catalogue of disadvantage for women in the labour market, the sphere of production continues. The past three decades have seen a dramatic growth in part-time work, mirroring the increase in the participation of married women in paid work. Most part-timers are women, (Robinson and Wallace, 1984) and conversely a large proportion of women are in part-time work (43 per cent in 1983). Women take part-time work to accommodate their domestic responsibilities, they take it as it becomes available, whatever it may be. In many cases this work is not covered by protective employment legislation,[10] is poorly paid, and is characterized by poor working conditions and extreme insecurity. For many women it also represents underutilisation of their actual qualification and skill level (Martin and Roberts, 1984), there is considerable evidence of downward occupational mobility in women coming back into part-time work after a period of absence from the labour market (Dex, 1987). Women also undertake homework, most of those working at home rather than from home are women (Cragg and Dawson 1981; Hakim, 1984). Conditions and levels of pay are variable, but most homeworkers are found in manufacturing, office and clerical work, and needlework. The largest concentrations of homeworkers exist in occupations that are themselves predominantly female. The work itself is characterized by 'extremely poor rates of pay and the hidden costs and hazards for the women who do it and their families' (Lonsdale, 1987).

Despite the Equal Pay Act (1975) women's pay remains resolutely below that of men. There are difficulties in calculating this figure precisely given the factors which we have discussed above, women work in different sectors from men, frequently part-time and are often unable to work overtime. The EOC has reported, however, that women's gross hourly earnings as a proportion of men's for full-time workers aged over 18, after an initial rise in the mid-seventies, have settled in the range 73–75 per cent. The average gross weekly earnings figure comes out somewhat lower at about 67 per cent (1983 figures). Since women are crowded into a limited range of work defined as women's work and so not directly comparable with men's jobs, and do work in less skilled, often part-time jobs, it is not really surprising that the Equal Pay Act has been largely ineffective. But just in case these structural constraints were insufficient to maintain the imbalance between female and male earnings, the five-year implementation period before the Act became law gave firms the opportunity to reclassify work in a way that ensured that women remained in clearly separated lower paid grades of work, in some cases collaborating with trade unions in this endeavour. Snell (1979) gives examples of these 'minimizing actions', for example changing the system of grading work so that women ended up on lower rates or grades regardless of their skill level, or bringing women up to the minimum level of a unisex salary scale, but tightening piecework rates to offset increases in their basic rates.

Women and the Family

The division of the labour market into women's jobs and men's jobs leaves women distinctly disadvantaged, but our brief review of the evidence on women's poverty indicates that the family itself does not necessarily offer 'a haven in a harsh world' (Lasch, 1977) for women. The second major sexual division between the public and the private, between work and production as the sphere of men and the family and reproduction as the sphere of women, places women primarily in the family. The classic image of the breadwinner male with dependent wife and two children under 16 years old is in fact a relatively rare household form — approximately 17 per cent of households could be accurately described as such at any one time. But most people in Britain will spend some periods in their lives in a nuclear family, and 'most women are housewives, whether or not they are in paid employment, and are mothers all their adult lives' (Leonard and Speakman, 1986). The family or household form and levels of obligation felt to different degrees of kin vary with region, class and ethnic group, but in general the domestic labour performed within the family is the responsibility of the woman, and childcare is seen as a natural extension and concomitant of childbearing.

The work which women perform in the family includes emotional and physical caring for all other family members, and socialization of children into the values and norms of the society. This work can also be described as reproduction in two senses. First, women reproduce the labour force in the here and now, by physically and emotionally servicing men and other family members who work in production; they also reproduce the labour force over time through their work of cultural and social reproduction preparing children for their expected future positions in the social and sexual divisions of labour. Class and gender relations are reproduced through the material conditions and interactional practices of families, and the ideologies which influence these familial practices. The work of servicing the labour force is seen as functional for capitalism by some socialist feminists. The second aspect of women's reproductive work is the most obvious, women biologically reproduce the next generation, and it is control over this aspect of women's labour which is seen as the root of their oppression by some radical feminists.

Over time with technological and social change, the physical labour and time required by some work in the home has been reduced, but numerous studies have indicated that the time women actually spend on housework has not declined for a range of reasons. Time budget studies, detailing the precise amount of time spent performing certain household tasks by women and men have indicated that the average number of hours spent on housework per household has remained constant at about 50–70 hours a week for the last fifty years, and that everywhere men do much less than women. Women regard housework as real work and Oakley's (1974) studies have indicated that by and large they do not enjoy it or at best feel ambivalent. Monotony, repetitiveness and fragmentation of tasks, number of hours worked (an average of seventy-seven hours a week), pressure of the pace, isolation, low status of the work and dislike of economic dependence were amongst the complaints from her sample of forty housewives. Women who do paid work in production merely add their domestic tasks to their workload, unless they can afford to buy replacement for their domestic labour. When men take on housework it is seen as 'helping' the woman, not part of their own domestic responsibility. When fathers play a role in childcare, the division of labour often leaves the woman with the basic physical and emotional caring tasks and men taking on play and outings.[11] Arranging childcare is a continuous problem for women, who are frequently excluded from the labour market when they would wish to take employment by the absence of adequate facilities for childcare.

Health and illness is an issue for women in the family. Their own health is affected by the demands of their domestic work, as Bernard (1973) has put it 'being a housewife makes women sick', and the health of their family is their responsibility. Brown and Harris (1978) found that one woman in three of their sample of married women was clinically depressed, and that working class women were more at risk in this than middle class women. When women complain to their doctors that they are suffering from severe tiredness, anxiety or depression, they are frequently treated with tranquilizers and anti-depressants. Feminists have criticized this overprescribing of psychotropic drugs to women (twice as many women as men were prescribed these drugs in the early 80s) arguing that they can be addictive and have serious side effects. The practice can also operate as a form of social control, keeping women passive and doing nothing to solve their problems or change the underlying social conditions responsible for their depression (Dale and Foster, 1986).

What Whitehead (1981) has called the 'ideology of maternal altruism' leads a woman to put the family or children first, denying herself resources to make scarce resources go round. A woman might eat less or different food for example, to ensure that other family members are adequately fed.[12] The pervasive demands of women's work in the home means that they are less free to take part in leisure pursuits of their own choice and interest, or indeed at all. Leisure must be slotted into spaces dictated by the leisure, work, needs and demands made by other household members. Women's 'leisure' may be taken at the same time as a work task — ironing whilst watching television for example (Deem, 1986). Analyzing the context of women's leisure, Deem concludes that 'women's leisure is much more constrained than men's and occurs relatively less often in proportion to work, whilst taking rather different forms and occurring in different locations and contexts'. Griffin (1981 and 1985) argues that men see leisure as a right, women do not, and that the ways in which women do take part in leisure are largely determined by men and on inferior terms to those enjoyed by men. And in relation to the health of others, the Equal Opportunities Commission (EOC) estimated in 1981 that there were about one-and-a-quarter million carers in Britain, most of whom were women, looking after the long-term sick, handicapped or elderly. This number will have increased in the intervening years due to explicit Government policies and financial cutbacks. There has been a reduction in institutional provision for these people, and a move to 'community care', which in effect means care in the family or community by individual women. The burden is increased by reductions in welfare services such as meals on wheels.

Many women are made more than sick in the family, they are subjected to physical abuse and male violence. Dobash and Dobash (1980) provide from their study of cases of violence reported to the police in two Scottish cities the disturbing figure that 26 per cent was assault against wives. Violence within the home is an event which most frequently involves a man attacking a woman (estimates put the reverse at about 10 per cent), but most sources of information are likely to underestimate the extent of violence towards women. There is a history of police reluctance to take domestic violence seriously. Social workers are inclined to perceive it as an extreme manifestation of a neurotic marriage relationship between inadequate people, requiring therapy, counselling and support rather than separation (Wilson, 1977). The inception and development of the Natonal Women's Aid Federation, setting up and running refuges for battered women, demonstrates amongst other things the desperate need of these women for a place to run to, and for support (Rose, 1985; Dale and Foster, 1986). The home can become a prison for a battered woman with dependent children and limited or no opportunity for employment which would provide sufficient income to support her and her children if she were to leave. In addition to providing horrifying first-hand accounts of 'the violent event' Dobash and Dobash conclude from the experiences of the women they interviewed that men who use violence consider it their right and privilege as men and as heads of households to make claims on their wives, and if their demands are not met, for example meals are not on time or there is an inadequate response to their sexual advances, punishment can be meted out. The Dobashes do not see this perception of male prerogatives and rights in violent men as any different from that of other men in Western society, what differs is the degree of violence with which they are prepared to enforce their desires and expectations, sometimes extreme. The incidence of male domestic violence is not associated with particular social class groups, poverty, lack of education or psychological disorder.

Ideological Support for Material Disadvantage

This discussion has been pitched largely at the level of women's material experience in the labour market and in the home, the material conditions under which they live and work. But almost more important in the maintenance of women's disadvantaged material position in Britain today are the ideological messages which support it. Stereotypes are powerful means of conveying ideological information, and crucial vehicles for socialization and for control over dominated groups (Perkins, 1979). We can think about ideology in the following way. There are a multiplicity of ideologies, in the sense of ostensible explanations for social facts and events often borne by stereotypes, operating within society. They are not necessarily in agreement, in fact they are often in tension and contradiction. Consider for example the conflicting stereotypes of women as madonna/whore, dumb blond/cunning minx. But they operate within the context of an overall dominant framework which provides legitimation and support for inequalities based primarily on gender, class and 'race'.

Ideology is both false and true — false in the sense that the purpose of the general dominant ideological framework and its more specific subvariants is to legitimize or disguise power relations, often converting arbitrary or power based distinctions or differences into 'natural' or 'innate' ones. We can see this, for example, in aspects of the ideology of the sexual division of labour. Ideology is true in the sense that it becomes incorporated into the individual's self identity, generated by and through their own actual lived experience of practices and institutions into which these ideological distinctions are incorporated. An example here is the individual's experience of their own gender identity. Ideology can also become part of the material conditions affecting women's lives, as for example when an employer has a stereotype of men's work for which he would not employ a woman, whatever her skills and qualifications. Or health, welfare and commercial organizations operating with the implicit ideology that a woman's place is in the home and being open or providing services only during working hours, at which times in fact many women are working.

We can identify some of the ideologies which support class, gender and 'race' inequalities and generate stereotypes which influence beliefs and behaviour. For class there are ideologies of inherited capacities, leadership, responsibility, individualism, meritocratic achievement and equality of opportunity. These general ideologies also operate to support inequalities of 'race' and gender. More specific racist ideology is incorporated into stereotypes associated with particular 'races' or ethnic groups.[13] At a general level these can refer to inferiority (often associated with levels of intellectual capacity), sexuality, relationship to the work ethic, and criminality. Specific patriarchal ideologies adhere around the sexual division of labour — women's work and men's work, female domesticity supported by the male breadwinner, the family, and characteristics and capacities attributed to femininity and masculinity. Some have argued for example, that the major importance of the family is ideological, a powerful force influencing those who live both inside or outside whatever remains of the 'traditional' family form (Barrett and McIntosh, 1982). And this 'traditional' form of family emerged only in capitalist society in the mid-nineteenth century, despite claims of universality and timelessness (Poster, 1978). Ellis (1983) argues even more radically that the family is a mythological construct. Despite its fundamental contradictions, not least the image of it as a private space, whilst it is deeply saturated with the public, the family can become in people's perceptions not just a particular living arrangement, 'but the institution that can cure all our social and personal ills, a metaphor for some private and public paradise lost'. The ideology of women's work and men's work enmeshes with that of femininity and masculinity to support and maintain occupational segration, almost constructing type of work undertaken as part of one's sexual identity (Willis, 1977; Cockburn, 1987).

Other Institutional Sites for Gender Inequality

Buttressing the workplace and the home, the central institutional sites in which gender inequality is constructed and maintained through the material conditions which exist in them, and the ideologies which support their practices (Holland, 1985 and 1988) stands the rest of the institutional structure of British society. Each institution, the education system, the political system, the media, religion, the law and the state is threaded through with ideologies and based on practices supportive or expressive of gender inequality.[14] A large and growing body of feminist literature exists, which describes, analyses, and attempts to explain the situation of women in each of these areas. The employment experience of women in these sites reflects the overall positioning of women in the labour market, they are in a limited range of jobs, low in the occupational/organisational hierarchy, with relatively low pay and inferior conditions compared with men. Women have limited, indeed negligible, access to power within these institutions, one is reminded of Millett's (1970) definition of patriarchy: 'Our society, like all other historical civilizations, is a patriarchy. The fact is evident at once if one recalls that the military, industry, technology, universities, science, political office and finance — in short every avenue of power within the society, including the coercive force of the police, is entirely in male hands'.

Both the state and the legal system tend to support the sexual division of labour and the basic patriarchal paradigm of the dependent woman and the breadwinner man. This situation is not without contradictons and dilemmas since both are multifaceted and vastly complex institutions. In a detailed description and analysis of the legal system in relation to women's oppression, Smart (1984) argues that 'legislation does not create patriarchal relations but it does in a complex and often contradictory fashion reproduce the material and ideological conditions under which these relations may survive' (p. 22). Brophy and Smart (1981) argue that although the formal legal rights of married women have improved during this century, the rights of men and women have not been equalized, and there is a limit to the effect which legal changes can have in improving women's structural location, given the sexual division of labour. Changes in family law have been increasingly based on children's rights and parental obligation, and serve to stabilize and support a family form which reproduces dependency and inequality between husband and wife. Family law and welfare law have moved closer together, with the former adopting interventionist strategies more common to the latter. The courts have increasing powers for example to investigate incomes, deduct money at source, and investigate families through welfare agencies. Dale and Foster (1986) argue that the State reinforces women's position in the home since it alleviates political, administrative and fiscal problems which would arise if they were not there, if for example their unpaid work as carers had to be paid for. Women can also operate as intermediaries between state services and the family. The way in which welfare provision is closely tied to a model of the dependent woman has been examined and described in detail by a number of authors (in, for example, Wilson, 1977; Ungerson, 1985; Dale and Foster, 1986).

Explanations for Gender Inequality

There have been a wide range of explanations for gender inequality, some of which see it as theoretically insignificant — this would include most mainstream sociological explanations, stratification theory and economic labour market theories. Feminist explanations place women at the forefront of the analysis and are concerned with change, and take the following forms:

1　They concentrate on either patriarchy (gender relations) OR capitalism (class relations) as the fundamental area in which these inequalities are created, maintained and reproduced.
2　They postulate two systems of social relations, sometimes seen as different modes of production: patriarchy and capitalism. These two systems are regarded either as (a) totally integrated; OR (b) separate, autonomous but interrelated.

Patriarchy was defined briefly above as male dominated gender hierarchy, but the concept has been the subject of considerable controversy within feminism. Two positions form the boundary of the range taken up on the issue: (i) patriarchy is an unnecessary, loosely and very variously defined concept with biologistic and universalistic overtones, which is of little or no value in attempting to come to grips with the problems associated with analysing and explaining the position and experience of women (Adlam 1979; Barrett, 1980; Rowbotham, 1979); (ii) patriarchy is a crucial and essential concept in the task of understanding women's subordination, potentially having the force which the concept of class has in the Marxist explanation of social relations, although further theoretical work may be necessary and appropriate to develop this critical concept (Eisenstein, 1979; Alexander and Taylor, 1980; Lown, 1983; Walby, 1986 and 1987). We will discuss feminist explanations for women's subordinate position below, but first consider briefly two economic labour market theories.

Labour Market Theories

Dual market theory (see for example Barron and Norris, 1976) postulates two distinct sectors in the labour market with certain characteristics:

(i)   a primary sector, with high wages, fringe benefits, skilled work with opportunities for training and promotion, employment stability, and high unionization;

(ii)   a secondary sector with low wages, few fringe benefits, unskilled work with no opportunity for promotion, employment instability and lack of unionization.

Various reasons are put forward for the existence of this division — some authors relate the division to employers' desire to create a malleable workforce through a policy of 'divide and rule' (Bowles and Gintis, 1976). Some consider that it is employers' desire for efficiency, particularly in relation to technological developments and the need for a stable, skilled labour force which generates the division (Doeringer and Piore, 1971). Others suggest that it is the result of negotiation between employers and organized labour (Rubery, 1980; Walby, 1983). Women and various ethnic groups are found in the secondary sector. One explanation offered for the clustering of women and other groups in the secondary sector is that it is the result of discrimination, which has been generated within the processes of the development of the labour market itself, or which has taken over divisions and distinctions based on 'race' and gender which already existed in the society. An explanation which connects with the human capital theory of labour is that this clustering is the result of choice, that a lower investment in training and education has been made by those in the secondary sector.

A general criticism of dual labour market theory is that it is descriptive, and provides no explanation for the growth of segmented labour markets and the actual organization of the labour process. In versions which focus on employer strategies it ignores the impact of organized labour on rational market strategies which has contributed to the positioning of particular groups in the secondary sector. The explanations for women's position in the secondary sector are inadequate, and by allocating women to a heterogeneous category of secondary workers, important differences between predominantly female occupations and the nature of horizontal and vertical segregation are also submerged. But the major problem in relation to gender is that the dynamics of the labour market are assumed to be the main factor determining the position of female labour and no link is made between the structure of the labour market and the sexual division of labour. Dex (1987) has developed a more elaborated model of the segmentated labour market for women, in which women appear in a primary non-manual sector (as teachers) and in sexually segregated women's primary and secondary sectors. She describes women's mobility between these sectors over the working life on the basis of the Women and Employment Survey.

Human capital theory suggests that the explanation for sexual division in the labour market is that women have lower educational attainment and less training (particularly on the job) than men and so are only suitable for work in the secondary rather than in the primary sector. From this perspective, women's commitment to the family causes them to 'choose' to make a smaller investment in human capital, and the rational employer will therefore select men for skilled, well-paid jobs because of their greater commitment to work.

Unfortunately for human capital theory women are frequently found in lower level, lower paid jobs than men with equal or even inferior qualifications (Morris and Ziderman, 1971; MacDonald, 1981). And at the level of skill, Craig *et al* (1982 and 1985) argue that many of the jobs in the secondary firm sector require as much skill as those in the primary sector, despite the fact that wages in this sector are much lower. These objections clearly also apply to the location of particular groups defined by 'race' in low level, low paid work. We had a glimpse of the processes which can create the skills which women have as non-skills, or at least less skilled than those of men during the pre-implementation period for the Equal Pay Act discussed above. And to what extent are low levels of human capital the cause or the effect of labour force instability — low wages due to discrimination might discourage women from investing in human capital, and low investments in human capital perpetuate women's lower earnings (Amsden, 1980). Finally, human capital theory can explain why women are in low skill jobs, but not why they are in such a limited range of occupations within skill categories.

Feminist Explanations for Women's Subordination

In radical feminist arguments which postulate patriarchy as an autonomous system the emphasis is on male power, male control over women, as the primary form of social inequality. Millett (1970) introduced the concept of patriarchy into feminist discourse, using it to refer to male domination over women and the power relations which sustain women's subordination to men. The family is seen as crucial in socialising children into gender specific roles, temperaments and statuses. Radical feminists emphasize particular aspects of women's oppression in the area of reproduction — for example childbirth, abortion, motherhood.

The emphasis on biological reproduction is taken one stage further by revolutionary feminists, who, following Firestone (1970), develop a theory of patriarchy and sex-class based on male ownership of, and control over, women's reproductive capacities. In this argument there are two systems of social class, one the economic class system based on relations of production, and the other the sex-class system, based on relations of reproduction. Patriarchy refers to this second system where women are subordinated to male control over their reproductive power (Jeffreys, 1977) and it is the constancy of this power which provides the unchanging basis of patriarchy. Socialist feminists have criticized the definition of reproduction used by radical and revolutionary feminists as too narrowly focussed on biological reproduction and argue against the idea of two autonomous systems of class (economic and sex-class) existing in parallel, with no discussion of the relationship between them.

Firestone puts the biology of reproduction at the core of women's subordination relating all other aspects of the organization of society to this fact, seeing reproduction as the material basis of women's oppression. But she does not believe that the relationship between men and women is unchangeable, arguing that the technical capacity to overcome the problems of the biology of reproduction already exists and that human embryos could be developed outside the woman's body. Women would, however, need to seize the means of reproduction in political struggle. Firestone appears to have undue faith in technology as a solution to women's reproductive problems, and in their capacity to seize power over new technologies of reproduction. There is, in fact, a strong radical feminist tendency to attack all recent developments in reproductive technology, which are seen as further control over women by men.

More recently radical feminists have argued that male power and control over female sexuality is a crucial mechanism of women's oppression, that male violence against women is an essential instrument in maintaining that control, and that both of these form an essential part of the construction of masculinity. Hanmer (1977) argues that force and its threat is the basis for hierarchical, power relations, the ultimate sanction for maintaining other forms of control, and applies this notion to male-female relationships. Others have delineated the extent and ubiquity of male violence against women, and the power that the threat of violence — from wife battering to rape — has to control women's lives. The role of the state and the law in maintaining male control over women through male threat and use of violence has been described in some detail, particularly in the study of rape, and wife battering (Brownmiller, 1976; Dobash and Dobash, 1980; Stanko, 1985; Hanmer and Saunders, 1984; London Rape Crisis Centre, 1984).

Radical and revolutionary feminists have been criticized for rooting their explanation of women's subordination in biology and emphasizing the universal nature of gender hierarchy. Claims of universality leave no way of explaining the different manifestations of gender hierarchy and patriarchy in different cultures, and at different historical junctures. The more recent versions, incorporating notions of the social construction of sexuality avoid this problem (Mahoney, 1985).

Socialist feminists focussing on capitalism as the primary source of oppression have drawn on various Marxist concepts to make the link between the labour market and the sexual division of labour, considering the ways in which the sexual division of labour is functional for capital, both in terms of production by looking at women as a reserve army of labour, and in terms of their domestic labour. Women have been analyzed as a floating reserve army of labour, a pool of labour drawn in and out of employment as required. Beechey (1977), for example, has argued that in the post-war period in Britain, married women may have become a preferred source of the reserve army of labour because they are dependent on the family (and the husband's wage) for part of the costs of their own upkeep and so not reliant on their own wage. This is advantageous for capital since they can therefore be paid at a lower rate, one which would not actually support them, and this will lower wages in general.

But are women available to be drawn into the labour market as the requirements of production change since, as we have seen, women are only actually available for a very limited range of work, given the existence of the sexual division of labour within production? Women could be a reserve army only for the types of work which women do, not as a substitute for men in 'men's work'.[15] Milkman (1976) rejected the notion of women as a reserve army of labour in the context of the 1930s depression in the USA, indicating that occupational segregation and the growth of the service sector protected women's employment from the worst impact of the recession. Similar results have been found in studies of more recent recessions (OECD, 1976; Breugel, 1979). Breugel (1979) did find some support for seeing women as a reserve army of labour by looking in more detail at women's work in different sectors, those who fit the reserve army of labour model most closely, were part-time workers in manufacturing industry. She also points out that the micro-electronic revolution is liable to undermine the protection from job loss which women in the service sector have experienced in the past. Buswell (1987) argues that the pattern of women's labour force participation, with a break for childrearing, and the availability of cheap youth labour through the YTS is being used by employers in a process of restructuring labour markets, drawing young unmarried women and older married women into the labour market as needed.

Another attempt to make the link between the sexual division of labour in reproduction and production which led to an extensive effort to apply Marxist categories and concepts to an analysis of women's work in the home and family was what has become known as the domestic labour debate. Much of this debate centred around two issues. First, how appropriate was the application of concepts developed to deal with production in a capitalist society to the issue of domestic labour, since labour performed in the home is outside the relations of production. Second, how adequate were the definitions of the particular concepts being used in the discussion. This was an attempt to conceptualize the material position of women as housewives, but the economistic tendency ultimately became a severe limitation, and led the debate into a cul-de-sac. What it did accomplish was to put housework, domestic labour, firmly on the agenda as work, to draw attention to the links between work inside the home and outside, and to indicate the contradictory demands on women as domestic labourers and as workers selling their labour power in the market place.[16] One thing omitted from the debate, however, was the issue of the interests of men in the perpetuation of domestic labour.

Eisenstein (1979 and 1984) is an exponent of an explanation based on capitalist patriarchy, arguing that capitalist and patriarchal relations are so intertwined that they form a mutually interdependent system. Capitalism needs patriarchal relations in order to survive and vice versa, the two systems not only shape each other but are fused into one and cannot be analytically separated. Her earlier work stresses the synthesis, but her later work does recognize that there may be tensions or even conflict between capitalism and patriarchy. Capitalism and patriarchy are fused for example at the level of the state where patriarchal interests are represented by male capitalists. There is separation around the rival demands for women's labour, with capital and patriarchy pulling in opposite directions: household or paid employment.

Those who see patriarchy and capitalism as autonomous systems and analytically independent, specify the ways in which the two systems interrelate. One form argues that different spheres of society are determined by either patriarchal or capitalist relations, capitalist relations are usually assigned to producton or the economy. Patriarchy may be confined to the sphere of ideology, culture and sexuality (Mitchell, 1975); or to reproduction or the family (Delphy, 1977; O'Brien, 1981). Another form argues that patriarchal and capitalist relations articulate at all levels and in all spheres of society (Hartmann, 1979 and 1981; Walby, 1986 and 1987).

Delphy (1977), for example has developed a materialist feminist analysis locating the source of women's subordination in marriage and the family. She argues that there are two modes of production in contemporary capitalist society: (i) the industrial mode of production defined by capitalist property relations and capitalist exploitation; and (ii) the family mode of production which is defined by patriarchal relations of production and the exploitation of women by men. For Delphy the family is the site of the economic exploitation of women where both their productive and reproductive labour is appropriated by men. It is women's position within the domestic mode of production which is the basis of their class oppression by men, and this is their main form of subordination. As a result of their common position in the patriarchal domestic mode of production, women form a distinct class irrespective of the class position of their husband, which is derived from his relation to the industrial mode of production.

Hartmann (1979 and 1981) provides a powerful analysis of gender inequality in terms of the interrelationship of patriarchy and capitalism. A socialist feminist, she considers that most Marxist analyses of women's subordination focus on women's relation to capitalism and ignore the independent role of male interest in the oppression of women. Patriarchy and capitalism should be seen as separate structures which have had important effects on each other historically; they can be analytically separated, but in contemporary western society operate in partnership. She locates the material base for patriarchy in male control over female labour power and sexuality and considers that patriarchy, operating through men in the interests of men at different historical points can be either in conflict with or coincide with the interests of the capitalist class. She provides a historical analysis of the interaction of patriarchy and the processes of capitalism emphasizing the role of the male worker in restricting women's participation in the labour market, with examples from both the UK and USA. Job segregation by sex and the family wage are crucial aspects of ways in which patriarchy and capitalism have interacted, combining to exclude women from much paid work. Occupational sex segregation lowers the wages of women in the jobs which do remain open to them and forces them to remain dependent on men within the family. The circle is completed by men demanding a family wage, which pushes women away from paid work and into unpaid domestic work from which men benefit, both in terms of wages and women's domestic labour. Capital gets labour services below cost! Hartmann considers that capital and patriarchy find a mutual accommodation in the family wage (see too Foreman, 1977; Humphries, 1977; Barrett and McIntosh, 1982 on the family wage).

Walby (1986) pushes the specification of the relationship between patriarchy and capitalism further, arguing that it should be seen as historically and spatially variable and riddled with conflict. She demonstrates her thesis by making a detailed analysis of gender relations in paid work in the UK from 1800 to the present day, focussing on three industries: cotton textiles, engineering and clerical work. She examines overlapping rounds of restructuring in employment, looking at the two main strategies by which men and patriarchy retain control: first that of excluding women from paid employment; and second that of confining women to jobs which are graded lower than those of men.[17] There has been conflict not only between patriarchy and capital at particular times but between particular groups of men and women as well. 'Some groups of men struggled to prevent women from entering their areas of work. Neither did women docilely withdraw from paid work when men wanted them to, on marriage, or at the end of wars, or during depressions. They were pushed vigorously, and vigorously resisted' (Walby, 1986).

Recent feminist writings have attempted to incorporate 'race' into their discussions and analyses in response to growing criticism from black feminists both in the US and in the UK (Davis, 1981; Hull *et al*, 1982; Carby, 1982; Giddings, 1984; Amos and Parmar, 1984; Bryan *et al*, 1985; Bhavnani and Coulson, 1986). The fact that 'race' needs to be incorporated into this body of work demonstrates the force of the criticisms of white feminist analyses which have been raised, and which centre around the following issues. First, are certain feminist concepts, theoretical constructs and analyses (for example relating to the family, reproduction, sexuality) universally applicable in the light of black women's different experiences? Second, doubts have been raised about the primacy of sexual divisions in the face of the institutionalized racism which is the experience of both black women and men. Thirdly, attention has been drawn to the invisibility of black women in the feminist retrieval of herstory and feminist theorising. Black women's history in the context of imperialism and racism, their political struggles and involvement in both black and predominantly white movements, and their daily experience are largely absent from the white feminist literature. And finally there has been the accusation of racism in the feminist movement (both historically and currently) and the difficulty for white feminists to accept that whilst as women they may be oppressed (by men, patriarchy or patriarchal capitalism) as whites they can be the oppressor.

As Amos and Parmar (1984) put it, 'Black feminism as a distinct body of theory and practice is in the process of development and debate both here in Britain and internationally and has begun to make significant contributions to other movements of liberation, as well as challenging the oppression and exploitation of black women'. Both black and white feminists are in the process of understanding the ways in which 'race', class and gender intersect to produce and reproduce women's position in society.

Conclusion

We have examined the position of women in Britain today and found it wanting. Gender inequality permeates every aspect of British society, with its own specific manifestations for different social class and ethnic groups, and those of a different sexual orientation to dominant, male defined, heterosexuality. We have considered a range of explanations for this phenomenon, which focus largely on the relationship between women's position in the home and the workplace, and on male control over female work and sexuality. These have elaborated the ways in which patriarchy, capitalism and racism interrelate to produce the continuing subordination of women.

Developments, adjustments, and advances in feminist analysis and theory are continuous, so that earlier formulations are frequently reviewed and reassessed. This kind of theoretical elaboration by successive authors, honing down the nature of the specific theoretical formulations and concepts can sometimes seem like so much academic nitpicking. But it is extremely important for theoretical clarification and development to take place in order to gain an understanding of women's position in society. What are also important are historical and empirical studies to further test and develop these formulations, and most important of all political action to change women's position for the better. This is the ultimate purpose of all feminist theoretical work, to identify areas in which action can and must take place.

Notes

1 See OAKLEY (1981) and NICHOLSON (1984) for a discussion of biological differences and similarities between the sexes and the ways they have been used to defend women's inferior social and economic position, and MACCOBY and JACKLIN (1975). The latter review of studies of biological differences undermined earlier biological theories of sex difference by demonstrating that the differences they sought to explain did not in fact exist. The weight of opinion now supports the idea that the similarities between the sexes outweigh differences. This does not of course prevent biological arguments supporting women's subordination from being used, and they do regularly reappear in various guises.

2 OAKLEY (1972).

3 For some the biological and the social are inextricably entwined, and so the distinction is unnecessary. MATHIEU (1979) argues radically that maternity is social, and EDHOLM (1982) gives further examples of the social definition of the biological. A growing literature exists describing the social construction of sexuality, for example GAGNON and SIMON (1973), FOUCAULT (1979), COVENEY et al (1984) and WEEKS (1986).

4 The classic examples come from MEAD (1950). One of the tribes she studied, the Tchambuli, had to some extent reversed the attributes assigned to males and females, men were skittish, artistic and decorative, women assertive and managing. In others, women and men had a wider range of activities and attributes in common than in highly gender differentiated societies such as ours, and the approved adult type approximated to our male stereotype in one case and female stereotype in the other. In Nepal the concept of female beauty has as an important component physical strength (SATOW, 1987). Whilst women may in fact be required to be physically strong in much of the work they undertake in our society and are biologically stronger (OAKLEY, 1981), a powerful ideology supports strength as part of the male stereotype and weakness as a feminine attribute.

5 Latest government estimates (DHSS, 1986) are that 950,000 people are living as lone parents caring for 1,500,000 children. Between 1979 and 1983 the proportion of these families living in poverty rose from 50 to 60 per cent.

6 Thirty per cent of married women with children aged under 5 years have paid work in the labour market, but only 7 per cent of them full-time.

7 The economic activity rate is the number economically active (employed, or unemployed but seeking employment) as a percentage of the total population in that age group.

8 Sixty per cent of women manual workers are in 'catering, cleaning, hairdressing and other personal services'; 15 per cent in 'painting, repetitive assembling, product packaging and related; and 11 per cent in 'making and repairing (excluding metal and electrical)'. Of non-manual women workers, 53 per cent are in 'clerical and related'; 27 per cent in 'professional and related work in education, welfare and health'; and 12 per cent in 'selling' (HOLLAND et al, 1985)

9 Examples at random are doctors, 23 per cent women, chartered accountants, 6 per cent, and architects, 4 per cent (figures from professional associations, (GAOC, 1987)). Of 160 top jobs in the BBC, six are held by women (radio discussion, 1988); of 635 Members of Parliament, forty-one are women.

10 The Women and Employment Survey (see MARTIN and ROBERTS, 1984) demons-

trated that there was a large peak in women's part-time hours at sixteen hours per week, above which level employers become liable for more overhead costs associated with the work (DEX, 1987) and employment rights accrue to the worker.

11 Recent fears that fathers in Sweden are not forming close relationships with their children has resulted in an addition to women's work in the family. It is seen as their task to provide the necessary emotional space and time, and to facilitate the development of close relationships between father and children (Kerstin Hägg, personal communication, 1988).

12 See too CHARLES and KERR (1987) for a discussion of power and authority relations in the family within which food consumption takes place. 'Often unwittingly, sometimes reluctantly, women are themselves instrumental in reproducing the social and sexual division of labour so clearly demarcated in the way in which food is distributed within the household' (p. 173).

13 For a useful description of stereotypes see Style Council 'The stand up comic's instructions', sung by Lenny Henry, *Our Favourite Shop*, London, Polydor Records, 1985.

14 I make these very general statements in relation to gender inequality, but they can be seen to apply to other forms of inequality, the most obvious being 'race', class and sexual orientation.

15 In times of national emergency, such as war, women substitute for men in 'men's jobs' and the state takes over some of their domestic labour by providing nurseries and canteens, removed once the need for their labour disappears, or, more accurately, men reappear.

16 For a discussion of the domestic labour debate and a collection of articles from it see MOLYNEUX (1979) and MALOS (1980).

17 See COCKBURN (1985) for a discussion of the interaction between the processes of gendering and subdivision of work during technological change, which in her view reproduces male dominance. As MCNEIL (1987) puts it, when women appear to be replacing men, you can almost always be sure that the job has been redesigned and devalued (in pay, status, conditions) in some way.

References

ADLAM, D. (1979) 'The case against capitalist patriarchy', *m/f*, 3, pp. 83–102.

ALEXANDER, S. and TAYLOR, B. (1980) 'In defence of patriarchy', *New Statesman*, 1 February p. 161.

AMOS, V. and PARMAR, P. (1984) 'Challenging imperial feminism', *Feminist Review*, 17, pp. 3–19.

AMSDEN, A.H. (Ed) (1980) *The Economics of Women and Work*, Harmondsworth, Penguin Books.

BARRETT, M. (1980) *Women's Oppression Today: Problems in Marxist Feminist Analysis*, London, Verso and New Left Books.

BARRETT, M. and MCINTOSH, M. (1982) *The Anti-social Family*, London, Verso.

BARRON, R.D. and NORRIS, G.M. (1976) 'Sexual divisions and the dual labour market' in LEONARD BARKER, D. and ALLEN, S. (Eds) *Dependence and Exploitation in Work and Marriage*, London, Longman.

BEECHEY, V. (1977) 'Some notes on female wage labour in capitalist production', *Capital and Class*, 3, autumn, pp. 45–66.

BERNARD, J. (1973) *The Future of Marriage: His and Hers*, London, Souvenir Press.

BHAVNANI, K.K. and COULSON, M. (1986) 'Transforming socialist-feminism: The challenge of racism', *Feminist Review*, 23, pp. 81–92.

BOURNE, P.G. and WIKLER, N.J. (1978) 'Commitment and the cultural mandate: Women in medicine', *Social Problems*, **25**, pp. 430–40.

BOWLES, S. and GINTIS, H. (1976) *Schooling in Capitalist America: Educational Reform and the Contradictions of Economic Life*, New York, Basic Books.

BRANNEN, J. and WILSON, G. (Eds) (1987) *Give and Take in Families: Studies in Resource Distribution*, London, Allen and Unwin.

BREUGEL, I. (1979) 'Women as a reserve army of labour: A note on recent British experience', *Feminist Review*, 3, pp. 12–23.

BROPHY, J. and SMART, C. (1981) 'Family law and the reproduction of sexual inequality'. Paper presented at the annual conference of the British Sociological Association 1981. (A shorter version appears as 'From disregard to disrepute: The position of women in family law', *Feminist Review*, 9, 1981, pp. 3–16).

BROWN, G.W. and HARRIS, T. (1978) *Social Origins of Depression*, London, Tavistock.

BROWNMILLER, S. (1976) *Against Our Will: Men, Women and Rape*, Harmondsworth, Penguin.

BRYAN, B., DADZIE, S. and SCAFE, S. (1985) *The Heart of the Race: Black Women's Lives in Britain*, London, Virago.

BUSWELL, C. (1987) 'Training for low pay' in MILLAR, J. and GLENDINNING, C. (Eds) *Women and Poverty in Britain*, Brighton, Wheatsheaf Books.

BUSWELL, C. (1988) 'Flexible workers for flexible firms?' in POLLARD, A., PURVIS, J. and WALFORD, G. (Eds) *Education, Training and the New Vocationalism: Experience and Policy*, Milton Keynes, Open University Press.

CARBY, H. (1982) 'White woman listen! Black feminism and the boundaries of sisterhood' in CENTRE for CONTEMPORARY CULTURAL STUDIES (Eds) *The Empire Strikes Back: Race and Racism in 70s Britain*, London, Hutchinson.

CHARLES, N. and KERR, M. (1987) 'Just the way it is: Gender and age differences in family food consumption' in BRANNEN, J. and WILSON, G. (Eds) *Give and Take in Families: Studies in Resource Distribution*, London, Allen and Unwin.

COCKBURN, C. (1985) *Machinery of Dominance: Women, Men and Technical Know-how*, London, Pluto Press.

COCKBURN, C. (1986) 'Sixteen: Sweet or sorry?', *Marxism Today*, **33**, December, pp. 30–3.

COCKBURN, C. (1987) *Two-track Training: Sex Inequalities and the YTS*, London, Macmillan.

COOK, J. and WATT, S. (1987) 'Racism, women and poverty' in MILLAR, J. and GLENDINNING, C. (Eds) *Women and Poverty in Britain*, Brighton, Wheatsheaf Books.

COVENEY, L., JACKSON, M., JEFFREYS, S., KAY, L. and MAHONY, P. (1984) *The Sexuality Papers: Male Sexuality and the Social Control of Women*, London, Hutchinson/Explorations in Feminism Collective.

CRAGG, A. and DAWSON, T. (1981) *Qualitative Research Among Homeworkers*, Research Paper No. 21, London, Department of Employment.

CRAIG, C., GARNSEY, E. and RUBERY, J. (1985) *Payment Structures in Smaller Firms: Women's Employment in Segmented Labour Markets*, Research Paper No. 48, London, Department of Employment.

CRAIG, C., RUBERY, J., TARLING, R. and WILKINSON, F. (1982) *Labour Market Structure, Industrial Organisation and Low Pay*, University of Cambridge, Dept. of Applied Economics, Occasional Paper no. 54, Cambridge, Cambridge University Press.

DALE, J. and FOSTER, P. (1986) *Feminists and State Welfare*, London, Routledge & Kegan Paul.

DAVIS, A. (1981) *Women Race and Class*, New York, Random House.

DEEM, R. (1986) *All Work and No Play? The Sociology of Women and Leisure*, Milton Keynes, Open University Press.

177

DELPHY, C. (1977) *The Main Enemy: A Materialist Analysis of Women's Oppression*, London, WRRC Explorations in Feminism No. 3.

DEX, S. (1987) *Women's Occupational Mobility: A Lifetime Perspective*, London, Macmillan.

DHSS (1986) *Low Income Families 1983*, London, HMSO.

DOBASH, R. and DOBASH, R. (1980) *Violence Against Wives*, London, Open Books.

DOERINGER, P.B. and PIORE, M.J. (1971) *Internal Labor Markets and Manpower Analysis*, Lexington, Mass., D.C. Heath and Co.

EDHOLM, F. (1982) 'The unnatural family', in WHITELEGG, E., ARNOT, M., BARTELS, E., BEECHEY, V., BIRKE, L., HIMMELWEIT, S., LEONARD, D., RUEHL, S. and SPEAKMAN, M.A. (Eds) *The Changing Experience of Women*, Oxford, Martin Robertson, in association with the Open University.

EISENSTEIN, Z.R. (Ed) (1979) *Capitalist Patriarchy and the Case for Socialist Feminism*, New York, Monthly Review Press.

EISENSTEIN, Z.R. (1984) *Feminism and Sexual Equality: Crisis in Liberal America*, New York, Monthly Review Press.

ELLIS, K. (1983) 'Can the left defend a fantasized family?', *Feminist Review*, **14**, pp. 45–9.

FIRESTONE, S. (1970) *The Dialectic of Sex: The Case for Feminist Revolution*, New York, Morrow.

FOREMAN, A. (1977) *Femininity as Alienation: Women and the Family in Marxism and Psychoanalysis*, London, Pluto Press.

FOUCAULT, M. (1979) *The History of Sexuality, Vol. 1 An Introduction*, London, Allen Lane.

GAGNON, J.H. and SIMON, W. (1973) *Sexual Conduct: The Social Sources of Human Sexuality*, London, Hutchinson.

GAOC (Girls and Occupational Choice Project) (1987) *Hidden Messages: An Equal Opportunities Teaching Pack*, Oxford, Blackwell.

GB (1909) *Report of the Royal Commission on the Poor Laws and the Relief of Distress*, Cmnd. 4499, London, HMSO.

GIDDINGS, P. (1984) *When and Where I Enter: The Impact of Black Women on Race and Sex in America*, New York, Bantam Books.

GRAHAM, H. (1984) *Women, Health and Family*, Brighton, Wheatsheaf Books.

GRIFFIN, C. (1981) 'Young women and leisure' in TOMLINSON, A. (Ed) *Leisure and Social Control*, Eastbourne Brighton Polytechnic, Chelsea School of Human Movement.

GRIFFIN, C. (1985) *Typical Girls?: Young Women from School to the Job Market*, London, Routledge & Kegan Paul.

HAKIM, C. (1979) *Occupational Segregation: A Comparative Study of the Degree and Pattern of the Differentiation Between Men and Women's Work in Britain, the United States, and Other Countries*, Research Paper No. 9, London, Department of Employment.

HAKIM, C. (1984) 'Homework and outwork', *Employment Gazette*, **92**, 1, pp. 7–12.

HANMER, J. (1977) 'Violence and the social control of women' in LITTLEJOHN, G., SMART, B., WAKEFORD, J. and YUVAL-DAVIS, (Eds) *Power and the State*, London, Croom Helm.

HANMER, J. and SAUNDERS, S. (1984) *Well-founded Fear: A Community Study of Violence to Women*, London, Hutchinson.

HARTMANN, H. (1979) 'Capitalism, patriarchy and job segregation by sex' in EISENSTEIN, Z.R. (Ed) *Capitalist Patriarchy and the Case for Socialist Feminism*, New York, Monthly Review Press.

HARTMANN, H. (1981) 'The unhappy marriage of Marxism and feminism: Towards a more progressive union' in DALE, R., ESLAND, G., FERGUSSON, R. and MACDO-

NALD, M. (Eds) *Education and the State Vol. 2: Politics, Patriarchy and Practice*, Lewes, Falmer Press.

HOLLAND, J. (1985) 'Gender and class: Adolescent conceptions of the division of labour' PhD thesis, University of London, Institute of Education. Also in *CORE*, 10, 1, 1986.

HOLLAND, J. (1988) 'Girls and occupational choice; In search of meanings' in POLLARD, A., PURVIS, J. and WALFORD, G. (Eds) *Education, Training and the New Vocationalism: Experience and Policy*, Milton Keynes, Open University Press.

HOLLAND, J., BLACKMAN, S.J., GORDON, T. and TEACHER TEAM (1955) *A Woman's Place: Strategies for Change in the Educational Context*, GAOC Working Paper No. 4, London, Institute of Education.

HULL, G., SCOTT, P. BELL, and SMITH, B. (Eds) (1982) *All the Women are White, All the Blacks are Men But Some of Us are Brave*, New York, Feminist Press.

HUMPHRIES, J. (1977) 'Class struggle and the persistence of the working class family', *Cambridge Journal of Economics*, 1, 1, pp. 241–58.

JEFFREYS, S. (1977) 'Sex-class — Why is it important to call women a class?' (with J. Hanmer, C. Lunn and S. McNeill); 'The need for revolutionary feminism', 'Male sexuality as social control' all in *Scarlet Women Five*, North Shields, Tyne and Wear.

JOSHI, H. (1987) 'The cost of caring' in MILLAR, J. and GLENDINNING, C. (Eds) *Women and Poverty in Britain*, Brighton, Wheatsheaf Books.

JOSHI, H. and OWEN, S. (1981) *Demographic Indicators of Women's Work Participation in Post-war Britain*, London, Centre for Population Studies.

LAND, H. (1976) 'Women: supporters or supported' in LEONARD BARKER, D. and ALLEN, S. (Eds) *Sexual Divisions and Society: Process and Change*, London, Tavistock.

LAND, H. (1983) 'Poverty and gender: The distribution of resources within families' in BROWN, M. (Ed) *The Structure of Disadvantage*, London, Heinemann.

LASCH, C. (1977) *Haven in a Heartless World: The Family Besieged*, New York, Norton.

LEONARD, D. and SPEAKMAN, M.A. (1986) 'Women in the family: Companions or caretakers?' in BEECHEY, V. and WHITELEGG, E. (Eds) *Women in Britain Today*, Milton Keynes, Open University Press.

LEWIS, J. and PIACHAUD, D. (1987) 'Women and poverty in the twentieth century' in MILLAR, J. and GLENDINNING, C. (Eds) *Women and Poverty in Britain*, Brighton, Wheatsheaf Books.

LONDON RAPE CRISIS CENTRE (1984) *Sexual Violence*, London, Women's Press.

LONSDALE, S. (1987) 'Patterns of paid work', in MILLAR, J. and GLENDINNING, C. (Eds) *Women and Poverty in Britain*, Brighton, Wheatsheaf Books.

LOWN, J. (1983) 'Not so much a factory, more a form of patriarchy: Gender and class during industrialisation' in GAMARNIKOW, E. *et al* (Eds), *Gender, Class and Work*, London, Heinemann Educational.

MACDONALD, M. (1981) *Class, Gender and Education*, Milton Keynes, Open University Press.

MACCOBY, E.E. and JACKLIN, C.N. (1975) *The Psychology of Sex Differences*, London, Oxford University Press.

MCNEIL, M. (Ed) (1987) *Gender and Expertise*, London, Free Association Books.

MAHONEY, P. (1985) *Schools for the Boys? Co-education Reassessed*, London, Hutchinson and The Explorations in Feminism Collective.

MALOS, E. (1980) *The Politics of Housework*, London, Allison and Busby.

MARTIN, J. and ROBERTS, C. (1984) *Women and Employment: A Lifetime Perspective*, Report of the 1980 DE/OPCS Women and Employment Survey, London, HMSO.

MATHIEU, N.C. (1979) 'Biological paternity and social maternity: On abortion and infanticide as unrecognized indicators of the cultural character of maternity' in HARRIS, C.C. (Ed) *The Sociology of the Family*, London, Sociological Review Monographs.

MEAD, M. (1950) *Male and Female*, Harmondsworth, Penguin Books.

MILKMAN, R. (1976) 'Women's work and the economic crisis: Some lessons from the Great Depression', *Review of Radical Political Economics*, **8**, 1, pp. 73–97.

MILLAR, J. (1987) 'Lone mothers' in MILLAR, J. and GLENDINNING, C. (Eds) *Women and Poverty in Britain*, Brighton, Wheatsheaf Books.

MILLAR, J. and GLENDINNING, C. (1987) 'Invisible women, invisible poverty' in MILLAR, J. and GLENDINNING, C. (Eds) *Women and Poverty in Britain*, Brighton, Wheatsheaf Books.

MILLET, K. (1970) *Sexual Politics*, New York, Doubleday.

MITCHELL, J. (1975) *Psychoanalysis and Feminism*, Harmondsworth, Penguin.

MOLYNEUX, M. (1979) 'Beyond the domestic labour debate', *New Left Review*, **116**, July–August, pp. 3–27.

MORRIS, V. and ZIDERMAN, A. (1971) 'The economic return on investment in higher education in England and Wales', *Economic Trends*, May.

NICHOLSON, J. (1984), *Men and Women: How Different are They?* Oxford, Oxford University Press.

OAKLEY, A. (1972) *Sex, Gender and Society*, London, Temple Smith.

OAKLEY, A. (1974) *The Sociology of Housework*, Oxford, Martin Robertson.

OAKLEY, A. (1981) *Subject Women*, Oxford, Martin Robertson.

O'BRIEN, M. (1981) *The Politics of Reproduction*, London, Routledge & Kegan Paul.

OECD (1976) *The 1974–1975 recession and the employment of women*, Paris OECD (authors: J. O'Neill and R. Smith).

PAHL, J. (1983) 'The allocation of money and the structuring of inequality within marriage', *Sociological Review*, **13**, 2, pp. 237–62.

PERKINS, T.E. (1979) 'Rethinking stereotypes', in BARRETT, M., CORRIGAN, P., KUHN, A., and WOLFF, J. *Ideology and Cultural Production*, London, Croom Helm.

POSTER, M. (1978) *Critical Theory of the Family*, London, Pluto Press.

ROBINSON, O. and WALLACE, J. (1984) *Part-time Employment and Sex Discrimination Legislation in Britain*, Research Paper No. 43, London, Department of Employment.

ROSE, H. (1985) 'Women's refuges: Creating new forms of welfare?' in UNGERSON, C. (Ed) *Women and Social Policy: A Reader*, London, Macmillan.

ROWBOTHAM, S. (1979) 'The trouble with patriarchy', *New Statesman*, 21–28 December, pp. 970–1.

ROYAL COMMISSION ON THE DISTRIBUTION OF INCOME AND WEALTH (1978) Research Report 6, *Lower Incomes*, London, HMSO.

RUBERY, J. (1980) 'Structured labour markets, worker organisations and low pay', *Cambridge Journal of Economics*, **2**, pp. 17–36.

SASSOON, A. SHOWSTACK (1987) *Women and the State: The Shifting Boundaries of Public and Private*, London, Hutchinson.

SATOW, M. (1987) talk given to the British Sociology Association Equality of the Sexes Committee 'Workshop on women and research'.

SCOTT, H. (1984) *Working Your Way to the Bottom: The Feminisation of Poverty*, London, Pandora Press.

SMART, C. (1984) *The Ties that Bind: Law, Marriage and the Reproduction of Patriarchal Relations*, London, Routledge & Kegan Paul.

SNELL, M. (1979) 'The Equal Pay and Sex Discrimination Acts: Their impact in the workplace', *Feminist Review*, 1, pp. 37–57.

SPENCER, A. and PODMORE, D. (1987) *In a Man's World: Essays on Women in Male-dominated Professions*, London, Tavistock.

STANKO, E.A. (1985) *Intimate Intrusions: Women's Experience of Male Violence*, London, Routledge & Kegan Paul.

STOLLER, R. (1968) *Sex and Gender*, New York, Science House.

THOROGOOD, N. (1987) 'Race, class and gender: The politics of housework' in BRANNEN, J. and WILSON, G. (Eds) *Give and take in Families: Studies in Resource Distribution*, London, Allen and Unwin.

UNGERSON, C. (Ed) (1985) *Women and Social Policy: A Reader*, London, Macmillan.

UNITED NATIONS REPORT (1980).

WALBY, S. (1983) 'Patriarchal structures, The case of unemployment' in GAMARNIKOW, E., MORGAN, D., PURVIS, J. and TAYLORSON, D. (Eds) *The Public and the Private*, London, Heinemann.

WALBY, S. (1986) *Patriarchy at Work*, Cambridge, Polity Press.

WALBY, S. (1987) *Gender and Inequality*, Oxford, Basil Blackwell.

WALLACE, C. (1986) 'From girls and boys to women and men: The social reproduction of gender roles in the transition from school to (un)employment' in WALKER, S. and BARTON, L. (Eds) *Youth, Unemployment and Schooling*, Milton Keynes, Open University Press.

WEEKS, J. (1986) *Sexuality*, London, Ellis Horwood/Tavistock Publications.

WEITZMAN, O.J. (1985) *The Divorce Revolution: The Unexpected Social and Economic Consequences of Divorce for Women and Children in America*, New York, Free Press.

WHITEHEAD, A. (1981) 'I'm hungry mum': The politics of domestic budgeting' in YOUNG, K., WOLKOWITZ, C. and McCULLAGH, R. (Eds) *Of Marriage and the Market: Women's Subordination in International Perspective*, London, CSE Books.

WILLIAMS, G., BLACKSTONE, T. and METCALF, D. (1974) *The Academic Labour Market: Economic and Social Aspects of a Profession*, Amsterdam, Elsevier.

WILLIS, P. (1977) *Learning to Labour*, Farnborough, Saxon House.

WILSON, E. (1977) *Women and the Welfare State*, London, Tavistock.

WILSON, G. (1987) 'Money: Patterns of responsibility and irresponsibility in marriage' in BRANNEN, J. and WILSON, G. (Eds) *Give and Take in Families: Studies in Resource Distribution*, London, Allen and Unwin.

Chapter 9

Gender and Primary Schooling

Jenny Shaw

Bruno Bettelheim, now a very distinguished psychologist and pediatrician working in the United States, describes in his book *A Good Enough Parent* an episode that happened to him at school in Vienna aged 15 at around the time of the First World War. By his own account he had been a good pupil, hard working and respectful, at least superficially, of his teachers. Yet on one occasion he appeared to act quite out of character, assaulted the teacher and pushed him out of the room. Much to his surprise he did not receive the severe punishment that he expected from the Director. On the contrary, the Director showed an understanding that Bettelheim did not fully comprehend until many years later. The Director did not question him about his motives and only punished him mildly. Rather, he dismissed the offending teacher and replaced him with a man who, writes Bettelheim,

> we all highly respected, not just for the excellence of his teaching ... but also for his inner security and obvious manliness ... Only years later did it occur to me that the director probably chose this man because he felt we were entitled to be compensated for the bad experience we had had with Dr X and so replaced him with someone who was his exact opposite.[1]

It would distort the significance of the story to fix uniquely on Bettelheim's description of Dr X's effemininacy and present it detached from its context in a book aimed at helping concerned parents to do better. Though today our first reactions might be shock at hearing of a teacher being dismissed for not being masculine or feminine enough (and dismay that over fifty years later some things have not changed) Bettelheim's story turns on the unspoken recognition between pupil and Director that Dr X had transgressed some rules about teaching and gender at a time when there was little or no open discussion of such issues. We live in a time when there is reasonably open discussion of gender and phrases such as 'the hidden curriculum' have been coined to help us understand the dynamics of a situation such as that described by Bettelheim where, finally, abiding by social rules was as important as curricular instruction. But there is still a long way to go in understanding just how fundamentally gender is inscribed into the organization of all our social institutions, including schools, and just what the significance of this is. For some time the effort to get gender taken seriously as an issue in education has consisted virtually of a campaign around the rights of girls to receive an education equal to that enjoyed by boys. In this sense it has not been directly about gender or girls and boys equally. Building on a framework of ideas about equality and citizenship achieved through education[2] relatively rapid progress has been made, in lip service at least, towards the principle of equal opportunity for both sexes in schooling. One review of organizational changes in secondary schools over the decade which included the passage of the Sex Discrimination Act even singled out changes relating to gender as amongst the most marked of all.[3]

Yet as feminists have sought to extend the concept of rights to women the issue of equality has taken on new and more complex meanings. On the one hand formal equality stated in terms of rights can be empty and hide inequalities unless accompanied by knowledge of the social structure and a concern for the real conditions of access. On the other the idea of a 'genderless' child, lying at the heart of measures aimed at improving educational fortunes, can deny pertinent sex differences and unintentionally damage each sex at various stages. Rights are of limited use if they are inscribed only in laws and not in minds and, if not mentioned explicitly, they remain pre-conscious. Under these circumstances the principle of equality can misfire when applied to a deeply gendered society. Precisely because free universal education generally underwrites progressive social change and access to that education is not formally governed by gender many people have difficulty in regarding schools as sexist institutions at all, or in recognizing that the informal social processes which operate within and without schools may have particularly enduring or amplified effects because of the school setting.[4]

Few teachers can honestly ignore the fact that gender has become an educational issue, indeed it shows signs of having become 'naturalized' rather than dealt with. Some may not like it and hope that it will turn out to be just a fad that will go away, or remain just an 'issue'. As such it can preserve a somewhat indeterminate status and academics can concern themselves with showing that schools are sexist institutions, meaning that they operate in a manner that systematically produces arrangements and results which advantage boys and men and disadvantage girls and women. We can show that the distribution of headships and senior teaching positions, especially in the primary sector, is so assymetrical or skewed that it demands an explanation and, moreover, one that is only possible in terms of sex discrimination.[5] Historians can remind us that Britain once had a marriage bar whereby women teachers were forced out of their jobs on marriage.[6] We can show that there is a form of sex stereotyping of subjects such that there are 'girls' subjects and 'boys' subjects and that this has consequences, for example, in weighting the chances of continuing in education.[7] We can record that at the time of the '11+' a form of positive discrimination for boys operated to ensure that boys got as many grammar school places as girls even though on the basis of their results they did not deserve 50 per cent.[8] We can argue that the switch from single sex schools to co-education has been regressive, rather than progressive, for girls and that girls are educationally better off in single sex sets and perhaps in single sex schools too.[9] And yet there is still considerable scepticism over the worth of such endeavours. This, I believe, derives less from a distrust of the feminism that has undoubtedly inspired much of the research than from the central dilemma underlying the study of gender and education (and one which is experienced acutely by the teacher in the classroom) namely, whether sex differences in education should be eliminated or accommodated.

Recently I had one of those brief conversations that took my breath away whilst giving a probably much needed shock and something to think about. I had been talking about the shortage of funds for in-service training to the Acting Head of my children's primary school whose application for funding had been rejected with the instruction to choose instead a course from a nearer institution. The teacher wryly commented on the unsuitability of what it offered as indicated by its course on 'Women and Education'. 'What use is that to me in the classroom?'

It is indeed a question worth asking and one that I shall try to answer although, as a tutor on that course, I am not on a recruiting drive and want to go beyond the merits of different types of in-service training. Clearly the keywords are 'use' and 'classroom'. Teachers are often accused of being interested first and foremost in tips and practical advice and only secondly in 'understanding'. This stereotyped view rests partly on the false but very common opposition between theory and practice and partly, I believe, on the social position of teachers, especially women teachers and even more especially primary school teachers. If sociologists can indicate why teachers formulate their professional concerns in the way that they do, then perhaps their claim that an analysis of the social context of schooling — including its gender divisions — is worth having, might be greeted more enthusiastically.

At this point it is worth noting that the teacher I had spoken to was a woman, the course which she had wanted to go on and the LEA had refused was in classroom studies and she had already done professionally qualifying courses in her own time and expense relatively late in her career. Her experience was in fact a typical one and the more we try to explain why women teachers do not get on the courses they want to do or get promoted as much as men the more we are forced to ask questions about the position of women in society generally. This leads us very quickly to consider the nature of most marriages as giving priority to husband's jobs, for example, in terms of geographical location or the distance that can be travelled to work,[10] to see that all parenting is immensely time consuming and demands an accommodation which interferes with labour market participation whatever the sex of the primary parent, though this is usually a woman.[11] To conclude, inescapably, that despite legislation the range and choice of alternative occupations and earning potential for men is substantially wider and higher than for women[12] and that most employers and unions, the tax and social security system are still sexist and discriminatory.[13] Under these circumstances many women teachers develop a pragmatic approach to themselves, their work and their educational philosophy which reflects their location in the classroom and not in the head's office, the conference circuit or the lecture hall. This may be, and often is, misrepresented as a lack of ambition and disinclination to apply for promotion or a lack of interest in managerial, financial and theoretical issues.

Some years ago two American researchers wrote an article entitled 'Why do women teach and men manage?'.[14] Although differences in local government between Britain and the United States prevent exact comparisons it was a good title and a fair question that is just as pertinent for Britain today. Men comprise about a quarter of the primary school teaching staff but they hold over half of the headships.[15] They get seconded to more courses (and get promoted thereafter more often too) although the courses they choose are rarely of the 'Women and education' or 'Classroom Studies' sort but 'Management' and 'Curriculum Development'. Are they more ambitious, less concerned with the pupils, or more favoured and sponsored? Are they cleverer and better qualified? Or do they have more time to put into their work?

Very briefly the answers to these questions are 'Yes', they do seem to be more ambitious, although the next question has to be 'ambitious for what?'. 'Yes' they are less concerned with pupils if this is interpreted in the pastoral sense and in terms of what teachers say they get out of teaching. 'Yes' they are more favoured, promoted and sponsored than women teachers.[16] 'No' they are not better qualified initially although they do become so and 'Yes' as they rise they do put more time into their work and 'Yes' they usually have wives (often teachers themselves) who underwrite their husband's careers. If the position of women in society generally can account for women teachers' inequitable treatment by their employers and colleagues, and in turn for the focus of their professional interests, can the same be true for pupils? Can knowing more about gender divisions outside school help us understand what goes on inside?

Many feminists have stressed that the labour market, divided, ghettoized and segmented, is crucial to any account of sexual divisions and disadvantage in education.[17] But the primary school is about as far as you can get from the labour market and no compulsory education system can ever be that responsive to fluctuations in demand for labour. Examples of 'men's work' and 'women's work' abound but the idea that sexual divisions in schooling can be traced back to economic institutions, though intuitively attractive, is hard to demonstrate. In the other direction attempts to measure the effect of education on later earnings have shown a weaker relation than perhaps those of us working in the sector fondly imagine or enjoy ourselves.[18] However, difficulties in showing exactly how the wider context (especially if interpreted narrowly to mean the labour market) converts into specific practices of concern to teachers is not the end of the story. For whilst any scrupulous researcher has to agree with Delamont's conclusion that there is a very 'shaky data base' at the heart of the discussion about gender[19] there have, nevertheless, been many singular, imaginative and thought-provoking pieces of research which have enlivened the debate and maintained a richer idea of social processes. For example, Spender's pioneering observation that teachers could not help themselves give more attention to boys than to girls, as measured by the amount of time that they talk to them, sticks in the mind and has probably been more effective in changing practice than many in impeccable, well controlled and replicated study.[20] Whatever criticisms are made of Spender's methodology or scepticism over whether this extra attention is such a bonus[21] more people are now conscious of variation in time spent talking to girls and boys than they once were, debate has been stimulated and so has further research and observation. Research, after all, is a jig-saw, and it requires, a playful attitude for the pieces to fall into place.

Students about to complete their training might expect to be regarded as rather up to date on current educational thinking. Yet if they want to take some of that thinking about gender into their work as teachers they will undoubtedly have problems.[22] They will enter in a junior position where that knowledge will eternally take second place to the 'experience' of older serving teachers. Their head, and or deputy head, will, in all probability, be a man. Their LEA just might, but probably will not, have declared itself an equal opportunity employer, but it will be hard to know what this means. Their colleagues, even if they are sympathetic to the idea that gender divisions in schooling exist, will baulk usually at the point of doing anything about them.[23] And plenty of parents, always 'wanting the best for their child', will watch with hawk eyes for signs of sexism if their child is a girl and will constitute the 'backlash' if their child is a boy and the newly-qualified teacher seems to be trying to do something which excludes him.

Understanding gender and avoiding sexist actions are neither the same nor easy for, as Morgan put it, 'gender is both ubiquitous and hidden', it also waxes and wanes in visibility.[24] We can very easily get into the position of fearing that every time we make any reference to gender differences as in 'Good morning girls and boys' that we are committing some sort of error and creating or at least reinforcing iniquitous social divisions.[25] And we can do very little about it if, in some subjects, children learn best with teachers of their own sex.[26] It feels like a very tricky and odd situation especially as most teachers entering a primary school are strongly committed to treating all children equally. For several years now primary education has, compared with other sectors, been relatively free of pressure to select and I strongly suspect that, amongst other things, it is this possibility of egalitarianism that draws many teachers to work in what is otherwise an underrewarded sector. A belief that all young children deserve equal treatment is a central component of recent primary school pedagogy[27] and it is hard to accept that one might, unwittingly, be failing to do just that at the very moment that one was trying hardest.

Research, however, alerts us to these possibilities and there are good reasons for grounding a discussion of the wider social context of gender in the primary school beyond the obvious one that a focussed argument is the only choice in a limited space. In the search for causal explanation there is a tendency to perpetually shift the enquiry back in time, especially when, in the case of sexual divisions, it appears that they increase over time. The less successful the quest in, say, using the technicalities of options schemes or the attitudes of pupils and staff to explain why pupils and their curriculum polarize along a gender continuum in secondary schools, the more likely we are to ask whether something had happened to determine this before the children even got to secondary schools, possibly in the primary sector. This gravity pull explains in part why the social sciences periodically find themselves back where they started, fighting off some variant of sociobiology.

Yet primary schools are interesting not just because they come first in the sequence of schooling but because they focus the argument on gender rather than just on what has been happening to girls. Things happen in primary schools which should not if sexual divisions are cumulative. To date a concern with gender has largely been a concern with the under-achievement of girls, especially in secondary and post-secondary education. But in primary education the most striking gender differences or 'problems', social and academic, tend to revolve around boys. They read less well and a significant minority pose more discipline or behaviour problems. Teachers are more worried about boys in primary schools and about girls in secondary schools.[28] As in so many areas we get interested only when something changes course, be it a star, a river or a social process, something has to attract our attention. That this happens so dramatically to boys and girls as they progress through the education system as a whole, with boys getting off to a distinctly less good start than girls but ending up seemingly more successful in educational terms, at least makes it easier for us to remember that neither gender nor its social consequences are fixed. Recent reports from the Soviet Union suggest that where there is an extremely strong egalitarian ideology girls and women maintain their early educational lead, become generally better educated and increasingly dissatisfied with their husbands as a result.[29]

In Great Britain, which is not a particularly egalitarian society, there is another aspect to primary schooling which is of general interest. Most primary schools are mixed. Fortunately this is uncontroversial in primary education and drawing attention to forms of social interaction characteristic of mixed settings does not get guillotined or diverted into a polarized and premature debate about support or not for single sex schools as the subject does in relation to secondary education. Furthermore the regularity with which descriptions of primary school classrooms register the fact that boys and girls distinguish themselves by different behaviour encourages generalization even by those firmly committed to treating each child 'as an individual' and hostile to claims about 'all boys' or 'all girls'. In the end it is the mixed setting and behaviour that is produced within it by teachers and pupils that forces us to go beyond the classroom walls for an understanding of what is going on.

The effect of single sex setting in improving girls' performance in mathematics and the natural sciences at the secondary school level has been widely reported.[30] But there are other reports, less well known perhaps, which lead out towards the social context. For example, in a review of classroom interaction and sex differences Sutherland refers to an 'unexplained but perplexing difference between co-educated and single sex pupils who, whatever their sex at the ages of 12 to 14 read fewer books if they attend co-educational schools than their counterparts in single sex schools'.[31] The first explanation that jumps to mind for this is quite simply that it is an effect of social class. In the past many single sex schools were grammar schools with a higher social class intake and in some areas now, where there is a strong demand, the few remaining single sex comprehensives may be becoming quasi-selective. The second is that there is an interaction between the inclination to read, the content of the books[32] and the social composition of what, after all, is the 'learning environment' which can have a profound effect on intellectual performance and behaviour. Tann, in summarizing some of the ORACLE research which considered grouping in the classroom, concluded that the

> most conspicuous finding ... relates to the problems which occurred in mixed sex groups. In these, the members at best tolerated each other and at worst swore at each other. Just as differences in the verbal behaviour relating to sex became increasingly acute amongst the older pupils so too the problems in mixed groups became sharper with older pupils; indeed in only one instance was it possible to persuade a mixed-sex group, in the secondary school, to participate at all.[33]

This process of sexual division, which somehow both accelerates with age and changes its basis, has been much noted and deserves close attention for it involves a complex interplay of social and psychological factors.

A gripping description of young children in the United States by Paley illustrates the processes well and opens with the statement:

> Kindergarten is a triumph of sexual self stereotyping. No amount of adult subterfuge or propaganda deflects the 5-year-olds' passion for segregation by sex. They think they have invented the differences between boys and girls and, as with any new invention, must prove that it works. The doll corner is often the best place to collect evidence. It is not simply a place to play; it is a stronghold against ambiguity.
>
> When the children separate by sex, I, the teacher, am more often on the girls' side. We move at the same pace and reach for the same activities, while the boys barricade themselves in the blocks, periodically making forays into female territory . . .
>
> If I have not yet learned to love Darth Varder, I have at least made some useful discoveries while watching him at play. As I interrupt less, it becomes clear that boys' play is serious drama, not morbid mischief. Its rhythms and images are often discordant to me but I must try and make sense of a style that, after all, belongs to half the population of the classroom.
>
> It is easier said than done. The further away a boy moves from fantasy play, the more I seem to appreciate him. Thus while appearing to value play, I seem to admire boys most when they are not playing as young boys play.[34]

In an unusually perceptive account this teacher extends the quite commonly held view that primary school classrooms, being 'feminized' insofar as they are dominated by women, are somehow inhospitable to boys.[35] Despite the even more widely held, though dubious, view that all primary schools are now 'progressive'[36] and appreciate the value of 'play' and 'fantasy' in encouraging learning, play occupies a subsidiary, not a central, role. Paley argues that its place in opposition to school 'work' has repercussions for each sex. For the boy who thinks that he is not very good at school work the relative inability to 'play' at work and the compression of the recognized 'playtimes' can be a disadvantage. Unlike small girls who can play 'pretend school' and take the feeling of pretend with them into real school work, boys switch away from table work if they are not soon successful. In her classroom boys only seemed able to 'play' at work two years later than the girls. If proper 'playtimes' were shortened for any reason, giving them less opportunity for their fantasy play (superheroes) boys worked even less at the tables and reverted to their 'block' or 'construction' preferences. For a teacher in a work setting where an 'open' door and a low level of noise are both signs of good practice there are

Jenny Shaw

subtle pressures to arrange the day in ways that the appearance of control is maintained, albeit at the expense of running, fantasy etc. In this context these costs were borne most heavily by young boys.

The boys in Paley's classroom spent as much time as they could in what she called aggressive 'superhero' play, more even than in their other preferred activity, building and construction. She observed that superheroes did not argue as much as building and construction workers, it was as if they had less need to prove their power for their

> label tells a story. A builder, confronted by a collapsed block structure, has no such sustaining symbol of confidence.

Worried that the girls might be missing out by not getting the experience of building she tried to engineer a situation where the girls built a house out of some older discarded blocks only to see it misfire and have the boys take over, clean up the blocks for their own purposes and the girls retreat:

> the boys drive the truck into the empty doll corner and call it a parking lot. They bring enough of the regular supply to make it a multi-level garage. My pilot programme has gotten out of hand. The abandoned doll corner is about to be swallowed up, the cubby room is impassable, and the girls are sitting on the ladder, under a blanket, chanting 'boys, boys, stop the noise'.
>
> Disappointed she sees that for girls the blocks are 'devoid' of image or purpose. Apparently the doll corner can be brought into the blocks, the blocks cannot be brought into the doll corner.

Several attempts to manipulate the fantasy play of either girls or boys fail. On one occasion involving a parade the boys' mock dragon gets pretty beaten up and whilst forbearing to comment on the roughness Paley recognized that

> the girls remained calm because their fantasies placed them in an enchanted garden, for which they received compliments plus the added bonus of an undamaged dragon. The boys took the dragon seriously as Jack would have. They confronted it, tricked it, and destroyed it. It is the teacher who does not take dragons seriously, who prefers and expects dragons — and heroes — to remain inside the fairy tale book.

Fairy tales indeed reveal much about gender. Paley notices that the girls do not play *Goldilocks* as they do *Snow White*, rather they pretend that they are either ordinary sisters in household dramas that have no wolves, bears or witches, or else they are princesses, Snow White, Sleeping Beauty — who are protected by magic. The same problem arises with the other stories. Like *Goldilocks* both the *Three Bears* and the *Three Little Pigs* are flawed by an absence of magic and the stories relate too

190

closely to primitive fears of abandonment. Commenting on the case of *Goldilocks*:

> She lacks all visible support, except perhaps the dubious ability to outrun the bears. If she is alone, to whom will she run? If she has a family, why don't they care about her? Lacking parents or siblings who protect her she needs a fairy godmother or at least glass slippers.

And in the context of a discussion conducted by the teacher on who might play *with* Goldilocks the replies came wholly along gender lines. The girls thought that they would play with her whereas the boys

Never in infinity.

No way, no way.

If she comes, shoot her up to the moon.

Blast her to Jupiter.

The differentiation in style of play is located in fantasy. As the year progresses a common story theme disappears for boys but remains for girls. 'Lost', vulnerable children once found by loving parents and taken home by them or, later, by 'nicer' substitute ones, give way to a less victimized persona who lives in an enchanted house until the proverbial prince comes along to marry her.

Meanwhile boys may search for their friends but they never settle down and, in that school, the absence of a permanent home is the most marked difference between girls' and boys' play. Paley also notices, though does not follow it up, that girls are more affected by the absence of the opposite sex than are boys, which is very similar to what happens much later and can be vividly shown by the dramatic effect single sex setting can have on girls' performance in science and mathematics, areas which have become distinctly 'boys' territory in the secondary school. I cannot spell out in detail the sequence but these sort of early emotional gender differences, long recognized[37] and clearly reinforced by aspects both of school organization and general cultural provision seem compatible with, and preliminary to, a range of later sex differences which have identifiable educational consequences.

Ten years ago I used to cheerfully oversimplify the differences between the sociology and psychology of education as being about understanding failure and success respectively. Sociologists studied the reasons why some pupils seemed not to fulfil their educational potential (in the main working class boys) while psychologists tended to be more interested in the cognitive processes underlying success, intelligence, creativity etc. Gender makes all that irrelevant.

Deaux, a social psychologist adapting 'attribution theory' to the differential educational performance of boys and girls at the secondary school stage, argued that girls characteristically view their successes as resulting from luck and their failures as the consequence of their innately limited abilities.[38] She speculated that the lessons girls would be likely to draw from such self interpretations would be that in the future failure could be expected whereas success could not. Boys on the other hand chose (bad) luck to explain their failures and (innate) ability to explain their successes. In each case the crucial factor was whether stable or unstable variables were used to explain good or bad educational outcomes. This account takes for granted a social structure in which both modesty is normative (expected) for girls and visible opportunities limited but it at least gives a clue as to why boys seem willing to go on with subjects which they find difficult whereas girls are keener to drop them and why boys, apparently have more autonomy and less need for approval. It also reflects the earlier pattern where a secure base was more necessary to girls than to boys.[39]

What is certain is that the cultural resources that the girls, the teachers and the boys respectively draw upon are both very different and unequally valued and we can more or less see in the schooling process how these become incorporated into moderately fixed individual identities. Some of these differences may simply correspond to differences between American and British culture, although both American and British boys seem to know and use television characters more than girls. These characters give boys what fairy tales and domestic events give to girls and their teachers, namely a continual flow of characters and actions, a resource which seems especially useful for low achieving boys.[40] But culture is most powerful when it corresponds to, and dovetails with, personal preoccupations. American researchers seem to have been more struck by the centrality of sexuality in the classroom than their British counterparts. Best's study proposes that learning about masculinity and toughness is quite as important as anything else learned by American junior school age boys.[41] Age for age her account can be compared to Armstrong's British study which does not mention gender or sexuality.[42] Although this might simply indicate the interests or gender of the researcher it is quite likely to reflect aspects of the culture that each observed. This is not to say that a preoccupation with sexuality in British schools is absent or more repressed. As a study of nursery school children showed, the means of sexual harassment based on sexuality are available to even very young males and can override the authority that a female teacher is supposed to have.[43] Rather, although harder to pin down in some contexts than others, a very coercive form of socialization around sexuality goes on in schools and is central to any understanding of gender. It operates at the informal level and is highly resistant to intervention of any sort which, of course, though depressing is no reason to stop trying to understand it.[44]

Progress has been made. For many years it was not self-evident that sex differences were important and worthy of further investigation. For a long time they were ignored, suppressed or 'overcome'. McGuiness has pointed out that when Binet and Simon first designed intelligence tests it was clear that boys predominated amongst the low scoring children, but rather than abandon a methodology based on chronological age and propose different scores for each sex they changed the test so that the sex difference disappeared, discarding items that favoured girls and adding more of those that favoured boys.[45] As this pattern of test construction has been continued the long-term consequences of this practice have been immense. McGuinness' view is that we should cease at once to measure boys and girls on the same scale and at a stroke we would solve many of the problems of the primary school classroom.

Whether or not all the problems of the primary school classroom truly stem from unacknowledged differences in cognitive development between girls and boys which then create social and management problems for the teacher there is considerable consensus that many boys are rowdier and often disruptive, certainly more active and less inclined to sit at tables and enjoy school work and distinctly less accomplished at drawing and at the reading, writing and language skills in general which predominate in the early years. There is also clearly scope for an unproductive sort of interaction between parents anxious and concerned about their children and the formal denial of sex differences which teachers are obliged to maintain in their official relations with parents (whatever their actual observations and theories). Whether parents of 'underachieving' boys could take comfort from the idea that their sons may be doing as well as boys in general though not in terms of the class as a whole if the cognitive and emotional differences in development were more generally recognized is perhaps an open question. What is certain is that viewing either teachers or children as genderless hinders rather than helps a search for better practice.

There may not be much to be done in the face of evidence that for some subjects each sex finds it easier to perform well when taught by a teacher of the same sex. But it is of some comfort to remember that individuals are not responsible for teaching in a mixed classroom, that is the result of policy decisions made largely in ignorance of their consequences, nor are they responsible for the hidden curriculum embodied in the 'staffing for sexism' and which affects the degree of official authority available to be added to personal authority for men and for women teachers.[46] But knowledge is power and better practice can come if we can see that both the behaviour that we face in the classroom and our own reactions to it are the products of the institutions that we live in.[47]

Jenny Shaw

Notes

1 BETTELHEIM, B. (1987) _A Good Enough Parent_, London, Thames & Hudson.
2 MARSHALL, T.H. (1950) 'Citizenship and social class' in _Citizenship and Social Class_, Cambridge, Cambridge University Press.
3 KING, R.A. (1982) 'Organisational change in secondary school', _British Journal of Sociology of Education_, 3, 1.
4 See DELAMONT, S. (1984) 'The conservative school' in BARTON, L. and WALKER, S. (Eds) _Gender Class and Education_, Lewes, Falmer Press; and MARLAND, M. (1983) 'Schooling as a sexist amplifier' in MARLAND, M. (Ed) _Sex Differentiation and Schooling_, London, Heinemann.
5 See ACKER, S. (1987) 'Primary school teaching as an occupation' in DELAMONT, S. (Ed) _The Primary School Teacher_, Lewes, Falmer Press.
6 ORAM, A. (1983) 'Serving two masters? The introduction of a marriage bar in teaching in the 1920s' in LONDON FEMINIST HISTORY GROUP (Ed) _The Sexual Dynamics of History_, London, Pluto Press.
7 PHILLIPS, C. (1969) _Changes in Subject Choice at School and University_, London, Weidenfeld & Nicholson.
8 See THOM, D. (1987) 'Better a teacher than a hairdresser? "A mad passion for equality" or, keeping Molly and Betty down' in HUNT, F. (Ed) _Lessons for Life: The Schooling of Girls and Women 1850–1950_ Oxford, Blackwell.
9 See DEEM, R. (Ed) (1984) _Coeducation Reconsidered_, Milton Keynes, Open University Press.
10 See WOMEN AND GEOGRAPHY STUDY GROUP OF THE INSTITUTE OF BRITISH GEOGRAPHERS (1984) _Gender: An Introduction to Feminist Geography_, London, Hutchinson.
11 See SILTANEN, J. (1986) 'Domestic responsibilities and structuring of employment' in CROMPTON, R. and MANN, M. (Eds) _Gender and Stratification_, London, Polity Press.
12 See BEECHEY, V. (1986) 'Women's employment in contemporary Britain' in BEECHEY, V. and WHITELEGG, E. (Eds) _Women in Britain Today_, Milton Keynes, Open University Press.
13 See COCKBURN, C. (1988) 'Brothers: Male dominance and technological change' in COLLINSON, D. _Barriers to Fair Selection_, EOC research series, London, HMSO.
14 STROBER, M. and TYACK, D. (1980) 'Why do women teach and men manage: A report on research on schools', _signs_, 5, 3.
15 See ACKER, S. (1987) op. cit.
16 See NUT and EOC (1980) _Promotion and the Woman Teacher_, London, NUT/EOC.
17 See BARRETT, M. (1980) _Women's Oppression Today_, London, Verso; and WOLPE, A-M. (1988) '"Experience" as analytical framework: Does it account for girls' education' in COLE, M. (Ed) _Bowles and Gintis Revisited: Correspondence and Contradicton in Educational Theory_, Lewes, Falmer Press.
18 See JENCKS, C. et al (1973) _Inequality: A Reassessment of the Effect of Family and Schooling in America_, London, Allen Lane.
19 DELAMONT, S. (1984) 'Sex roles and schooling or 'see Janet suffer, see John suffer too"', _Journal of Adolescence_, 7.
20 SPENDER, D. (1980) _Man Made Language_, London, Routledge & Kegan Paul. See also 'Telling it like it is' in MARLAND, M. (Ed) (1983) _op cit_. For criticism and extension of the issues see CAMERON, D. (1985) _Feminism and Linguistic Theory_, London, Macmillan.
21 WOLPE, A.M. (1988) _op cit_.
22 See JOYCE, M. (1987) 'Being a feminist teacher' in LAWN, M. and GRACE, G. (Eds) _Teachers: The Culture and Politics of Work_, Lewes, Falmer Press.

23 See WHYTE, J., DEEM, R., KANT, L. and CRUICKSHANK, M. (Eds) (1985) *Girl Friendly Schooling*, London, Methuen, especially the chapters by PRATT, J. 'The attitudes of teachers', SPEAR, M. 'Teacher attitudes towards girls and technology' and ADAMS, C. 'Teacher attitudes towards issues of sex equality'.

24 MORGAN, D. (1986) 'Gender' in BURGESS, R. (Ed) *Key Variables in Social Investigation*, London, Routledge & Kegan Paul.

25 DAVIES, L. (1987) 'Racism and sexism' in DELAMONT, S. (Ed) *op cit.*

26 See STANWORTH, M. (1981) *Gender and Schooling: A Study of Sexual Divisions in the Classroom*, London, Hutchinson.

27 See CACE (1967) *Children and Their Primary Schools* (The Plowden Report), London, HMSO; and STEEDMAN, C. (1985) 'Mother made conscius: The historical development of primary school pedagogy', *History Workshop Journal*, **20**.

28 See LAWRENCE, J., STEED, D. and YOUNG, P. (1984) *Disruptive Behaviour: Disruptive Schools*, London, Croom Helm.

29 WALKER, M. (1988) *The Guardian*, 12 February.

30 See SMITH, S. (1984) 'Single sex setting' in DEEM, R. (Ed) *op cit*; and MARLAND, M. (1983) 'Should the sexes be separated?' in MARLAND, M. (Ed) *op cit.*

31 Quoted in SUTHERLAND, M. (1985) 'Sex differences and classroom interaction' in BENNETT, N. and DESFORGES, C. (Eds) *Recent Advances in Classroom Research*, Edinburgh, Scottish Academic Press. But see too BARRS, M. (1986) 'Gender and reading', *Language Matters* No. 1, who points to a distinction between fiction and non-fiction underlying the apparently greater appetite for reading amongst girls. If non-fiction is included then the gap between the sexes narrows.

32 See RUSTIN, M. and RUSTIN, M. (1987) *Narratives of Love and Loss*, London, Verso for a discussion of how the content of popular children's fiction corresponds to stages in emotional growth. The predominance of women writers in the books selected both follows and reinforces gender differences in reading habits.

33 TANN, S. (1981) 'Grouping and group work' in SIMON, B. and WILLCOCKS, J. (Eds) *Research and Practice in the Primary Classroom*, London, Routledge & Kegan Paul.

34 PALEY, V. (1984) *Boys and Girls: Superheroes in the Doll Corner*, Chicago, IL, University of Chicago Press.

35 See SEXTON, P. (1974) 'Schools are emasculating our boys' in STACEY, J.B. and DANIELS, J. (Eds) *And Jill Came Tumbling After: Sexism in American Education*, New York, Dell.

36 See DELAMONT, S. (1987) 'The primary school teacher 1945–1990: Myths and realities' in DELAMONT, S. (Ed) *op cit.*

37 See KLEIN, M. (1923) 'The Role of the school in the libidinal development of the child' in KLEIN, M. (Ed) (1988) *Love, Guilt and Reparation*, London, Virago.

38 DEAUX, K. (1977) 'Sex: A perspective on the attribution process' in HARVEY, J.H. *et al* (Eds) *New Directions in Attribution Research Vol 1*, Chichester, Wiley.

39 See PALEY, V. (1984) *op cit.*

40 See TANN, S. (1981) *op cit.*

41 BEST, R. (1985) *We've All Got Scars: What Boys and Girls Learn in Elementary School*, Bloomington, IL, University of Illinois Press.

42 ARMSTRONG, M. (1980) *Closely Observed Children*, London, Writers and Readers.

43 WALKERDINE, V. (1981) 'Sex, power and pedagogy', *Screen Education*, **38**.

44 LEES, S. (1986) *Losing Out: Sexuality and Adolescent Girls*, London, Hutchinson.

45 McGUINNESS, D. (1985) *When Children Don't Learn: Understanding the Biology and Psychology of Learning Disabilities*, New York, Basic Books.

46 MARLAND, M. (1983) 'Staffing for sexism: Educational leadership and role models' in MARLAND, M. (Ed) *op cit.*

47 DOUGLAS, M. (1987) *How Institutions Think*, London, Routledge & Kegan Paul.

Chapter 10

Chaining the Brain: Structural
Discriminations in Testing

Brian Matthews

Answer the following questions:

1   A racing track is 2.54 km long. A car goes round the track six times. How far has the car travelled?
2   Who was the king or queen in 1652?

How can the above questions be sexist, racist or classist? At first sight it seems impossible, but there are numerous ways.

As other chapters in this book have pointed out, education occurs in a social context. In the same way every question is given and received in a social situation.

Suppose that every question given to a group of pupils referred to white men doing professional jobs. Boys who come from such a background have their lives validated, and hence can relate more easily to the questions. At the other extreme, a girl from an ethnic minority, whose parents are unemployed, would have more difficulty in relating to the questions. Underneath this level of discrimination in questions lie structural discriminations and this is the area on which I wish to focus.

The first question I asked was given to girls and boys at age 11 (Mason, 1986). Boys did better at the question: 47 per cent getting it right, as opposed to 42 per cent of girls. However, if the question is asked as 'What is 2.54 × 6?', then girls do better: 64 per cent getting it right, compared with 54 per cent of boys. (*ibid*, p. 2). The work of the Assessment of Performance Unit (APU) has shown that at age 11 girls and boys differ in performance in certain areas of mathematics. For example, girls do better at number patterns (*ibid*). This example illustrates a general point. Questions, even when they do not contain an obvious social context (for example, 2.54 × 6) can still discriminate. No question is in fact neutral, but is always given and received in a social framework. It is possible to standardize tests so that they do not, overall, discriminate against groups of pupils. In the past this has been done for girls and boys, but not for different ethnic and/or cultural backgrounds. For example, IQ tests were supposed to be a measure of intelligence, and were constructed and standardized by white people. They were adjusted so that boys and girls performed, on average, the same. This was not done for people from different ethnic groups who, not surprisingly, did less well. White people then argued that black people were less intelligent! As Heather (1976) puts it, 'The black filling in whitey's IQ test sees it as part of the racial prejudice and injustice he [sic] is confronted with every day of his life. In this, he [sic] is correct!' (p. 125). Levidow (1987) expands on this point and explains how concepts of ability have been racist. The way that discriminations have been incorporated into tests and ideas of intelligence have been well covered. Block and Dworkin (1977), Jencks (1975) and Rose *et al* (1984) are good places to start reading about the debate.

The usual position taken by teachers and testers is that the answers given to questions are an indication of intelligence, and that they are neutral and objective. The terms 'neutral' and 'objective' mean that the items are free of bias, and so give an indication of ability *irrespective of sex, 'race'[1] or class*. We can see that while this may be true for some items, it is *not* generally true, and to assume that it is, is likely to reinforce discriminations.

As a general point, any assessment that is assumed to be neutral and objective, and so ignores that tests are social constructions that will be received differently by different people, will be discriminatory in effect if not in intention (Hextall, 1984).

Task Group on Assessment and Testing

The Conservative Government has set up a National Curriculum (DES, 1987a). A committee was set up to advise on criteria for national tests at ages 7, 11, 14 and 16. This was the *Task Group on Assessment and Testing*, or TGAT (DES, 1987b). There are only two paragraphs in the report specifically on gender and ethnic bias, and no mention of class bias (paras 51 and 52). They state:

> We recommend that assessment tasks be reviewed regularly for evidence of bias, particularly in respect of gender and race.[2]

This is at least an advance on other reports, and TGAT must be commended for the inclusion of 'race', but its exclusion of class is significant. However, the above recommendation refers to analysing questions and their outcomes. In other places in the report it totally ignores the social setting of tests and assessments and assumes that test items are objective.

TGAT recommend that a variety of techniques should be used, and these will include tests, which, it is assumed, are 'objective'. Let us look at this assumption. Can a test item, given across the country, like 'What is the water cycle?' give valid information on the attainment of a pupil? Suppose one teacher covered it well; suppose another did not like teaching this topic, and had the pupils on a Friday afternoon; another school had just lost their teacher due to the cuts; another had no money for videos, apparatus etc. We can see that such a test item has little validity as far as each pupil goes *because*:

(a) the subjective assessment of the teacher and school is not taken into account;

(b) schools do not have about the same resources (Fairhall, 1988).

The TGAT report assumes the comparative validity of test items. All this occurs when the gap between schools is increasingly growing in terms of resources. Independent schools are spending more on pupils, while at the same time ILEA is being split up by the Government for spending too much. Teachers' pay is being held low and their numbers reduced, while in many independent schools they are paid more than in the State sector. Schools are being allowed to opt out of local control, and parents allowed to take ethnic composition into account when selecting schools. This is likely to result in sink schools with less resources and educational apartheid (Matthews, 1987). Increasingly parents are being expected to contribute to educational costs. Already the effect of this is in evidence; children in well-off areas have parent associations that fund equipment, while in other areas schools lack basic equipment.

Child poverty is now rife. The DHSS (1986) has published figures that show that about 30 per cent of children are living on or below the margin of poverty.[3] Clearly these children must suffer educationally. They will not have the access to books and equipment that others do. They will also have poorer diets, be ill more and so miss schooling. To assume that if these children do less well on a national test they are less able is invalid and classist. Whitehead (1987) provides a good outline of the variation of health in Britain.

It is at such structural levels that racism, sexism and classism operate, and are supported by tests that are held up as being 'objective'. Any attempt to gauge attainment outside such a material context is essentially discriminatory.

Classroom Structures

There are other levels at which tests are discriminatory. Let us look at one of the ways in which racism and sexism is propagated. Psychological studies have argued that:

> The *authoritarian* personality is ... said to arise out of extreme parental rejection or domination in childhood, leading to re-

pressed hostility. This hostility finds expression in adult life in attacks on minority groups, as in anti-Semitism. The authoritarian personality pattern includes highly conventional behaviour, superstition, destructiveness and cynicism, desire for power, concern over sex. (Hilgard, 1953, p. 480)

This is an extreme that can be contrasted with democratic upbringing and personalities. We know from child development studies that children have to work out that they are a separate person from the parent(s) who take the role of carer. This is a difficult process and for the child to achieve a sense of 'self' she or he needs to grow up with a sense of security. However, authoritarian parents tend to promote certain attitudes in children. Because of the emphasis on power the child associates a gain in affection and self-worth with control. This is often combined with judgmental attitudes towards self and others. Children brought up by parents whose rule is law, and allow little argument or discussion, will tend to develop a strong belief in the idea that 'might is right'. This leads to the view that in the future they will become adults who can push others around, with little regard for opposing perspectives. Thus the child can learn to live in an unfair world, where right and wrong, fairness and justice, and listening to the oppressed, are less important than who has the power to ensure their point of view prevails.

The child brought up in an authoritarian atmosphere has little chance to develop a complex moral framework. The stress is on obedience, and so right and wrong seem simple dichotomies. The vital aspect of moral and intellectual growth, the ability to deal with ambiguities, is made very difficult for the child. He or she needs to learn the complexity of moral decisions, and if discussions of the ambiguities and contradictions are not held in a non-authoritarian framework, it is extremely difficult for the child to move from a simplistic judgmental attitude. The child tends to remain searching for certainties, and comes to stress 'facts' and 'truths'. The importance of understanding other points of view before making decisions is negated. It is these aspects; not giving validity to different points of view, the inability to deal with ambiguity and the need for unambiguous facts, which, when combined with might is right, are a powerful generator of discriminations.

Children who are brought up by parents who are *democratically* orientated are more likely to have a sense of worth based on shared feelings, a wider moral framework with more tolerance and respect for others. They are more likely to listen to others and to voice their own opinions, since they should have learnt that love is not conditional on strict obedience. A sense of self worth can grow out of being accepted as a person who can both question and be questioned.

Kegan (1982) in *The Evolving Self* gives a good account of how the moral framework of the child develops; Winnicott (1974) *Playing and*

Reality is essential reading on the development of children, while Chodorow (1978) and Richards (1984), while more difficult, are vital for understanding the wider significance of child-rearing patterns.

In schools, if we are to fight discriminations, we must provide an atmosphere that will help children develop their moral framework. If we are to encourage pupils to mature and see as valid others' points of view, they have to be in a supportive atmosphere that is not judgmental. Hence it is important that some areas of work are not assessed, and that formal assessment is not a constant feature of learning. It helps a great deal if pupils can be encouraged to work in cooperation with each other, so that each can learn and benefit from the others. An emphasis on competition has the reverse effect. Authoritarianism is linked with competition, for it encourages obedience, getting 'the' answer, accepting the teachers' point of view, and not questioning authority. Pupils are split from each other, and this provides a fertile ground for finding reasons for differences and using them to try to gain esteem. An emphasis on tests and ranking that are presented as a measure of ability, so that others can be judged, fits well into this pattern.

Against this we can see that an educative environment should be one that emphasizes informal self-assessments, accepts that intelligence is not only an individual property, but also a group one. Hence assessments would include group work, for all work is done with others, through discussions and debate. This is true even when alone with a book, for the book was written in a social context. I set one of my classes a problem-solving exercise. Most groups did well, but one group, which contained four pupils the school generally considered to be very intelligent, achieved very little. They could not work constructively together. Part of the reason was that they were in competition with each other, rather than in cooperation. If one has knowledge it is of little use unless it can be used and applied, which this group did not do. Cooperative working is very useful because ideas can be genuinely shared, bounced off each other, and so improved. Group intelligence is important in many ways for getting jobs done, and can have disastrous effects if not present. For example, analysis of 'black' boxes after aeroplane accidents have shown that a major cause has been the pilot's wish to be the leader and so be in competition with the crew. The recordings have, in many cases, shown clearly that warnings given by the co-pilot and crew were ignored by the pilot. If they had worked together cooperatively as a team the accidents and deaths would probably have been avoided. Intelligence and ability are very complex ideas. The ability to achieve things in the world is always dependent on a mixture of individual attainment *and* social or group intelligence. Conventional examinations and testing procedures in no way tap such complexities.

Hence we can see from the above discussion that assessments are structurally discriminating if they encourage authoritarian classrooms, competition, restrict the range of viewpoints and see attainment as a property of an individual only.

Aims and Objectives

We can now return to the TGAT report and look at one of its important assumptions. The report says that it starts from the following propositions.

> A school can function effectively only if it has adopted:
> — clear aims and objectives;
> — ways of gauging the achievement of these;
> — comprehensive language for communicating the extent of those achievements to pupils, their parents and teachers, and to the wider community ... (DES, 1987b, para 2)

Since these are the starting assumptions they are very important; the rest of the document is informed by them.

The document uses the 'aims and objective' model of curriculum development for education. On this model 'aims', which can be quite general, are stated, and then 'objectives', which are specific statements, are described. Typical objectives would be 'The ability to use the following terms: (a) dissolve; (b) solution ...' and 'An awareness of the wide range of uses of water in the world ...' (ILEA, 1978, p. 5).

Objectives tend to be facts, skills or processes that can be tested, and hence an aims and objective approach to education tends to emphasize small segments of knowledge. This is precisely what the TGAT report states. This means that much of what is essential in education, if it is to combat discrimination, is actively excluded.

This model has some major drawbacks (MacDonald-Ross, 1973; Stenhouse, 1975; Blenkin and Kelly, 1981). It generally leads to a view of education as being concerned with ends. Definitions are invariably hierarchical, and content included that reflects the purposes of the people who produce the curriculum. As a result education is seen as being specified in terms of the outcomes to be assessed. The greater the detail outlined, the less the freedom for education. The teacher becomes like a technician whose professional skills become subsumed under the mechanical aspects of teaching. Active learning, which requires adaptation to the pupils' needs, critical awareness, autonomy and empathy *requires* that the learner and teacher have control over the learning environment. Self-exploration and growth become more and more difficult as objectives are specified. One could argue that every child at 11 should be able to paint a portrait. Of course, to ensure 'objectivity' the person could be specified. This would lead to an art that was little more than painting by numbers. But this destroys the educational reasons for doing art. Similarly in science courses skills and processes are being identified and then split up for assessment of outcomes. But in science, skills and processes are insepar-able. Science could increasingly be assessed as a whole instead of being defined through objectives. What is happening at present is like deciding that as a picture is made up of colours each colour should be assessed on its own! This is possible but destroys the point of painting. It is easy to see how stupid this is, as is painting by numbers. It is equally stupid in other subjects.

The aims and objectives model, and all the Government proposals, assume that if levels of attainment rise then education is also getting better. It may, but the reverse may be happening. To set attainment targets in a reading scheme may help levels rise, while at the same time inhibiting love of reading. In general, the more specific and narrow the attainment targets, the more likely it is that education will suffer. Saying what pupils should do assumes that it is legitimate to mould pupils according to specified aims, not taking into account the wishes and desires of the pupils. Pupils are seen as essentially passive and all having the same interests. Hence education is restrictively reduced to training and the brain is chained.

Clearly education, as an alternative to this, must encourage pupils to organize their own behaviour, to set, pursue and achieve their own ideals. This process model is explored by Blenkin and Kelly (1981). The means and outcomes of education would not be separated and education would be seen as a complex evolutionary process. The importance of education would lie in its intrinsic interest, rather than being for external rewards. The pupils must have the freedom to explore, with the teacher as a catalyst to facilitate development. Hence, a measure of power must lie at the site of learning. At heart this is a radical difference to an aims and objectives model, where the power resides with the curriculum definers. This is why this latter model is so liked by those who wish to control pupils.

On the other hand in seeing education as process the whole experi-ence of intellectual and emotional development is emphasized. The educa-tional environment and how it fosters a wide range of perspectives, dispositions and understanding is seen as central, that is, the *whole* process the pupils experience is stressed, and *not* the objectified and split up 'processes' and 'skills'. Instead of focussing on small bits of knowledge, processes are seen as more important than knowledge. This model of education is one that places the processes — like the ability to find things out for oneself — as being the focus of education. When one starts to think about what processes are important, one soon realizes how far such a curriculum would differ from an aims and objective one. For example, one process would probably be 'The ability to question evidence for the bias of the person presenting it', and another, 'The ability to understand the differing viewpoints that exist in society on major issues'. Another should be 'That pupils develop an interest in the subject that continues after leaving school'. Clearly these guiding principles, while they may be asses-sed, could *not* be measured by an exam and certainly not by nationally prescribed tests.

The last part of the paragraph 2 of the TGAT report quoted above, says that a school can only function properly if it communicates the 'extent of those achievements to pupils ... and the wider community'. For those pupils and schools who are doing well, this will be beneficial. But what will be the effect on those pupils who are not doing well, and are now officially told so through a national test? Similarly, what will happen to the schools who do not do well, perhaps because they have limited resources and are set in a poor area? The argument that national testing will help identify these schools is spurious, since they are already known, and anyway much more effective ways of identifying them could be intro-duced.

The next paragraph of the report states:

> Promoting children's learning is a principal aim of schools. Assess-ment lies at the heart of this process. It can provide a framework in which educational objectives may be set, pupils' progress charted and expressed ... (DES, 1987b, para 3)

I find it difficult to conceive that a national assessment programme based on a nationally prescribed course lies at the heart of the learning process when all the other factors that are important are considered. Here are some which come way ahead of testing: (a) teachers who are up to date; (b) teachers who have a high morale, because they are valued and included in decision making; (c) teachers who are non-classist, non-racist and non-sexist; (d) good resources and school buildings; (e) an emotionally safe environment for the pupils; (f) an environment that validates the child's experiences and hence *must* be non-discriminatory; (g) an environ-ment where children are not afraid of failure, but can use it to learn; and (h) flexibility so that the curriculum can be changed to follow interests.

This list could be very long, and we can see that the achievement of many of these items is made more difficult by the TGAT proposals, even though they have tried, in places, to allow flexibility. By focussing atten-tion on objectives, and its definition of the curriculum, it means that 'facts' are emphasized and what is covered in schools becomes less flexible.

In such ways structural discriminations are built into education the more an 'aims and objectives' model of education is used, especially when combined with breaking knowledge down into small parts for the purpose of 'objective' tests.

Pupils' Self-esteem

In every school there is a wide range of people: from different cultures, classes and sexualities, and both genders. Diverse dialects and also languages can be spoken, and some people have particular special needs. Each person has a different range of experiences from others. As other chapters in this book have shown, the way each pupil is treated affects their learning. Urry and Lee, in chapters 4 and 5, have shown how social class affects attainment. As Lee points out, schools have a particular set of values. These are mainly middle-class, and so pupils from different backgrounds are at a disadvantage because their culture, knowledge and learning processes are not validated, but negated. They have to take on the middle-class norms. Similarly, for example, learning history, which looks mainly at men and wars and ignores women's contributions to progress, makes it more difficult for girls to relate to it. Also many pupils are, through the history of colonialism, and their experience of institutional racism, presented with an image of themselves as inferior. The Eggleston Report (1986) (Runnymede Trust, 1986) has shown how teachers' racist attitudes have negatively affected the performance and aspirations of black pupils.

In order to encourage pupils to learn, *their* background must be legitimated. The more an education system emphasizes that there is only one way of seeing things, the more this becomes impossible. To be truly educative other perspectives *must be given legitimacy and explored*, particularly the viewpoints of the oppressed. As it stands, for example, Caribbean girls know that the school system will not help them as much as white middle class boys, even if they get the same exam results. As Matthews and Roberts (1987) point out:

> To assume that all pupils should strive for the same aims means that it is taken for granted that everyone is working for a 'success' that will help all. This obscures educational differences and their relationship with 'race', sex and class and the economic structure. So, for example, it hides that for girls to accept existing school values necessarily means accepting a subordinate role in society. Hence it also reinforces the myth of educational opportunity and obscures the need for structural and power changes. (p. 45)

The more that, for example, a girl from a working-class Caribbean background sees her interests in school as being the same as a white, middle class boy, the less likely she is to see the source of her oppressions. Indeed, a considerable number of pupils reject the values of the school because its definition of success does not have much meaning for them and even denies the validity of their experience. If an education system can help all to see the forces of oppression at work, and see how complex and ambiguous the situation is, the more each individual will be encouraged to learn, since it will relate to them and their feelings.

But what is happening in schools at the moment, and how does national testing and assessment affect the range of meanings available? Let's look first at the general picture before referring to TGAT.

Inequalities and Meanings

The present Government knows that there are inequalities in Britain. However, it believes, to a great extent, that it is right that they should exist. One basis of its philosophy is that people should compete to get to the top of society, and those that get there should have more wealth. In confirming the status quo therefore, it does not centrally confront the injustice of the system that it is maintaining. It has to either justify the inequalities, or deny that they exist, or pretend that they are the fault of the oppressed.

> We talk a lot about social class in British society, but I think its significance socially is very small. (Norman St John Stevas, 1980, Conservative MP.)

> They [young people] are quite unwilling to put in a day's work. (Jeffery Archer, 1985, Conservative MP. He was 'explaining' why some people were unemployed.)

In these ways it tries to hide that the unacceptable inequalities are an inherent part of the system they support. Hence, for example, it supports independent schools, even though it knows that these schools deny any chance of equality of opportunity, since not only do they have superior resources and funding, they also have unfair links to universities and other powerful institutions.

One way of avoiding confronting the injustices that exist is to pretend that the many different views on society do not exist by promoting the 'cult of consensus'. Hence it tries to pretend that there is only one set of views and values and seek to impose this set on the country (Levitas, 1986; Matthews and Roberts, 1987). Here are some examples:

> Together we are building One Nation ... (Margaret Thatcher, 1987)

Kenneth Baker (Secretary of State for Education and Science) even sees the National Curriculum as a way of furthering the idea that there is only 'one nation':

> I see the National Curriculum as a way of increasing our *social coherence*. There is so much distraction, variety and uncertainty in the modern world that in our country today children are in danger of losing any sense at all of a *common* culture and a

common heritage. The *cohesive* role of the national curriculum
will provide our society with a greater sense of identity. (Baker,
1987, my emphasis)

This is explicit social engineering towards Conservative ideals.

People from different cultural backgrounds are seen as a threat:

There is no way of understanding British and English history that
does not take seriously the sentiments of patriotism that go with a
continuity of institutions, shared experiences, language, customs,
kinship ... English patriotism ... has at its centre a feeling for
persons of one's own kind.

... the West Indian community is structurally likely to be at
odds with English civilization. (Casey, 1982)

The words 'one's own kind' are particularly significant. They carry the
message that anyone who is different in any way cannot expect to be seen
as British, and hence contain a deep racism, as it justifies disliking people
who are different. Barker (1981) and Gordon (1988) elaborate on this
point.

The Conservatives have made similar statements in respect to education. '... I believe (it is) wrong to turn our education system upside down
to accommodate ethnic variety ...' (Joseph, 1986). Sir Keith Joseph went
on to argue that we must not subvert our fundamental values and institutions, and then attacked the Institute of Race Relations cartoon book that
questions the attitudes of the police. His main point was that schools exist
to transmit 'our (meaning his) culture' and not those of other ethnic
groups. This is why the Conservatives give token support to multicultural
education, which tends to see other cultures through the eyes of white
people, but they strongly attack anti-racist education. Anti-racist education is concerned with recognizing the perspective of other cultures, and
acknowledging how they feel. In making valid such interpretations one is
involved also in showing that British people have very different views on
how society should be organized, and this involves debates on power (see
chapter 7). This is incompatible with the idea of one nation. The Government's attempt to ban the booklet 'How racism came to Britain' by the
Institute of Race Relations illustrates this (ALTARF, 1987). In doing this
it was trying to suppress the views of the people who were colonialized,
and to deny their validity. In the same way the Government's attack on
anti-sexist education arises out of a wish to suppress those who wish to
make valid the voices of women who feel oppressed. The attempt to
proscribe homosexual relations through the Local Government Act, and
other related attacks on lesbian and gay people, are also about suppressing
and controlling difference.

The Education Reform Act makes the teaching of controversial issues
very difficult indeed. This is of great political significance, since it means

that opposing political views to the Government's cannot easily be expressed (Gill, 1988).

It has been pointed out that the Education Reform Act places education in a strait-jacket. Browne (1988) argues that parts of the Act appear to say 'Thou shalt not experiment without permission' and goes on to say that the Government seems to have moved to a mode of public confrontation which seems sometimes so blinkered that it is ready to deny the self-evident when it emanates from any source other than itself.

The present proposals for a National Curriculum help to ensure that what is taught in schools is what the Government wants. The Government has made compulsory an emphasis on science and technology. It has completely left out areas like social studies that provide a way of discussing democracy in our society. Education is being imposed from the top down, and the voices of those who have been in education for many years are, when consulted, ignored (Haviland, 1988).

Kenneth Baker has asked subject groups to 'recommend attainment targets which provide objectives specific enough to offer a sound basis for the assessment and testing of pupils' progress and performance; and programmes of study detailing the content, skills and processes pupils need to be taught' (DES, 1987b, appendix B). This provides a stipulated course, for much of the time, which teachers will have to concentrate on for fear that unless the school does well it will suffer. Time and time again it has been shown that areas of study that are outside 'official time' tend to suffer. These areas will particularly affect primary schools, who, partly because they teach a wide range of subjects, will be involved in a lot of formal assessment. This is bound to affect teaching styles. If we compare primary and secondary schools we can see the effect this may have. Pupils arrive in secondary schools eager to learn. By the time they have moved to the fifth year they have often been turned off learning. One reason for this is the constraining effect of exams.

We can see that the present trend is towards suppression of different meanings and the enforcement of specific, stated objectives. This also reinforces the position of those who wish to move towards authoritarianism. We have seen that the more an education system is authoritarian, or encourages it, the more it is racist, sexist and classist. *If we wish to fight discriminations we must move away from authoritarianism in education.*

One only supports authoritarianism in education if one has a concept of human nature based on competition, and one wants to encourage a society where people will follow and obey, rather than think, care and be democratic.

There are many ways of encouraging authoritarianism. For example:

1 Emphasize tests, especially formal ones. The present National Curriculum is therefore discriminatory in principle.

2   Stress the academic learning of 'truths' and 'facts'. Do not value that which cannot be 'objectively measured'.
3   Devalue the pastoral side of education.
4   Ensure teachers do not have time to talk and discuss with pupils; overload curricula, make teachers do a lot of administration, increase class sizes.
5   Centralize curricula so teachers have less space to respond to individual interests. This also restricts curriculum development.
6   Stress the management of teachers, so they can be controlled more easily, and so not question authoritarian decisions made by heads etc.
7   Reduce the money for schools, so that resources are scarce and teacher-centred teaching has to become the norm.

These can all be seen in recent proposals for education. We can now see that the Government's policy on education is to make it serve its political interests. Education is becoming part of preparing students for Conservatism and is hence highly political (Hextall, 1988). It is, at the hidden and therefore most powerful levels, designed to produce people who will search for 'truths' and certainties so that through competition they may be the ones to dominate others. This, in turn, makes it more difficult to provide an educational atmosphere that validates the experience and background of the wide variety of children in school. Thus structural discriminations are being built into the education system.

We know that for an education system to be democratic, it *must* allow for social contexts to be made explicit, and for different viewpoints to be heard. In light of the views on this from the Conservative Government, an assessment system becomes very political if it allows suppression of other views. How does TGAT stand on this issue? Quite simply, it does not address the issue at all. It does not make any statements about the teaching of controversial issues, and how important they are, it does not argue that the subject working parties must not be racist or sexist or classist in their syllabuses by ignoring other viewpoints.

At this stage I would like to point out that the TGAT Report is a complex mixture. What I have indicated is that when we look to see the discrimination built into an assessment system, we have to look at its social context. Both the social context and the framework of the TGAT report is discriminatory. Against this the TGAT report has, it appears, tried to make the assessment system educational to some degree. Here are three examples (DES, 1987b):

1   Paragraphs 64–90 are concerned with moderation. The report argues that teachers' rank orders of pupils' performance vary from those provided by tests (para 66). The report rejects having a written test to form the basis of moderation, although this would

be simpler. The report argues for a system of groups of schools discussing results together.

2   Tests are seen as only part of the assessments, which are to be diagnostic and formative, and hence provide a basis for future decisions, rather than summative — i.e., able to give standardized and publishable results (paras 23–30).

3   The report argues that there must be a wide range of forms of assessments (paras 40–50). It argues that there should be a wide range of modes of presentation, operation and response.

We will have to wait to see just how wide these will be when the subject working parties' proposals are accepted or rejected. Appendices D and E are samples of tests that could be given. These cover a wide range and are *not* just written tests for knowledge. However, the examples are sexist, where women take the passive/nurturing roles. After having the paragraphs on not discriminating on the grounds of sex and 'race', they could, at a minimum, have provided examples of questions that did not follow sexual stereotypes. Or, at least commented on the stereotype and pointed out the need to change such questions.

I would like to stress that on first reading the TGAT proposals seem to be good. They have made a real effort in many cases to try not to constrict education. I am sure many other groups would have made a much worse job. However, one must look deeper at the framework.

If one takes the framework of a saloon car, and tries to turn it into a racing car, one will make it go faster, but not do as well as starting with one designed for racing in the first place. The Government has designed a framework that is discriminatory. The TGAT report has accepted this framework and hence, no matter how hard it may try to make the assessments reasonable, it cannot do much, since it is the Government's car they have decided to ride in. Three assumptions ensure discrimination. These are (i) the acceptance of an aims and objectives model of education; (ii) accepting that test items can be given across a country and remain 'objective' and 'neutral', and (iii) the idea that assessment on a national scale is a main way of helping educational standards. On top of this, the better aspects of the TGAT report are already under attack from Mrs Thatcher (*The Guardian*, March 10, 1988).

We can now outline the structural conditions likely to promote discriminations, including the view on ideas of intelligence. On page 197 I referred to reading on these issues. In brief, the concept of intelligence was defined very narrowly, and the people who constructed the tests not only saw themselves above bias, but also came from a small social range. Clear biases were, in fact, built into the tests.

Brian Matthews

Structural conditions for equal opportunities.

INTELLIGENCE taken to be a very broad concept, with all sections of society involved in saying what is important about it. Seen as a SOCIAL as well as individual property, and will vary in different situations. Cannot be measured meaningfully, but attainment can be assessed.

Learning to take place in a CHILD-CENTRED way and in an EMOTIONALLY WARM and supportive environment.

Teacher-pupil relationship to be as DEMOCRATIC as possible.

Emphasis on COOPERATION.

A lot of time spent DISCUSSING AMBIGUITIES.

VALIDITY given to a wide range of points of view, especially of the oppressed.

The BACKGROUND of the child held in esteem and given validity.

PROCESS model of education used. WHOLE view of learning is stressed.

Stress on INFORMAL assessment, with discussion, problem solving and group work as part of overall apprasial.

Economic and social factors seen as crucial.

Structural conditions for propagating sexism, racism and classism

INTELLIGENCE defined as an INDIVIDUAL property, in a NARROW way. Its definition can rest in the hands of experts who can be at the top of society.

Learning to take place in a DIDATIC way, with EMOTIONAL DISTANCE.

Teacher-pupil relationship to be AUTHORITARIAN.

Emphasis on COMPETITION.

Most time spent learning 'facts', with little discussion.

Only one point of view emphasized, others IGNORED, suppressed or placed in a hierarchy.

ONE cultural viewpoint given great status over others. This is part of maintaining power.

AIMS and OBJECTIVES model of education used. Knowledge split up into small parts for assessment.

A strong emphasis on EXAMS and MEMORY, with THE RIGHT ANSWERS. Exams assumed to be NEUTRAL and OBJECTIVE.

Social and economic factors seen as having little effect on pupils' performance, since 'ability' is independent of these factors.

It is essential to realize that the above chart only indicates *tendencies*. One could organize an education system on the left hand column and it still be discriminatory. All it does is to provide a backcloth against which documents, like the TGAT, can be judged.

Le Crunch

On the basis of the arguments above, I believe that it is clear that the present proposals are more about *control* of education than helping to raise attainment. To really improve education it is essential that many factors are tackled. These must include a strong commitment to equal opportunities, equal resources in all senses, an up-to-date and confident teaching profession and taking into account recent research. All of these involve a democratization of power, and this is really what it is all about — power. If we look at the two columns above there are obviously many factors involved. However, as a general trend, the left-hand column is about *spreading* power, and more people, including the pupils, having a say about the educational process, its definitions and how it feels to be in it. The right-hand column is about the *concentration* of power in the hands of people who occupy a place, at whatever level, in a hierarchy, and to ensure that those below have little say. This is also true of the wider educational proposals that are being put forward in the Education Reform Act. Those in power are consolidating their power, (Sarup, 1986).

The powerless, who are always those who suffer most, have the least power to change society. The more oppressed, the less the chance of lifting the oppression by oneself. This is something educators cannot ignore, if for no other reason than that it is our responsibility to ensure the most attainment in schools.

One indicator of the reasons for the Act is that independent schools are exempt from the National Curriculum. If it was *really* believed that these proposals helped educational standards then all schools would be involved.

Finally, to return to the beginning of the chapter. In order to see discriminations one *always* has to place the assessment itself in its social context.

Notes

1 'Race' is a concept that has little biological meaning, even though it is often used as if it were grounded in biology. An article that explains this well is *Are the races different?* by LEWONTIN, R. (1987) in GILL, D. and LEVIDOW, L. (Eds) *Anti-racist Science Teaching*, London Free Association Books. Hence I put 'race' in inverted

commas because it is a problematic category being a social and not biological concept.

2 It is significant that TGAT does not put 'race' in inverted commas, and treats it as if it were an unproblematic category — see my note 1 above. It is an indication that the Committee is not aware of these issues.

3 There is no definition of a poverty line. Sixteen per cent of children live in families that are on or below supplementary benefit level. In 1983 31 per cent of children lived on the margin of poverty, which is defined as 140 per cent of supplementary benefit level. It is probable that the numbers are now higher.

References

ALTARF (1987) 'Baker attempts book ban', *ALTARF Newsletter Nos 27/28*, London, ALTARF, September/November.

BAKER, K. (1987) Speech given at the University of Manchester and reported in *The Times Educational Supplement*, 25 September 1987.

BARKER, M. (1981) *The New Racism*, London, Aletheia/Junction Books.

BLENKIN, G. and KELLY, A. (1981) *The Primary Curriculum*, London, Harper & Row (2nd edn 1987).

BLOCK, N. and DWORKIN, G. (1977) *The IQ Controversy*, London, Quartet.

BROWNE, S. (1988) *The Times Educational Supplement*, 8 January, p. 10.

CASEY, J. (1982) quoted in LEVITAS, R. (Ed) *The Ideology of the New Right*, London, Polity Press.

CASEY, J. (1982) 'One Nation: the politics of race', *The Salisbury Review*, 1, Autumn.

CHODOROW, N. (1978) *The Reproduction of Mothering*, CA, University of California Press.

DES (1987a) *The National Curriculum 5–16: A Consultation Document*, London, HMSO.

DES (1987b) *Task Group on Assessment and Testing: A Report*, London, HMSO.

DHSS (1986) *Low Income Families: 1983*, London, DHSS, July.

EGGLESTON, J. *et al* (1986) *Education for Some*, Stoke-on-Trent, Trentham Books.

FAIRHALL, J. (1988) 'The curse of the black spot', *The Guardian*, 1 March.

GILL, D. (1988) *Curriculum Indoctrination and the Law*, London, Association for Curriculum Development.

GORDON, P. (1988) 'The new right: Race and education — or how the Black Papers became a White Paper', *Race and Class*, **XXIX**.

The Guardian (1988) 'Leak exposes Thatcher rift with Baker', 10 March.

HAVILAND, J. (1988) *Take Care Mr Baker! The Advice on Education Reform the Government Collected But Withheld*, London, Fourth Estate.

HEATHER, N. (1976) *Radical Perspectives in Psychology*, London, Methuen.

HEXTALL, I. (1984) 'Rendering accounts: A critical analysis of the APU' in BROADFOOT, P. (Ed) *Selection, Certification and Control*, Lewes, Falmer Press.

HEXTALL, I. (1988) 'Education policy in England and Wales: The impact of the new right' in GUMBERT, E. (Ed) *The Politics of Educational Reform*, Georgia, GA, University of Georgia Press.

HILGARD, E. (1953) *Introduction to Psychology*, London, Brace Jovanovich.

ILEA (1978) *Insight to Science: Water Unit*, London, Addison-Wesley.

JENCKS, C. (1975) *Inequality*, London, Penguin.

JOSEPH, SIR, K. (1986) *Educational Aims for Ethnically Mixed Society*, press release from DES 124/86, para 5. See also *Multicultural Teaching*, 4, 3, summer 1986.

KEGAN, R. (1982) *The Evolving Self*, Boston, MA, Harvard University Press.

LEVIDOW, L. (1987) 'Ability labelling as racism in anti-racist science teaching' in GILL,

D. and LEVIDOW, L. (Eds) *Anti-racist Science Teaching*, London, Free Association Books.

LEVITAS, R. (Ed) (1986) *The Ideology of the New Right*, London, Polity Press.

MacDONALD-ROSS, M. (1973) 'Behavioural objectives — A critical review' reprinted in GOLBY, M. *et al* (Eds) (1975) *Curriculum Design*, Beckenham, Croom Helm.

MASON, K. (1986) 'Areas of mathematics in which girls are ahead', *Assessment of Performance Unit Newsletter No 8*, London, APU.

MATTHEWS, B. (1987) 'Oh to be in England now that apartheid's here', *ALTARF Newsletter Nos 27/28*, London, ALTARF, September/November.

MATTHEWS, B. and ROBERTS, S. (1987) 'A case study of concealment: The Hargreaves report', *Multicultural Teaching*, 5, 2.

RICHARDS, B. (Ed) (1984) *Capitalism and Infancy*, London, Free Association Books. An understanding of the issues raised by Chodorow (1978) would be very useful before reading this book.

ROSE, S., LEWONTIN, R. and KAMIN, L. (1984) *Not In Our Genes*, London, Penguin.

RUNNYMEDE TRUST (1986) *Education for Some: A Summary*, London, Runnymede Trust.

SARUP, M. (1986) *The Politics of Multicultural Education*, London, Routledge and Kegan Paul.

STENHOUSE, L. (1975) *An Introduction to Curriculum Research and Development*, London, Heinemann.

THATCHER, M. (1987) 'Foreword', *Conservative Party Manifesto*, London, Conservative Central Office.

WHITEHEAD, M. (1987) *The Health Divide: Inequalities in Health in the 1980s*, London, Health Education Council.

WINNICOTT, D.W. (1974) *Playing and Reality*, London, Pelican.

Part 4

Class, 'Race' and Gender:
A Comparative Example

Chapter 11

Class, Gender and Ethnicity as Influences on Australian Schooling: An Overview

Bill Cope and Scott Poynting

An Egalitarian Society?

There is a pervasive and abiding myth of Australia that it has an egalitarian and virtually classless society. Donald Horne wrote *The Lucky Country* in 1964, in which he claimed, 'There is no evidence that there exists in Australia a small clique of people — certainly not a whole "class" of people — who "run" the place' (p. 182). To Horne, it was evident that:

> In outward form, and as far as ordinary people know or care, Australia is the most egalitarian of countries, untroubled by obvious class distinctions, caste or communal domination, the tensions of racialism or the horrors of autocracy ... The spirit of fraternalism permeates the nation ... Whatever kind of a bastard the boss might be, he usually rolls up his sleeves and looks like one of the boys. Usually he does not outwardly contest the belief that those who work for him are as good as he is. (*ibid*, pp. 11–12)

Twenty-four years later, in a quite different economic climate, the Prime Minister finds it useful to perpetuate this myth:

> Now I came to power and I said, 'Look, this is nonsense, we are great people, we Australians'. Employers are great blokes, workers are great blokes, farmers are great blokes — and I use blokes to encompass men and women. (Hawke, 1988, p. 30)

This was and is, to use Horne's own words on another subject, 'ideology that has almost always been "bullshit"' (Horne, 1964, p. 38).

Australian culture is in fact based on fundamentally unequal social relations of class and of gender. These are compounded by ethnicity; since 1788, racism has been a crucial feature of Australian society. As in all modern class societies, the education system plays an important role in reproducing these unequal social relations and the ideology which arises from and secures them. In this chapter, we focus in turn upon class,

217

gender and ethnicity in Australian society, and their relationship with the process of schooling.

Class

The richest 1 per cent of Australians own a quarter of the nation's wealth. Ten per cent of the population own 60 per cent of the wealth. There are over 30,000 millionaires in Australia, yet two million of the total sixteen million people live below the poverty line (Raskall, 1987, pp. 21–4).

Private ownership and control of industry is the key to these disparities; in Australia this is highly concentrated. Crough (1981) found that, of the ninety-eight largest publicly listed companies, the top twenty shareholders owned about 51 per cent of the shares. Much of this is overseas controlled. According to Crough and Wheelwright (1981, p. 1), Australia is a 'client state', with 'the highest level of foreign ownership and control of all advanced countries of the world except Canada'. (They point out that the section of the Australian Bureau of Statistics (ABS) which monitored the degree of foreign ownership was closed in 1978 (*ibid*, p. 2).)

The schooling system serves vitally to reproduce key class aspects of this society, important among which is the prevailing ideology, including the fiction of an egalitarian Australia. Central features of this system are: the divide between public and private education, unequal provision of education resources, streaming within and between schools, pedagogy and curricula ('hidden' and manifest) which disadvantage the working class, discriminatory methods of assessment, and processes of selection into higher education which militate against working class students.

Private Schools

About 27 per cent of Australian school students attend fee-charging private schools. These are of two types. There is a relatively small élite of non-Catholic church, non-denominational and a few Catholic schools which may charge up to $4800 per annum tuition fees (median household after-tax income for 1984 in Australia was $15,454 per annum), with most receiving substantial State Aid as well (Australian Bureau of Statistics, 1988, p. 373). These are virtually exclusively ruling class in their clientele, and influential out of all proportion to their numbers in Australian society. The real bulk of the 27 per cent is comprised of local parish ('systemic') Catholic schools, charging fees of the order of $250 per annum (primary) and $600 per annum (senior secondary), the lion's share of their recurrent expenses being met by subsidies from federal and state governments. Most students in the latter type of school come from working class families, though there is some recent evidence to indicate that the Catholic system may be moving towards catering for more élite class fractions with commensurate improvements in retention and matriculation rates (Preston, 1984, p. 6; Anderson and Vervoorn, 1983, pp. 64–80). Lamb (1985) found 48.3 per cent of 1983 year 10 students in Victorian Catholic schools with fathers in 'lower clerical and manual — skilled and unskilled' occupations, compared to 62 per cent in public schools.

Many official statistics fail to disaggregate the two types of private school (or the two types of Catholic school) thus obscuring to some extent the class differences in outcomes. It is nevertheless instructive to compare the rates of 'apparent retention' in secondary schools across the various sectors ('apparent' because the figures do not allow for those relatively few who cross from one sector to another). In government schools in 1983, the total number of students who remained until the final year represented 33.7 per cent of those who had begun in the first year; Catholic schools retained 51.3 per cent of their students until the final year; the retention rate at other non-government schools was 92.9 per cent (Commonwealth Schools Commission, 1985, p. 199).

Private schools, though largely publicly funded, are not open, as are state schools, to all suitably aged members of the public within their area. They are exclusive, that is, selecting 'clients' on academic, religious and other criteria. They do not, therefore, have to cater to all, including those with learning difficulties, those who present discipline problems, and so on, who create extra demands on the resources of a school. It is not surprising, therefore, that they are able to deliver higher credentials to those whom they do accept. Ashenden (1987) records that the rate of enrolment in universities of students from 'independent' schools is five times that of students from state schools (p. 59).

Catholic 'systemic' schools are organized around central administration and funding allocation from their own education authorities, which derive most of their running costs, however, as we have noted, from federal and state governments. In some 60 per cent of private schools, mostly these Catholic diocesan schools, government subsidies provide for 85 per cent of all operating expenses (Junor, 1987). Such parish Catholic schools are able to remain more 'organic to' — a living part of — their community, through religious and other social ties (sport is important, especially for boys). This counteracts, to some extent, the distancing of working class parents experienced in state schools, which occurs following the transition from primary to secondary education, when parents are less able to help with the homework, subjects become specialized and their children have many different teachers who are inevitably less familiar with each of their charges (Connell, Ashenden, Kessler and Dowsett, 1982, pp. 52–3).

Ruling-class schools are kept organic to 'their' class primarily through the operation of the market (*ibid, passim*). Their bourgeois clients are very much at home in the market; they are buying a valuable commodity and they are able to demand a high quality. They are powerful, confident and articulate, and do not hesitate to intervene if the product does not meet their expectations. The charging of expensive fees, as well as providing for a high level of resources, is a very exclusive mechanism for selection of students. Families of 'old boys' and 'old girls' are invariably accorded entrance priority. Sometimes, IQ-style tests are also used to screen applicants. Teachers and principals are chosen carefully to be compatible with the school's 'product' (and are dismissed if they prove not to be); they are generally fitted neatly into the social networks of the members of the school 'community' (*ibid*). These schools deliver the goods for their class. Dunn (1982) showed statistically that the State of Victoria's Higher School Certificate (HSC) results are 'biased against state school students [and consequently in favour of private school students] when used to select entrants to the University of Melbourne' (p. 202). About half the students in medicine faculties in major Australian universities come from non-Catholic private schools (Williams, 1982) (see figure 11.1).

That this pattern reflects social class is indicated by the findings of Anderson, Boven, Fensham and Powell (1980), in their consideration of the social composition of students enrolling to begin undergraduate degrees or diplomas in Australian universities in 1976 (p. 87). Their study shows a clustering in the highest income level of fathers (over $16,000), particularly for the prestigious professional faculties of Law and Medicine. (Note that average male earnings for 1975/76 were about $8,800.)

Since the early 1960s, there has been a powerful and successful political alliance between the constituents of predominantly working class Catholic schools and the ruling-class private schools, to demand that State Aid be extended to private schools. As many working class Catholics in Australia have a historic allegiance to the dominant right wing of the Labor Party, while the conservative Coalition of Liberal and National/Country Parties holds the 'natural' champions of the élite private schools, this alliance has resulted in a bipartisan approach to the maintenance and expansion of private schools. The onset of the recession from the mid-1970s onwards, and the ensuing fiscal crisis of the state, has meant that increased funding to private schools has necessarily entailed corresponding cuts to state school funding. (Marginson, 1982). This process has continued apace since the election of the Hawke Labor Government in 1983 (Junor, 1987).

Inequalities Between State Schools

State schools are largely, although not solely, schools for the working class (Connell, *et al*, 1982, p. 207). (We stress *for*, rather than *of* the working class; this aspect is discussed below.) Indeed, some authors have postu-

Figure 11.1

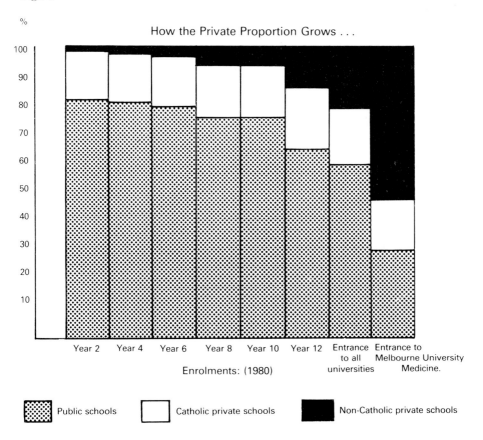

%

How the Private Proportion Grows . . .

Enrolments: (1980)

Entrance to all universities

Entrance to Melbourne University Medicine.

Public schools   Catholic private schools   Non-Catholic private schools

Source: Australian Bureau of Statistics 'Schools 1980', and Williams, C with Page, T. (1982) 'The Early Experiences of Students On Australian University Campuses'.

lated a process of 'residualization' in train since the early to mid-1970s, whereby the state schooling system increasingly moves towards a residual, stigmatized last resort, utilized only by those who cannot afford the private option (Preston, 1984).

As yet, however, there are a number of élite schools in the state system. Some of these are selective schools, many originating historically as the early state high schools for the academically 'talented', which grew up from the mid to late nineteenth century alongside the private schools for the wealthy, adopted their curriculum, and continue to share some similar élitist traditions. Having parents who attended, for example, can help to gain entry. Such schools have produced a good many notable

221

politicians, judges, academics, and so forth, often associated with the Labor Party, who staunchly defend them on 'egalitarian' grounds, arguing that the private system should not have a monopoly on 'excellence', while assuming on meritocratic or pragmatic grounds, that such standards cannot be available to all. Many selective schools have thus successfully resisted efforts by teacher unions and some state education departments to phase them out as inequitable. They certainly are 'excellent', or 'inequitable'. (These are the same thing, viewed from different standpoints over equity; the few 'excel' in competition with, and to the detriment of, the many — a clear inequality which some justify as 'equality of opportunity'.) A New South Wales (NSW) Education Department survey (1984) concluded, on the basis of the 1982 HSC results, that students at selective government high schools 'performed significantly better on the Best 10 Aggregate (matriculation score) than would be expected on the basis of their IQs' (p. 11).

Other inequalities within the state system arise from geographic differences. Access to a particular state school is generally tied to a local 'catchment' area. This, of course, advantages students from privileged suburbs, where the offerings of the schools, both curricular and infrastructural, differ markedly from those in working class localities. As with élite private schools, parents of students in these schools tend to have more formal education and are more confident to engage with the workings of the schools, both on an individual basis, and through parents' and citizens' organizations, which can be a significant source of extra funding as well as influence on these schools. These schools, as well as selective schools, achieve far higher rates of retention and matriculation than state schools in working class areas.

Working Class Schooling

Most working class schooling takes place in comprehensive, co-educational, local state schools. Not all are comprehensive; some selective schools remain, as we have seen. Similarly, some single-sex schools are retained by the various states' education departments, often despite their preferred policy, because of combined pressure from traditionalists, feminists believing them to be better for girls, and certain ethnic communities who prefer the sex-segregation of their children at school. Within the public sector, and with very few exceptions, local schools are attended by all schoolchildren who neither gain entry to a selective school nor have a case for attending a single-sex school. Such a case would have to be made by the parents to an officer of the Department of Education in the state concerned. This exemplifies the fact that all contact between working class families and state schools, be it with the principal, headteacher, or whoever, is in contact with the state itself, through its employees working within a huge bureaucracy. Connell *et al* (1982) show that, while the ruling class are articulated to their schools via the market, the working class are articulated to state schools via a state bureaucracy (pp. 133 and 137–9). This produces a good deal of alienation of working class people from 'their' schools, with at best token and often nil input to, or control over, the content and processes of their children's schooling.

Working class public schools in Australia are characterized by a similar sort of opposition to the school's authority to that found by Willis (1977) in British working class (boys') education — 'authority' both in the sense of its *power* over them and of the *source of knowledge* of the type it deals in (Connell, *et al*, 1982; Hawkins, 1982).

> There is a lot more noise, movement and mess in the working-class comprehensives. The kids rush, slouch, stroll and huddle around, in a mixture of uniform, part-uniform and anti-uniform clothes. At breaks, the grounds give off a tremendous babble punctuated by yells (some from the teachers), with a general air of undisciplined energy. (Connell, *et al*, 1982, p. 79)

This contrasts starkly with the 'effortless good order' pervading private, ruling class schools (*ibid*; Dowsett, G., Kessler, S., Ashenden, D. and Connell, B., 1982, p. 9).

Working class girl 'school resisters' direct their opposition against prevailing gender, as well as class, relations. In doing so, they defy the dominant models of femininity, thus becoming targets in a process of sexual labelling which renders their early and empty-handed exit from school as likely as Willis' 'lads' (Samuel, 1982 and 1983).

Outright opposition may only be practised by a minority of students in working class schools, and is not unknown in ruling class schools, either, as Connell *et al* (1982) rightly point out (pp. 82–100). The point is that this resistance stamps its character on working class schools, resulting for teachers in the experience of only just (or not quite) keeping the lid on an ever-present potential boilover: the 'discipline problem'.

Opposition, moreover, can take less confrontational forms. The most common mode of relating to school is a form of resignation to, rather than positive adoption of, the values and practices of schooling. Connell *et al* term this 'pragmatism', seeing it as characterising 'most kids most of the time', who are neither 'troublemakers' engaging in 'resistance' (roughly, Willis' 'lads') nor 'stars' opting for 'compliance' (Willis' 'ear'oles') (Connell, *et al*, 1982, pp. 82–8; Willis, 1977, *passim*). It is these kids who comprise the 'bedrock of busyness' identified in the progressive state primary school in Britain by Sharp and Green (1975), which allows the normal running of the class, with teacher attention focussed on the troublesome and the 'bright', to the advantage of the latter and the detriment of the busy-workers (p. 122 and *passim*: Sharp, 1976, p. 15). The 'dim' child present-ing few behaviour problems will receive less attention. The advantaged child perceived as 'bright' tends to be the school's 'ideal client', matching the teacher's 'ideal for children "from a good area" or a "middle class district"' (Sharp and Green, 1975, pp. 123 and 218–19 and *passim*).

Streaming

The question of the identification of 'bright' children and of curricular provision for them is a central one in the relationship between class and schooling in Australia as in Britain or the United States. As well as disparities between schools, differences within schools are important for the perpetuation of class privilege and indeed the reproduction of class relations. Streaming and competitive assessment are key inter-related processes in producing this outcome.

Virtually all Australian schools engage in streaming of one form or another. That is, they sort students according to perceived 'ability' and, on this basis, allocate different curriculum content, and perhaps employ different teaching strategies, accordingly. This sorting process can range from the informal teacher identification of the 'bright' or 'non-academic', to the deployment of batteries of standardized, IQ-type tests. Either form has been shown to discriminate against working class, Aboriginal and migrant kids of non-English-speaking background.

Until the post-war expansion and restructuring of the education system, most working class kids who went to high school at all went to schools for the 'non-academic': junior high schools with a three-year course leading to an 'intermediate' certificate or the like. There were 'technical' junior high schools for boys and 'domestic science' junior high schools for girls, with 'vocationally' oriented curricula. Most got jobs after that, some (mainly boys) training for trades in technical colleges. There was very little 'leakage' from this stream into the academic stream.

The relatively few 'academically inclined', selected by tests in primary school, could attend selective high schools, with five-year courses leading to a 'leaving' certificate or equivalent, and the possibility of competing for matriculation to university. Their curriculum was academic, a close copy of the private schools', laying the foundation for higher education. It is worth pointing out that this is also a 'vocational' education — one for quite a different vocation, or 'calling'.

The post-war economic boom allowed, and indeed needed, a mass extension of secondary education, which developed in the late fifties and early sixties. Comprehensive education was to become freely available to all as part of the post-war settlement. All high schools were deemed equal (barring a small, prestigious vestige of selectives), with ostensibly similar curricula, and the possibility of matriculation, through the HSC examination or its variously named analogues in different states. There was a common 'core' of compulsory curriculum, supplemented by various 'electives'.

In practice, streaming continued, with the different curriculum 'tracks' now accommodated under the one roof in the comprehensives. In a wealthy suburb, the 'A', 'B' and 'C' classes might resemble the selectives in their offerings; in working class areas, only the 'A' class would attempt to do so. For the rest, the 'core' would be watered down, and the 'choice' of electives guided or their availability limited, to produce quite distinct and disparate streams.

The Whitlam Government was elected in 1972: the first federal Labor government in twenty-three years. It had a strong platform of social reform, including a firm commitment to equality of opportunity in education. As education is constitutionally a state (rather than federal) responsibility in Australia, it could best direct such change through funding. University fees were abolished through providing the necessary federal funds. The Schools Commission and its Disadvantaged Schools Program were initiated to use supplementary funding to compensate for some of the class-based discrimination in schooling which had continued despite the expansion of the system, and, importantly, to 'seed' reforms in the system which might redress some of the discrimination against the 'disadvantaged'.

Many of the reforms to the schooling system were flawed from, the outset, as they were based on an attempt to encourage schools to 'value' working class 'cultural difference' in a society in which 'the disadvantaged lack political and economic power and inhabit a cultural world which reinforces their subordination' (Sharp, 1980). The funding, moreover, was a drop in the ocean, an ocean which was rapidly undergoing a sea change.

The Whitlam Government foundered on the rocks of the recession in 1985. The succeeding conservative Fraser Government used the Schools Commission to favour private schools, capitalizing on this mechanism for increasing state aid to these, opened up through the Labor Government's massive funding increases to 'poor' Catholic schools. The strategy of 'seeding' system reform was now applied to 'transition education' (transed), officially to facilitate the problematic transition form school to work said to be responsible for much youth unemployment. As well as introducing more directly work-related 'vocationally relevant' courses, 'Transed' sought to maintain work-discipline in young people who might be unemployed for long periods. Of course, it was only ever aimed at working class students; the privileged continued to make the 'transition' to higher education or well connected employment.

'Falling standards' and incompetence in 'the basics' through the 'failure' of schools, were blamed by employers, Conservative politicians and the media for the increasing numbers of 'unemployable' youth. Young people themselves responded to the economic crisis by remaining at, or

225

returning to school in vastly increased proportions, as they proved unable to find work and unemployment inflated the necessary credentials. This produced a 'discipline problem' in the senior years, as the 'non-academically inclined' encountered the predominantly academic HSC curriculum. This exacerbated the appearance of falling standards.

From the early 1980s, the system has responded to the crisis by diversifying the curriculum; reports recommending this proliferated around the country (Noble *et al*, 1985, pp. 21–31). Ironically, there is a *de facto* return to aspects of the bipartite secondary system which existed prior to the post-war reforms; terminal, non-matriculation, vocational courses for most working class kids, and a broad, liberal, academic schooling leading to higher education for the ruling class and the 'deserving poor'. The seeds of this bifurcation were sown, unfortunately, by the apparently progressive attempts at curriculum reform in the 1970s, with their enthusiasm to make schools 'relevant' to working class kids (Poynting, 1986).

The election of a corporatist, right-wing Labor government in 1983 has done nothing to halt this process. The dismantling of comprehensive education is now justified in the rhetoric of 'participation' and 'equity'. 'Efficiency', defined in narrow, economic terms, is the watchword, and 'relevance' means relevance to the needs of industry in its restructuring.

The Government has recently turned its attention to higher education to effect its economic 'rationalisations', and supposedly to build a skills base for the wished-for 'reconstruction' of the Australian economy. Tertiary tuition fees are in the process of being reintroduced, with the fallacious claim that their abolition never benefited the working class. Courses are being skewed towards the more vocational, and research funding is to be directed towards short-term economic return and areas of 'national priority'. Private universities and colleges are being encouraged, as are private, fee-charging courses in public ones. The net result will clearly be to make universities even more the domain of the ruling class and the tools of big business.

Gender

Women in Australian Society

Women's role in Australian society has changed quite dramatically since the Second World War. In 1947, 22 per cent of the workforce were women. Thirty years later, this had risen to 36 per cent and whereas 15 per cent of the female workforce were married in 1947, 61 per cent were married in 1979. This is but a crude indicator of a move away from traditional full-time housework. This move was not simply a matter of choice, but is linked, especially by the 1970s and 1980s to the growing fact that 'the family wage' was becoming less and less viable: no longer is it possible for the majority of waged or salaried husbands to maintain a non-waged wife and children on one income.

The most significant document linking the social context of gender to schooling was of a major report put out by the Commonwealth Schools Commission in 1975 called *Girls, School and Society*. Its base point was that increased female workforce participation did not necessarily mean that women were better off, or that they were coming to enjoy the same range of privileges as men.

> Nearly all women have children, but mothers have fewer than they once did. They complete child bearing earlier and live longer than they did even thirty years ago. They increasingly return to work as their children grow older, and many of them only with-draw from paid work for a short period after the birth of children ... Yet, despite the fact that paid work is more important in women's lives than it was, working women are still heavily concentrated in a few occupations. Few ever rise to senior posi-tions in these and it is still expected that women will bear main responsibility for domestic activities and child rearing although over 40 per cent of married women now work. Women have acquired new roles in paid work in addition to those they pre-viously had as wives and mothers. (Schools Commission, 1975, pp. 6–7)

Labour force participation, this report also pointed out, has directly related to educational qualifications. In 1966, for example, 62.4 per cent of women graduates were employed compared with 25 per cent of women who had only primary education. Yet, even though those women in the workforce were likely to be well educated, the median income for women was only 60 per cent of the median male income. This was partly because women were concentrated in lower paying, lower prestige 'female' occupations (pp. 24–7). But, most importantly, education seemed to be foreshadowing, reproducing and reinforcing this situation of inequality. Census figures linking the educational participation of 16–17 and 18-year-olds with their parents' occupations clearly showed that participations in full-time education increases or declines according to the occupational status of their fathers. Yet at every level of occupational status, females showed lower rates of educational participation than their male equiva-lents (pp. 35–6). However, by the time of the publication of a follow-up report in 1984, *Girls and Tomorrow*, this situation had changed. Girls had 'clearly overtaken boys in participating in formal post-compulsory school-ing' (Schools Commission, 1984). This seemed, to some, to indicate that there was no longer any problem of gender in education in Australia.

Bill Cope and Scott Poynting

Gender in Australian Education

In the post-compulsory years of schooling, 1981 census material showed a turnaround from 1975. There were 86.2 per cent of 15 to 16-year-old females involved in education compared to 85.8 per cent of males. But, reflecting differential rates of higher and technical education participation, only 39.2 per cent of 17 to 19-year-old females were continuing their education compared to 54.7 per cent of males, and 16.2 per cent of 20 to 24-year-old females compared to 24.1 per cent of males. In addition gender-based educational pathways emerged, with males moving proportionately more into apprenticeships and universities, and thence to potentially much more lucrative traditional male realms of employment (*ibid*, pp. 4–6). And even those females 'in' universities, despite significant inroads, were still much less likely to be studying medicine, law, dentistry, or economics than teaching, the humanities or social work (Powles, 1987).

So, how does this latter performance reflect upon the apparent parity of school participation? Looking back over the previous decade, the 1984 Schools Commission report answers this question in the following way:

Girls continue to be afforded for less opportunity than boys to realize their potential. The quality of girls' education does not match that of boys in terms of developing confidence and self-esteem or marketable skills. There are still fewer resources for girls' schooling than for boys'. Teachers continue to allocate less of their time to girls than to boys. Teacher interaction with girls does not encourage creativity and enquiry to the same extent as with boys. Teacher education courses for both teachers in training and practising teachers do not give detailed attention to non-sexist curriculum development and non-sexist teacher behaviour. School hierarchies are providing even fewer role models for girls than in 1975 (p. 2).

In other words, it is argued that, despite the appearances of school retention rates, schools compound the problem of gender inequality in education. Retention rates, in fact, may well only be a result of the declining availability of jobs traditionally performed by 15 to 16-year-old females. Females do not necessarily stay on at school because it provides a valuable experience rewarded in the long term by employment possibilities equal to males, but because they lack other alternatives (Johnson, 1988, p. 99).

Non-Sexist Education

What is being done to reduce the inequitable social outcomes of educaton around the gender divide?

A *National Policy for the Education of Girls in Australian Schools* was issued by the Schools Commission in 1987 (Schools Commission, 1987). In terms of school organization, the sorts of things to be tackled include putting girls and boys in situations in which they face similar expectations and have the same range of subject choices, and ensuring the equitable distribution of women through the educational hierarchy as role-models for girls. Behind these moves lie a number of fundamental principles, including that:

* Gender is not a determinant of capacity to learn.
* Girls and boys should be valued equally in all aspects of schooling.
* Equality of opportunity and outcomes in education for girls and boys may require differential provision, at least for a period of time.

But educational change cannot be brought about by simple statements of principle or intention, no matter how self-evident or important these seem. For a start, special programs require special funding, which is becoming hard to secure in the fiscal context of the late 1980s. But then, it is not simply the case that gender produces inequality. Jane Kenway's research on an all-girls school shows how, in certain, very specific privileged contexts, a female culture is constructed through schooling which is very different to, though just as compatible with, academic success and social power as that of privileged boys' schools (Kenway, 1988). To compound this complexity and difficulty, there is dissention about how to approach the problems of girls and schooling. The majority of interventions to meet the challenge of gender differences have aimed at social equity. Hence the prevalent concept of 'inclusive' curriculum: girls can participate as equals in subjects that were the traditional preserve of male culture. The politics of equality of genders means active support of the trend towards the erasure of the difference. Self-esteem for women is achieved by using education as a means to help them join the world of men on an equal footing.

Already, however, there has been a reaction to this. Should not schools aim to preserve female culture as much as they give girls the chance to join the 'male' world of power manipulation and competitive individualism? Are not skills and values of caring and domestic competence, for example, equally important? Affirmative action to place more girls in traditional boys' subjects implicitly reproduces the broader social devaluation of what was traditionally female culture and female work. Women's history for example, is as important as getting more girls into technical and scientific courses. Self-esteem is created by celebrating rather than erasing female cultural difference (Cope and Kalantzis, 1988).

These dilemmas remain far from resolved, even amongst those who support non-sexist education. Meanwhile, girls face unequal gender-specific challenges in schools. And, at least as importantly, boys' sexism and lack of skill in traditional female domestic and work roles are not significantly influenced by schooling.

Ethnicity

Concepts of 'ethnicity' or 'race' or 'culture' in Australia refer to two very different sorts of historical problems. One is the place of Australia's indigenous peoples, the Aborigines, in Australian society; and the other is the place of immigrants, particularly those of non-English speaking background. The concept 'race' is not used as frequently as it is in Britain. This is partly because Australia's mass immigration program has included large numbers of people who came from non-English speaking backgrounds, but who do not appear strikingly different physically (Northern and Southern Europeans, South Americans, etc.). Recently, the numbers of immigrants from South East Asia have increased dramatically, but still, the public debate both for and against the very large ongoing immigration program, has centred around the terminology of 'multiculturalism' rather than 'race relations'. This is also largely true of current concerns about Aborigines. The issues are conceived more to be ones of culture than 'race' (for example, maintaining Aboriginality rather than having to assimilate or adopt the culture of the now-dominant group).

There are nearly 200,000 people of Aboriginal origin in Australian society. This is over 1 per cent of Australia's population. Their history has been one of genocide and social marginalization. No-one knows precisely how many Aborigines were living in Australia when Europeans first established a settlement here in 1788. Estimates now put the figure at 500,000. Within a century, this had dropped to about 100,000 as blacks died in the guerilla war against the colonizers and died of European diseases against which they had little resistance or access to adequate medical facilities. To give an idea of the extent of the devastation, over 700 different languages were spoken in Australia in 1788. More than half of these languages have been lost or almost entirely lost, and only about 150 still have more than ten speakers. Today, there are no Aborigines who live in a purely traditional hunting and gathering economy, yet Aborigines are the group least well integrated into Australian society. Over one-third live in fringe-dweller camps in rural areas, which are equal to many of the worst of Third World conditions (Cole, 1986). Youth unemployment is often as high as 90 per cent. In NSW, Aboriginal male unemployment is estimated at 75 per cent (Castles, Cope, Kalantzis and Morrissey, 1988, pp. 20–3).

Australia's post-war immigration, in international comparative terms, has been quite extraordinary. Only Israel has experienced more immigration over the same period relative to the size of the existing population, but in the quite unusual circumstances of setting up a new state. More than three million immigrants have arrived since the post-war migration program began in earnest in 1947. The population has increased since then from under eight million to over sixteen million. One person in three is an immigrant or the child of an immigrant.

Over the decades, the composition of this immigrant population has become increasingly diversified. The original intention had been to draw as many immigrants as possible from the United Kingdom. This intention was based on the racist White Australia Policy and the idea that only people who could assimilate quickly should come to Australia. But, to meet targets, recruitment of refugees from war-torn Central and Eastern Europe grew. This was extended to increasing recruitment in Southern Europe, and by the 1960s and 1970s, to Turkey and the Middle East. In the 1980s the largest sources of immigrants are South East Asia and Central and South America.

How have immigrants fared in Australian society? Collins divides the Australian labour market into four major segments. The first consists of Australian-born and English-speaking male immigrants who earn the highest pay and who are employed in the tertiary sector of the economy or in skilled jobs in the manufacturing sector. They have clearly defined career structures and are disproportionately represented in power structures, such as the trade unions and politics. The second segment of non-English speaking immigrant males is located mainly in semi-skilled and unskilled jobs in manufacturing and construction. This is the 'factory fodder' of industry, frequently poorly paid, in exhausting and dirty jobs, with very low participation in power structures and little hope of career advancement. The third segment is Australian-born or English-speaking immigrant women, who are paid less than first or second segment men and tend to work in traditional areas of women's employment in the tertiary sector. In a fourth segment, women immigrants from non-English speaking countries are concentrated in the parts of the manufacturing sector hardest hit by economic restructing. Their pay is lowest and working conditions poorest, frequently being involved in piece work or outwork (Collins, 1984, pp. 10–11). To this categorization De Lepervanche adds fifth and sixth segments of Aboriginal men and women respectively, many of whom are marginalised to permanently unemployed, fringe dweller status (De Lepervanche, 1985, p. 18).

Ethnicity and Education

To a large degree, education reproduces this situation of inequality in Australian society. Or, at least, much of the time, it fails to make any significant changes. So, for example, only 11 per cent of Aboriginal students in New South Wales continue through to the end of school, and only a very small percentage of those go on to tertiary education. This compares with a national retention rate of about 50 per cent.

The situation of many non-English speaking background immigrants is similar. Having parents with low levels of education, who work in poorly paid blue collar jobs, and suffering language difficulties on entry to school — these are factors which make success in schooling extremely difficult for students in some neighbourhoods.

But the situation of non-English speaking background immigrant children in Australian education systems is not so clear as it is for the majority of Aboriginal students. For many immigrants (although still only a relatively small proportion of the total) education has proved to be a path to upward social mobility. Their own struggles to make a new home in Australia seem to have paid off in terms of their children's school results.

This has led some influential neo-Conservative social commentators to criticize multicultural education programs which have tried to improve the chances of non-English speaking background children at school. They argue that specialist education servicing is no longer needed as people of non-English speaking background appear, on average, to be doing as well as the rest of the population. (For a detailed analysis of this debate, see Kalantzis and Cope, 1988.)

But, if we look at the situation more closely we can make no valid generalization about non-English speaking background immigrants as a single social group. Some groups, for example, achieve tertiary qualifications more frequently than others. Some 7.8 per cent of Australians have an educational qualificaton of diploma or better. Yet 14 per cent of second generation Asian Australians and 13.3 per cent of second generation Polish Australians have achieved this level of education. On the other hand, the same figures for Italian Australians are 5.3 per cent, Maltese Australians 2.3 per cent (Hugo, 1987) and Aboriginal Australians almost zero.

Furthermore, all ethnic groups are themselves significantly divided along class and gender lines. Even generalization about each particular ethnic group is hardly valid. Even if 10 or even 15 per cent of a particular group go on to tertiary education, what about the remaining 85 to 80 per cent? The reasons for the relative lack of success of the vast majority of students are very different according to whether they are of English or non-English speaking background (NESB). Certain aspects of working class context for people of English speaking background — such as family poverty, cultural context or school situation — often mean limited education. The reasons for limited education for NESB students are not necessarily the same: language learning difficulties, racism, problems of family understanding of the education system, and so on. School strategies to meet the needs of these students have to be varied accordingly (Kalantzis and Cope, 1988).

And when we bring gender into the question, the difficulties are often compounded. There is considerable evidence that the chances of success of many non-English speaking background girls are lower than English speaking background girls and non-English speaking background boys. In some cases, schooling for a girl is valued highly but only because it enhances her prestige and manageability, rather than because it lays a foundation for career choices and alternative futures. Girls are also placed in a particularly difficult context of culture clash in which wildly contradictory pressures all collide: for example, their parents' high educational expectations; their exposure to the liberal culture of personal freedom, romance and individual self-determination; the official non-sexist stance of education systems; the traditional role-model of a 'good' mother and wife; and sexism and racism in the world around them: often the traditional role seems a comfortable and familiar retreat (Kalantzis, 1987).

Multicultural Curriculum Strategies

In the first decades of the post-war period, the official Government policy, both for immigrants from various backgrounds and for Aborigines, was 'assimilation'. What this meant was that everyone was expected to be thoroughly integrated into the project of economic development and post-war reconstruction, with immigrants drafted into major industrial projects such as the steel mills or the massive Snowy Mountains hydroelectric scheme. To placate the existing popular tradition of racism, the Government adopted the assimilation policy, as an assurance that, at least by the second generation, immigrants would speak English without an accent and would have become culturally 'Australians'. In schools, this meant that there would be no special programs. The quickest way to ensure assimilation was to throw immigrant children into the education system, to sink or swim according to how quickly they assimilated. As the years went on, special English-as-a-Second Language programs were introduced to assist the 'assimilation' process, or, as it came to be called later, integration'.

By the early 1970s, however, assimilation was beginning not to work. Many immigrants were obviously staying culturally different, as distinctive ethnic and local communities emerged. There was also a concern that many migrants were coming to Australia, only to become disillusioned and to return to the so-called 'economic miracle' in Europe. Finally, there was the emergence of 'ethnic' community organizations and lobby groups, and possibly even a 'migrant vote'. A more sophisticated approach was needed. Similarly, assimilation simply wasn't working for Aborigines, and Aboriginal political leaders increasingly demanded that the tens of thousands of years of Aboriginal cultural tradition be recognized and respected, rather than changed into the image of the dominant group by means of assimilation. Here too, a more sophisticated approach was obviously needed.

From the mid-1970s then, we see the emergence of a new policy of multiculturalism. It tried to right the ignorance and racism of assimilation, but, as we will now show, it too has had many limitations and has not improved the lot of many immigrants and Aborigines.

By and large multiculturalism has worked with a very narrow understanding of culture, viewing it as just those folk traditions, those symbols of difference which we can comfortably celebrate in Australia. So, far too often, schools have considered multicultural education to involve 'national' days (food, national costume and dance festivals), a taste of 'community' languages or themework on the different cultural traditions in the school. But, as well-intentioned as their programs often are, they can also create as many problems as they solve.

First, they appear tokenistic, as the real function of schooling, and many parents perceive this quite clearly, is grounding in the 'basics' and achieving credentials that allow social mobility. No amount of song and dance, in order to raise cultural tolerance and self-esteem alone, will do this. The song and dance is cheap, but programs to bring about equitable results from schooling, are not.

Second, this sort of multiculturalism creates or reproduces cultural stereotypes, by trivializing culture and reducing it to visible and colourful differences. In fact, children often find it hard to dredge up the remnants of traditionalism that will make them obviously different for the purposes of the multicultural curriculum. Having to do this often creates senses of social division and racism in a social reality in which the cultural boundaries are not that clear. There are also cultural things which many students share — jeans, or McDonalds, or popular music — which are not deemed to be cultural for the purposes of multiculturalism.

Third, multiculturalism implies that we want to preserve traditions, in a kind of cultural museum or national estate. But what about heartfelt traditions, in both dominant and minority cultures in Australia, which include racism and sexism — both contrary to the official stance of education systems and schools?

Fourth, a celebration approach to multiculturalism — one that is happy with all our colourful cultural differences — neglects the fact that behind these differences are unequal relations of social and economic power which need to be changed, not celebrated, if Australia is to become a fair, let alone more equal society. Multiculturalism, in other words, is frequently deliberately apolitical and requires little of schools and education systems.

We have called this a simple pluralist model of multicultural education. In its place, we have argued that multicultural education, to be effective, needs to place a much greater emphasis on social equity (Kalantzis and Cope, 1989). Thus, in the teaching of English as a second language, it should not simply cater to the differences, with, for example, non-English speaking background students doing euphemistically named 'communications skills' courses (how to conduct oneself in a job interview or fill out a dole form), whilst middle class students of English speaking background go on with the traditional English literature curriculum which leads to tertiary entrance. In the teaching of so-called 'community languages' it is not enough to teach short-term, poorly funded and intellectually unambitious programs as a token to raise community self-esteem. Rather, these should be taught to the same degree of intellectual seriousness and with the same expected results in terms of academic prestige and school credentials, as the traditional 'foreign' languages. And in the area of sociocultural, programs, the 'spaghetti and polka' approach needs to be replaced by anti-racist strategies to reduce discrimination in the school system and address the issues of racism and cultural identity to all students throughout mainstream curricula.

Conclusion

This chapter has attempted to analyze three major lines of social division in Australia — class, gender and ethnicity — to show in each case the ways in which the school system reproduces these divisions. We have also tried to outline and evaluate critically some of the attempts that have been made to make Australian education more equitable. As we have indicated, this is an ongoing project and many of the attempts at educational reform have been flawed and frustrated in various ways.

Unfortunately, in this short space we have not been able systematically or comprehensively to link class, gender and ethnicity. Suffice it to say, every person is simultaneously defined by these three social processes, which overlay each other as social factors which influence and determine educational outcomes. This does not imply that the three factors are necessarily equally weighted in social significance at any particular moment (Kalantzis, 1989). But, the education system, in every day of every student's life, in one way or another actively constructs skills, attributes and aspirations which determine each individual's destiny.

Note

We are grateful to Anne Junor, Research Officer of the NSW Teachers Federation, for her invaluable help in providing materials for this chapter.

Bill Cope and Scott Poynting

References

ANDERSON, D.S., BOVEN, R., FENSHAM, P.J. and POWELL, J.P. (1980) *Students in Australian Higher Education: A Study of their Social Composition Since the Abolition of Fees*, Australian Research and Development Committee Report No. 23, Canberra, Australian Government Publishing Service.

ANDERSON, D.S. and VERVOORN, A.S. (1983) *Access to Privilege*, Canberra, Australian National University Press.

ASHENDEN, D. (1987) 'Private or State?', *Time*, 4 May.

AUSTRALIAN BUREAU OF STATISTICS (1988) *Yearbook Australia 1988*, Canberra, Australian Bureau of Statistics.

CASTLES, S., COPE, B., KALANTZIS, M. and MORRISSEY, M. (1988) *Mistaken Identity: Multiculturalism and the Demise of Nationalism in Australia*, Sydney, Pluto Press.

COLE, M. (1986) 'The Aboriginal struggle: An interview with Helen Boyle', *Race and Class*, **XXVII**, 4.

COLLINS, J. (1984) 'Immigration and class: The Australian experience' in BOTTOMLEY, G. and DE LEPERVANCHE, M. (Eds) *Ethnicity, Class and Gender in Australia*, Sydney, George Allen and Unwin.

COMMONWEALTH SCHOOLS COMMISSION (1984) *Girls and Tomorrow: The Challenge for Schools*, Canberra, Commonwealth Schools Commission.

COMMONWEALTH SCHOOLS COMMISSION (1985) *Quality and Equality: Commonwealth specific purpose programs for Australian schools*, Canberra, Commonwealth Schools Commission.

COMMONWEALTH SCHOOLS COMMISSION (1987) *The National Policy for the Education of Girls in Australian Schools*, Canberra.

CONNELL, R.W., ASHENDEN, D.J., KESSLER, S. and DOWSETT, G.W. (1982) *Making the Difference: Schools, Families and Social Division*, Sydney, George Allen and Unwin.

COPE, B. and KALANTZIS, M. (1988) 'Cultural differences and self-esteem: Alternative curriculum approaches' in KENWAY, J. and WILLIS, S. (Eds) *Hearts and Minds: Self-Esteem and the Schooling of Girls*, Canberra, Department of Education, Employment and Training.

CROUGH, G. (1981) *Financial Institutions and the Ownership of Australian Corporations*, Sydney, Transnational Corporations Research Project.

CROUGH, G. and WHEELWRIGHT, T. (1982) *Australia: A Client State*, Ringwood, Penguin.

DE LEPERVANCHE, M. (1985) 'Women and the state in Australia', mimeo, Department of Anthropology, University of Sydney.

DOWSETT, G., KESSLER, S., ASHENDEN, D. and CONNELL, B. (1982) 'Effortless good order? How a study of private schools throws light on the nature of discipline', *Radical Education Dossier*, **17**, autumn.

DUNN, T.R. (1982) 'An empirical demonstration of bias in HSC examination results', *Australian Journal of Education*, **26**, 2.

HAWKE, R. (1988) cited in the *Sydney Morning Herald*, 16 July.

HAWKINS, G. (1982) *Resistances to School*, Sydney, Sydney Inner City Education Centre.

HORNE, D. (1964) *The Lucky Country: Australia in the Sixties*, Ringwood, Penguin.

HUGO, G. (1987) *Australia's Changing Population: Trends and Implications*, Melbourne, Oxford University Press.

JOHNSON, L. (1988) 'On becoming an individual: A reassessment of the issue of gender and schooling', *Discourse*, **8**, 2.

JUNOR, A. (1987) *New Private Schools*, Sydney, NSW Teachers Federation.

236

KALANTZIS, M. (1987) 'Aspirations, participation and outcomes: From research to a curriculum project for reform' in FOSTER, V. (Ed) *Including Girls: Curriculum Perspectives on the Education of Girls*, Canberra, Curriculum Development Centre.

KALANTZIS, M. (1989) 'Ethnicity meets gender meets class in Australia' in WATSON, S. (Ed) *Australian Feminist Interventions*, London, Verso.

KALANTZIS, M. and COPE, B. (1984) 'Multiculturalism and education policy' in BOTTOMLEY, G. and DE LEPERVANCHE, M. (Eds) *Ethnicity, Class and Gender in Australia*, Sydney, George Allen and Unwin.

KALANTZIS, M. and COPE, B. (1988) 'Why we need multicultural education: The "ethnic disadvantage" debate', *Journal of Intercultural Studies*, 1.

KALANTZIS, M. and COPE, B. (1989) 'Pluralism and equitability: Multicultural curriculum strategies for schools', *Curriculum and Teaching*, 4, 1.

KENWAY, J. (1988) 'Privileged girls, private schools and the culture of success' in KENWAY, J. and WILLIS, S. (Eds) *Hearts and Minds: Self-Esteem and the Schooling of Girls*, Canberra, Department of Education, Employment and Training.

LAMB, S. (1985) 'Percentage of year 10 students with fathers in various occupational categories', from a survey in *Statistics Bulletin*, 10, Education Department, University of Melbourne, cited in SLATTERY, B., WOOD, B. and HANNAN, B. (1987). 'The public responsibility of private schools', *The Victorian Teacher*, June.

MacCANN, R.G. (1984) *The Performance of Selective High Schools at the 1982 HSC*, Sydney, Assessment and Evaluation Unit, New South Wales Department of Education.

MARGINSON, S. (1982) 'The privatisation of Australian schools', *The Australian Teacher*, 2, September.

MARGINSON, S. (1983) 'Perpetuating privilege', *Radical Education Dossier*, 18.

NOBLE, G., et al (1985) *Making Futures for Young People*, Sydney, Common Ground.

POWLES, M. (1987) *Women's Participation in Tertiary Education*, Melbourne, Centre for the Study of Higher Education, University of Melbourne.

POYNTING, S. (1986) 'Flies and elephants: The common sense of relevance', *Curriculum Perspectives*, 6, 2, October.

PRESTON, B. (1984) 'Residualization: What's that?', *The Australian Teacher*, 8, May.

RASKALL, P. (1987) 'Wealth: Who's got it? Who needs it?', *Australian Society*, May.

SAMUEL, L. (1982) 'Labelling under a miss-apprehension': Working class girls and discipline', *Radical Education Dossier*, 17.

SAMUEL, L. (1983), 'The making of a school resister: A case study of Australian working class secondary schoolgirls' in BROWNE, R.K. and FOSTER, L. (Eds) *Sociology of Education: Australian and New Zealand Studies* (3rd edn), Melbourne, Macmillan.

SCHOOLS COMMISSION (1975) *Girls, School and Society*, Canberra, Schools Commission.

SHARP, R. (1976) 'Is progressive education the alternative?', *Radical Education Dossier*, 1, October.

SHARP, R. (1980) 'The culture of the disadvantaged: Three views', Schools Commission Discussion Paper No. 5.

SHARP, R. and GREEN, A., with LEWIS, J. (1975) *Education and Social Control: A Study in Progressive Primary Education*, London, Routledge & Kegan Paul.

WILLIAMS, C. with PEPE, T. (1982) *The Early Experiences of Students on Australian University Campuses*, Sydney, University of Sydney, cited by Marginson (1983).

WILLIS, P. (1977) *Learning to Labour: How Working Class Kids Get Working Class Jobs*, Farnborough, Saxon House.

List of Contributors

Mike Cole taught in Inner London schools for five years. He has been lecturing at Brighton Polytechnic since 1976 during which time he also taught at St Thomas University, Canada (1980/81) and Macquarie University, Australia (1985/86). He is currently a Senior Lecturer in Sociology in the faculties of Education and Health and teachers courses on class, 'race' and gender. He has published widely in these areas both in academic and committed journals and books. He is the editor of *Bowles and Gintis Revisited: Correspondence and Contradiction in Educational Theory* (1988) and *Education for Equality: Some Guidelines for Good Practice* (1989).

Bill Cope is a Research Fellow at the Centre for Multicultural Studies, University of Wollongong, Australia. He has worked for nearly ten years on a major social education materials development project (the Social Literacy Project), written numerous reports and papers on education and questions of ethnicity and race in Australian history. He has co-authored a book, *Mistaken Identity: Multiculturalism and the Demise of Nationalism in Australia* (1988).

Clive Griggs has taught in a secondary technical school in Middlesex, a language school in Sofia and a comprehensive school in Sussex. He was Education Correspondent for *Tribune* (1975–82), has contributed articles on education to numerous journals, written chapters in RUBINSTEIN, D. (Ed) (1979) *Education and Equality* and BROWN, K.D. (Ed) (1985) *The First Labour Party 1906–1914* and is author of *The Trades Union Congress and the Struggle for Education 1868–1925* (1983), *Private Education in Britain* (1985) and co-editor, with Max Morris, of *Education: The Wasted Years? 1973–86* (1988). At present he is a Senior Lecturer in Education at Brighton Polytechnic.

Janet Holland is a Research Officer in the Sociological Research Unit, University of London Institute of Education. In a long contract research career she has focused particularly on the experiences of young people, and the intersection of gender and class. She has lectured and taught in sociology of education, women's studies and gender issues in education. She has published widely including *Work and Women* (1981), *A Bibliographic Guide to Studies on the Status of Women* (1983), *Children, Work and Ideology: A Cross-cultural Comparison of Children's Understanding of Work and the Social Division of Labour* (1987) (with G. DAHLBERG and G. VARNAVA-SKOURGS) and numerous articles and research reports, most recently in connection with the Girls and Occupational Choice project.

Jan Lee is a Senior Lecturer in Education at Goldsmiths' College, University of London. She teaches on the language and multicultural/anti-racist education courses for the primary BEd (Hons) students. She has initiated and developed an INSET course on anti-racist education for teachers from the outer London boroughs. She was previously a primary school teacher in the ILEA, a research officer on the Schools' Council funded 'Vertical Groupings' project and a Lecturer at the West London Institute of Higher Education. Her major interests are with the issues of 'race, class and gender', particularly within the urban inner city context.

Peter MacDonald is an Associate Professor in the Department of Social Sciences at St Thomas University, Fredericton, New Brunswick, Canada. His graduate work was in the sociology of education at the Ontario Institute for Studies in Education. His research interests are in historical sociology in general and in the area of the origins of state schooling in particular, especially at the comparative level.

Barbara McKellar taught in London schools for twelve years and has been lecturing at the Polytechnic of the South Bank since 1985. She is a Senior Lecturer in Multicultural Education, Faculty of Science, Technology, Health and Society, and teaches courses on class, 'race' and gender in education. She has written a chapter entitled 'Black women in education' which appeared in ACKER, S. (Ed) (1988) *Teachers, Gender and Careers*.

Brian Matthews has taught science for nineteen years. He is now a Senior Lecturer in Science Education at Goldsmiths' College, University of London. He is especially interested in changing science education, to dispute its supposed objectivity and neutrality, and to show it is inherently politicial.

Scott Poynting taught in New South Wales secondary schools for five years. He has since taught in Education at Macquarie University, during which time he was a member of the Editorial Collective of *Education Links*. He is currently lecturing in Sociology at Macarthur Institute of Higher Education, Western Sydney. He has written a number of articles on social class and schooling. He is presently writing a PhD thesis on the Australian peace movement, new social movements and class politics.

Jenny Shaw is a sociologist in the School of Cultural and Community Studies, University of Sussex. Prior to coming to Sussex she taught at North East London Polytechnic. Her research interests are in the fields of gender, education, the family and politics. She has two primary school aged children.

John Urry is Professor of Sociology at the University of Lancaster. He was educated at the University of Cambridge. Among his books are *Social Theory as Science* (with R. KEAT), *The Anatomy of Capitalist Societies, Capital, Labour and the Middle Classes* (with N. ABERCROMBIE), *The End of Organized Capitalism* (with S. LASH) and *Contemporary British Society* (with various colleagues at Lancaster). He has recently been appointed Editor of the *International Library of Sociology* published by Routledge.

Index

Aborigines, 230, 233–4
Adlam, D., 167
Afro-Caribbeans, 119–20, 134–6
Alexander, R., 106
Alexander, S., 167
All Things Bright and Beautiful (King), 105–6
ALTARF 206
Althusser, L., 91
Amos, V., 173, 174
Amsden, A.H., 169
Anderson, D.S., 219, 220
Anti-Nazi League, 151
anti–racist education, 138, 147–52, 206
Anyon, J., 12–14
Apple, M., 29
Archer, Jeffrey, 205
Armstrong, M., 192
ARTEN (Anti-racist Teacher Education Network), 152
Ashendon, D., 102, 106–7, 219
Assessment of Performance Unit (APU), 196
Assisted Places Scheme, 66
Association of Cinematographic and Television Technicians (ACTT), 122
Atkinson, A.B., 79
attendance, 5, 17, 35, 42–3, 47
attribution theory, 191–2
Australia, 102, 217–37
Australian Bureau of Statistics (ABS), 218
authoritarianism, 198–9, 207–8

Baden Powell, 49
Baker, Kenneth, vii, 26, 142, 205–6, 207
Balfour, Arthur, 56
Ball, S., 103

Ballantyne, Robert, 49
Banks, O., 129
Barker, M., 206
Barnet Council, 65
Barrett, M., 165, 167, 173
Barron, R.D., 167–8
Barton, L., 99
Becker, H.S., 111
Beechey, V., 171
Bell, Andrew, 37
Bennett, N., 106
Benton, T., 114
Bereiter, C., 90
Bernard, J., 162
Bernstein, B., 23, 101, 103, 109–10, 113
Best, R., 192
Bettelheim, Bruno, 182
Bhavnani, K.K., 144, 173
Bhavani, R., 144
Binet, Alfred, 56, 193
biography, 6
black feminism, 174
blacks: discrimination against women, 129–31; patronizing by teachers, 144; representation in TV/film, 128
Blackstone, T., 98
Blenkin, G., 201, 202
Block, N., 197
Bourdieu, P., 100
Bourne, P.G., 159
Bowles, S., 10–16, 20, 45, 90–1, 168
Bradford School Board, 45
Brannen, J., 158
Braverman, H., 84
Breugel, I., 171
Brice Heath, S., 101–2
Britain, Victorian, 39–41

women, 166–7
Wells, G., 101
Wells, H.G., 45
West, E.G., 45–6
West Ham teachers' strike (1907), 57
Wheelwright, T., 218
White Australia Policy, 231
white collar work, deskilling of, 85, 86
White Paper (1943), 59
Whitehead, A., 163
Whitehead, M., 198
Whitlam government, Australia, 225
Wiener, M., 78
Wikler, N.J., 159
Wilderspin, Samuel, 38
Wilkinson, Ellen, 61
Williams, C., 220
Williams, G., 60, 98, 160
Williams, Shirley, 66
Willis, P., 14–16, 17, 30, 103, 165, 223
Wilson, E., 164, 167

Wilson, G., 158
Winnicott, D.W., 199–200
Wolpe, A.M., 99
women: in Australia, 226–7; and the family, 161–4; and paid work, 159–61; subordination of, explanations for, 167–74
Wood, Robert, 60
workhouse system, 44
working class: change in, 83, 87; culture, 14–16, 23; 'failure' legitimatized and institutionalized, 90–116; schooling in Australia, 222–4; schooling for girls, 41–2
world system, 24–5

Young, F., 103

Ziderman, A., 169